Hauptschule Bayern

New Highlight 3

Cornelsen

New Highlight
Hauptschule Bayern, Band 3

Im Auftrage des Verlages erarbeitet von
Raymond Williams, York
unterstützt von Richard Martin (Story-Abschnitte), Darmstadt
Auf der Grundlage der ursprünglichen Ausgabe ENGLISH H • Highlight, Band 3
(herausgegeben und erarbeitet von Roderick Cox, Aachen • Raymond Williams, York)

Anhang
Chris Caridia, Publishing Services, Berlin
Wißner-Verlag, Augsburg

Verlagsredaktion
Susanne Döpper (Projektleitung) • Grit Ellen Sellin (verantwortliche Redakteurin)
Christine Maxwell (Bildredaktion) • Natasha Doerrie • Stefanie Dalhoff sowie Martina Krause (Assistenz)

Beratende Mitwirkung
Prof. Dr. Heiner Böttger, Nürnberg • Petra Fiedler, Forchheim • Kunigunde Fraas, Würzburg
Martina Goßler, Bayreuth • Ute Kempf, Würzburg • Sonja Sonnauer, Postau
Hella Tinis-Faur, Bad Kissingen • Ludwig Waas, München • Petra Würschinger, Regensburg

Illustration
John Batten, London • Carlos Borrell, Berlin • Jeongsook Lee, Berlin • Andy Peters, Norfolk

Umschlaggestaltung
Klein und Halm, Berlin, unter Verwendung eines Fotos von Matthew Ford

Layoutkonzept
Christoph Schall

Layout und technische Umsetzung
Heike Freund, Berlin

Begleitende Tonträger zu diesem Band
Text-CDs zum Schülerbuch
ISBN 978-3-464-34430-9

www.cornelsen.de

1. Auflage, 3. Druck 2007 / 06

Alle Drucke dieser Auflage sind inhaltlich unverändert und können im Unterricht nebeneinander verwendet werden.

Druck: CS-Druck CornelsenStürtz, Berlin

ISBN 978-3-464-34429-3

Inhalt gedruckt auf säurefreiem Papier aus nachhaltiger Forstwirtschaft.

INHALT

[] 1. Vorkommen von Strukturen, die nur verstanden werden sollen (rezeptive Strukturen)

* wahlfreie Bestandteile des Lehrwerkes (fakultativ)

[] 1. Vorkommen von Strukturen, die nur verstanden werden sollen (rezeptive Strukturen)

* wahlfreie Bestandteile des Lehrwerkes (fakultativ)

5

five

ANHANG

Als Hörtext oder Song auf der CD vorhanden

1◉2 = CD 1, Track 2

▸ W 1 = Workbook, Übung 1 der Unit

● schwierige Aufgabe

Wiederholungsübungen

[] 1. Vorkommen von Strukturen, die nur verstanden werden sollen (rezeptive Strukturen)

* wahlfreie Bestandteile des Lehrwerkes (fakultativ)

Five teenagers

Three are British, ...

1 ⊙ 2

Hi, I'm Darris.
I live in London.
Do you live in a big city too?

Unit 1 London, England

Unit 2 Aberdare, Wales

I'm Katie.
I love sport.
Do you love sport too?

My name is Graham.
I have a new MP3 player.
Do you have an MP3 player too?

Unit 3 Edinburgh, Scotland

two are American, ...

Unit **4** Denver, Colorado

Hi! I'm Belle.
I like music and I play an instrument.
Do you play an instrument too?

Hi. I'm Gary.
My family goes camping.
Do you go camping too?

Unit **5** Detroit, Michigan

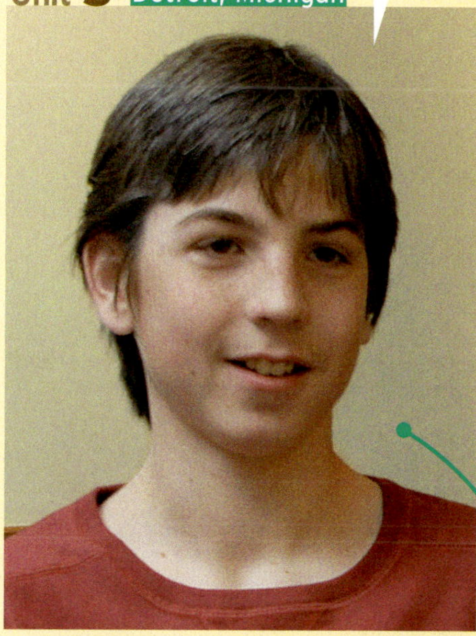

and they all speak English.

Unit 1

In London

Why are you in London?
1 ◉ 3

Lots of people visit London every year for business or on holiday.

Every day a million people travel from other towns to jobs in London.

People from all over the world study or learn English here.

London is the biggest city in Europe. More than 7 million people live here.

WE KNOW ...

- **what people do in towns:** They work. They ...

FAYE and DARRIS WESTON (13, 14) live in London.
1⊙4 This week their cousin Grace, from Manchester, is visiting them. She's with the family in the photo.

FAYE

Our house is in Brixton.
It's a very busy part of London.
Brixton has some problems: poor houses, a lot of traffic and some crime.
But the houses where we live are OK.

DARRIS

I'm proud to be a Londoner.
People from all over the world live here.
There are good shops and cool activities for teenagers in Brixton.
I'm mad about skateboarding.
You should see me!
We have students from lots of different backgrounds in our school.
My teacher says you can hear a hundred languages in Brixton.

GRACE

It's my first time in London.
I'm on holiday.
I think Brixton will be fun.
I'd like to see the sights of London.

ACTIVITY* – Radio interviews

You and a partner: Make an interview with Darris or Faye.

a) Here are some questions.

- Where do you live in London?
- Do you like Brixton?
- Do you have a flat or a house?
- What's your house like?
- What's Brixton like?
- Who lives in Brixton?

b) Make notes for Darris or Faye's answers.

- Brixton
- Brixton – great
-

c) Then act a radio interview.

Sights of London

Madame Tussaud's

A French woman started this waxworks museum over 200 years ago. You can see lots of famous people here.

Nelson's Column

Nelson was a famous admiral. The column is 51 metres high and this Nelson is 5 metres high!

The museums

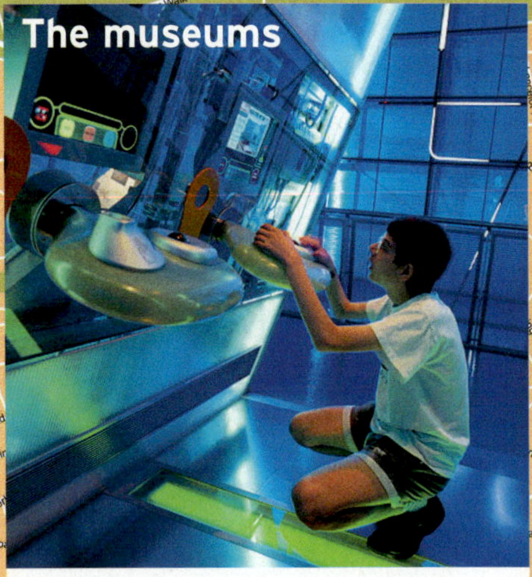

London has lots of great museums. Children like the Science Museum with its experiments and the dinosaurs in the Natural History Museum.

Buckingham Palace

This is the Queen's home in London.

Covent Garden

The old fruit and vegetable market has shops and cafés now. There are jugglers and dancers too.

The Tower of London

Parts of this old castle are about 1000 years old. You can see the Crown Jewels here.

The London Eye

This is a big wheel next to the river. You can see all over London. It's 135 metres high.

Tower Bridge

The River Thames has lots of bridges, but this is the most famous one.

Big Ben

The clock in the parliament building has a bell. Its name is Big Ben.

▸ W1, 2

A–C
1 6–8

A Grace's plans for sightseeing in London:

DARRIS You'll like London. It's the best city in Britain.
GRACE You Londoners! I like Manchester.
But I want to see the famous sights here.
I have a good guide book.
FAYE The sights are in central London.
We don't often go there.
But you and I will go there today.
DARRIS I always skateboard on Fridays.
I can come at the weekend.
And I can show you Brixton too.
GRACE Here's my list of sights for today.
FAYE Wow, that's a big list!
DARRIS It's a lot for one day.

Look at the River Thames.
Cross Tower Bridge.
Walk round the Tower.
Look at the Crown Jewels.
Visit a museum.
Visit Covent Garden.
Watch the jugglers and bands.
Visit Madame Tussaud's.
Visit Big Ben and Parliament.
Go to the London Eye.
See Buckingham Palace.

B

Later that day ...
The girls travelled by underground.
They travelled to central London.
They started at Tower Bridge and the Tower.
They visited a big museum with dinosaurs.
They stopped at Covent Garden for lunch.
Then they travelled home.
They enjoyed the day.
But London was so big.
And they were very tired ...

CHECKPOINT

Sagen, was in der Vergangenheit geschah (regelmäßige Verben):

I visit London every month.	Pat often walks to school.
I visit**ed** London last month.	She walk**ed** to school yesterday.

started (Wdh.)

Exercise 1: Grace and Faye had a busy day in London yesterday. What did they do?

Look at the River Thames. ✔	They looked at the River Thames.
Cross Tower Bridge. ✔	They crossed Tower Bridge.
Walk round the Tower. ✔	They walked ...
Look at the Crown Jewels. ✔	They ...
Visit a museum. ✔	They ...
Visit Covent Garden. ✔	They ...
Watch the jugglers and bands. ✔	They ...

C At breakfast on Saturday Grace told Mrs Weston about her day in London.

MRS WESTON What did you see yesterday?
GRACE We saw lots of things.
We saw the River Thames.
We saw Tower Bridge.
We saw the ...

Exercise 2: At Brixton library Grace wrote an email to her mum.
Setze die passenden Vergangenheitsformen für Grace ein.

Hi Mum,
London is cool! We ... a great day yesterday.
We ... the house in the morning.
Faye and I ... to central London.
I ... lots of photos of Tower Bridge.
We ... some dinosaurs – in a museum!
I ... a London T-shirt.
We ... lunch at Covent Garden.
We ... two German teenagers there.
Do you like my photo?
Love, Grace
PS More sightseeing today – with Darris.

→ bought
had (2x)
left
met
saw
took
went

AND YOU?

What things did you do yesterday?

In the morning	I	went to • bought	school. • my friends. • lunch.
In the afternoon		met • saw	a magazine. • a text message.
In the evening		sent • had	my homework. • my friend's house.
		wrote • did	a film. • an email. • ...

CHECKPOINT

Sagen, was in der Vergangenheit geschah (unregelmäßige Verben):

I take photos on every holiday.
I **took** a lot of photos last year.

Jack buys a magazine every week.
He **bought** a magazine yesterday.

▸ W 3, 4

saw (Wdh.)

D–E

1 9, 10

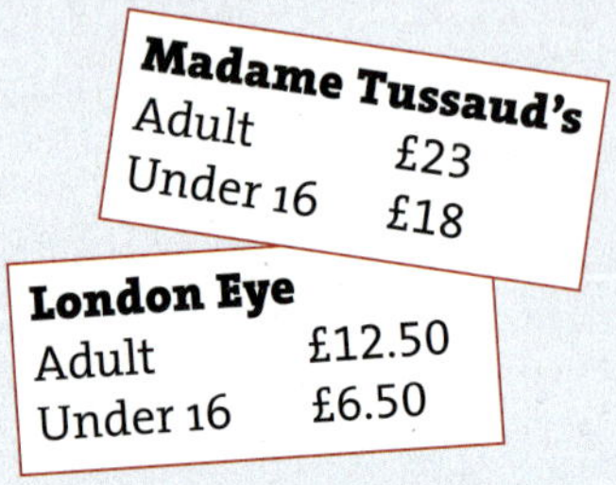

D Grace enjoyed the first day in London.
But the girls didn't see all the sights on her list.
They didn't have enough time because London is so big.
And they didn't have enough money.
– Some things in London are very expensive!

Exercise 3: Grace and Faye didn't do everything on the list.

- Visit Covent Garden. ✔
- Watch the jugglers and bands. ✔
- Visit Madame Tussaud's. ✘
- Visit Big Ben and Parliament. ✘
- Go to the London Eye. ✘
- See Buckingham Palace. ✘

1 They didn't go to all the places.

2 They ... go to Madame Tussaud's.

3 They ... to Big Ben.

4 ... to Parliament.

5 ... to the London Eye.

6 ... to Buckingham Palace.

CHECKPOINT

Sagen, was nicht geschah:

I **didn't go** to the cinema yesterday.
We **didn't have** a holiday last summer.
My brother **didn't like** the party yesterday.
You **didn't send** me an email yesterday!

Exercise 4: Make a report about Grace and Faye's day in London.

1 They (visited / didn't visit) central London.
2 They (travelled / didn't travel) by undergound.
3 They (went / didn't go) to the Tower.
4 They (saw / didn't see) some dinosaurs.
5 They (had / didn't have) lunch at Covent Garden.
6 They (went / didn't go) skateboarding.
7 They (bought / didn't buy) tickets for Madame Tussaud's.
8 They (saw / didn't see) all the sights on Grace's list.

AND YOU?

Your holidays:
What things did you do?
What things didn't you do?

I went to ...	I didn't go to ...	I met ...	I didn't meet ...
I visited ...	I didn't visit ...	I bought ...	I didn't buy ...
I watched ...	I didn't watch ...	I ...	I didn't ...
I played ...	I didn't play ...		

didn't see (Wdh.)

E

GRACE And what did you do yesterday, Darris?
DARRIS I had a terrific day.
I met my friends.
We went to the skateboard park.
FAYE Darris is always at the skateboard park.
DARRIS We can go there tomorrow, Grace.
It's fun.
But today you and I can do some sightseeing.
– And we'll see lots of London!
I have an idea ...

Exercise 5: What did Grace and Darris do in London on Saturday?

1 by – travelled – underground – They
2 walked – they – to – Then – the river
3 for – two tickets – bought – They – the London Eye
4 went – They – on – the – big wheel
5 all the – looked at – They – roads and buildings
6 some photos – took – Big Ben – They – of
7 saw – of – lots – They – London
8 didn't go – And – they – tired – home

POEM* – The economy flyer

1 ⊙ 11

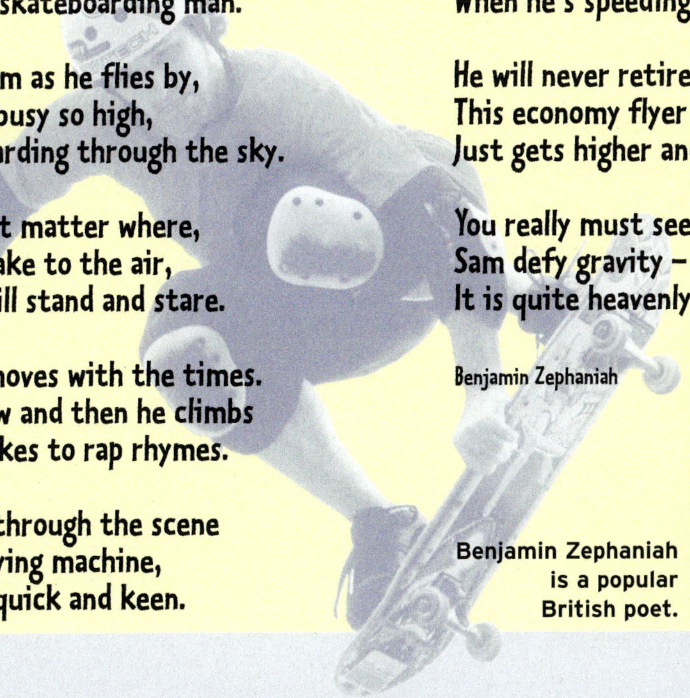

You will need a good plan
If you want to catch Sam –
He's the skateboarding man.

Watch him as he flies by,
Getting busy so high,
Skateboarding through the sky.

It doesn't matter where,
He will take to the air,
People will stand and stare.

Yes, he moves with the times.
Every now and then he climbs
And he likes to rap rhymes.

He flies through the scene
Like a flying machine,
He is so quick and keen.

He just cannot conceal
How exciting it feels
When he's speeding on wheels.

He will never retire –
This economy flyer
Just gets higher and higher.

You really must see
Sam defy gravity –
It is quite heavenly.

Benjamin Zephaniah

Benjamin Zephaniah is a popular British poet.

LISTENING – A famous Londoner

1 ◉ 12

Tipp:
Bevor du zuhörst, schau dir die Bilder an. Dadurch findest du heraus, worum es in der Geschichte geht.

1 Before you listen: Look at the four pictures. What do you think the story is about?

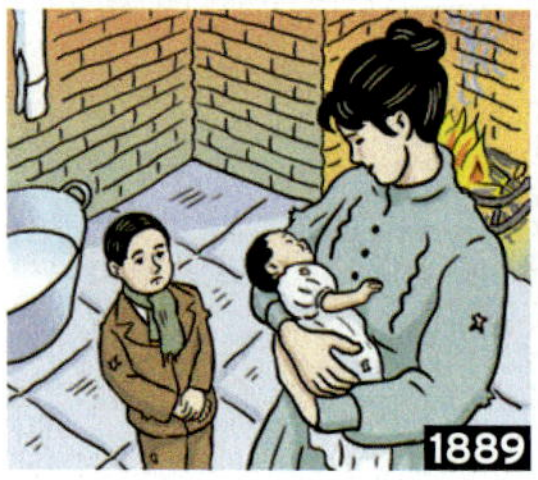

2 Listen to the story. Follow the story in the pictures. Look at the photos. Who's the famous Londoner?

Sherlock Holmes

Winston Churchill

Charlie Chaplin

Charles Dickens

3 Read these questions. Listen to the story again and write notes for the answers.

1 What year was the boy born?
2 Where was the boy's first job?
3 What country did the man go to?
4 Did he enjoy the journey on the ship?
5 He worked in a new industry. What was it?

▸ W 5, 6

READING – A brochure

Tipp:
Bevor du einen Text zum ersten Mal liest, lies die Überschriften. Sie verraten dir schon, worum es im Text geht.

Look at the brochure on page 17. Is it for tourists or Londoners?

1 Basic reading: Right or wrong?

1 The brochure is only about London.
2 It has information for people in cars.
3 It has tips about hotels in London.
4 It has tips about sightseeing.

2 Reading for details: What's right?

1 Taxis *are/aren't* cheaper than buses.
2 London taxis are usually *white/black.*
3 *Some/All* museums in London are free.
4 *Few/Lots of* people go to the London Eye.

3 Find the English sentences.

1 Besorge dir einen kostenlosen Plan.
2 Sei vorsichtig!
3 Essen in London kann teuer sein.
4 Du wirst 10% einsparen.

4 Language tasks

1 Find the English words: Fahrkarte, Stadtplan, Einbahnstraße, Reiseführer.
2 How can you go to places in London? Find five ways in the brochure: *by bus, ...*

▸ W 7

Tip: New words on page 17 are in the dictionary (page 118–136).

Tips – Some ideas for your visit

By bus

For most buses you buy your ticket before you get on. Or buy a travelcard and travel all day by underground or bus.

By tube

The tube (the Londoners' name for the underground) is the fast way to travel in London. It's big – 416 km long, with 275 stations. Get a free map. Most stations have them.

On foot

Be careful. Traffic is on the left, so look right first before you cross the road. But be very careful in one-way streets – there are lots in London.

By taxi

Taxis are more expensive than buses. But taxi drivers are London experts – they know every road. London taxis are usually black.

Saving money

London has lots of great museums. Some of the biggest and most interesting ones are free. (More than a hundred!) Check in a guide book first.

Sightseeing tours

You can go by bus, of course. But you shouldn't forget the river. By boat you can see lots of interesting places: Parliament, the MI6 building (home of James Bond) and the famous bridges.

Food

Eating in London can be expensive. For lunch, buy sandwiches in a supermarket or a small shop. Lots of people eat their sandwiches in London's big parks.

The London Eye

A fantastic way to see London from the air. It's 135 m high! But it's popular, so you often have to wait a long time. Tip: You can book online. (You'll save 10 %.) Or book by phone.

The Queen

How do you know when the Queen is at home in Buckingham Palace? Look for her special flag above the building.

Travelcard – *Your friend in London*

- *For underground and bus*
- *One or three days*
- *Buy one at a tube station*

Transport for London

ACTIONS – At a tourist office

1 13

What does Julia want?

JULIA Hello. I want to go to the zoo. When's it open, please?
WOMAN It's open from 10 a.m. till 5.30 p.m. today.
JULIA Can I have a brochure, please?
WOMAN Yes, of course. Here you are.

How can Julia get to London Zoo?

JULIA How can I get to the zoo, please?
WOMAN You can go by underground or bus.
JULIA What number bus goes there?
WOMAN You need the number 274.
JULIA Thanks for your help. Bye.

1 Look again.

1 Wie fragst du nach den Öffnungszeiten?
2 Wie bittest du um einen Prospekt?
3 Wie kannst du dich nach dem Weg zum Zoo erkundigen?
4 Wie fragst du nach einer Buslinie?

2 At a London tourist office: Find the answers for tourists' questions.

1 When's the London Eye open?
2 What number bus goes to the London Eye?
3 How much is a ticket at Madame Tussaud's?
4 How can I get to the waxworks?
5 What's the tube station for the waxworks?
6 Do you have a brochure about the zoo?
7 I'd like *Time Out* magazine. How much is it?

- Here you are. It costs £2.50.
- Of course. Here you are.
- A ticket costs £23.
- Baker Street is the nearest station.
- You can go by underground or bus.
- You need the number 13 or 18.
- It's open from 9.30 a.m. to 10 p.m. today.

SPEAKING

1 14

1 Intonation: Listen and say

1 I want to go to the zoo. I want to go to ...

→ the waxworks. • the Museum of London. • the Tower of London. • the London Eye.

2 Can I have a brochure, please? Can I have a ..., please?

→ map • ticket • badge • guide book • postcard • sticker

2 Make dialogues at a tourist office. Get information about places.

YOU Can you help me, please? I want to go to ...
When's it open, please?
A PARTNER It's open from ... till ...
YOU Is it open every day?
A PARTNER Yes, it is.
YOU Do you have a brochure, please?
A PARTNER Yes, of course. Here you are.
YOU Thank you.

OPENING TIMES	
The Museum of London	10 a.m. – 5.50 p.m.
London Zoo	10 a.m. – 5.30 p.m.
The British Museum	10 a.m. – 6 p.m.
Windsor Castle	10 a.m. – 5.30 p.m.
The Tower	9 a.m. – 5 p.m.

3 Make dialogues at a tourist office. Then act the dialogues for your class.

Transport for London

	Underground station	Bus number
London Zoo	*Camden Town*	274
Wimbledon	*Southfields*	493
Big Ben	*Westminster*	24
The Science Museum	*South Kensington*	9 or 10

Erkundige dich nach dem Weg.
How can I get to ..., please?

Sage, man kann mit der U-Bahn oder dem Bus fahren.
You can go by ...

Frage nach der U-Bahn-Station.
What's the nearest station?

Nenne die U-Bahn-Station.
The nearest station is ...

Frage nach der Buslinie.
What number bus goes there?

Sage, welche Buslinie man braucht.
You need the number ...

▸ W 8, 9

WORDPOWER

1 Find the nine simple past forms.

present	past
write	drove
drive	lay
say	left
lie	ran
leave	said
think	saw
go	thought
run	went
see	wrote

2 When? Find the past phrases.

Finde die Ausdrücke, die sagen, wann etwas geschehen ist.

Example: last year

I started skateboarding last year.
I got my skateboard last summer.
I met a new skateboarder last week.
Sam came to Brixton a month ago.
He started skateboarding two years ago.
I saw him at the park yesterday.
We tried some new tricks yesterday afternoon.
I did them last night too. They're great!

3 Make a sign with ten things for a souvenir stall in London.

Achtung: Auf diesem Schild haben sich auch andere Dinge eingeschlichen!

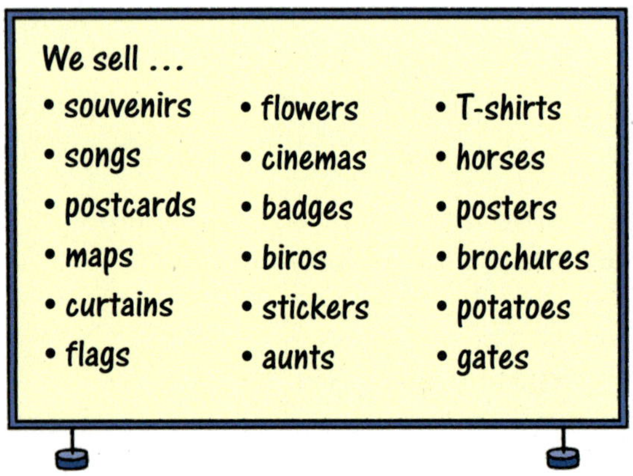

• **4 That isn't right! One word is wrong. What's the right word?**

1 Londoners call the underground the tool.
2 Tourists want to see all the famous sides in London.
3 It isn't fair from Big Ben to the river.
4 They have lots of fruit and villages at Brixton market.
5 People from all over the wood live in Brixton.
6 Brixton isn't boring – it's very interested.

► W 10–12

SITUATIONS

Wie kannst du auf Englisch ...

1 ... sagen, dass du im Urlaub bist?
2 ... fragen, was jemand gestern sah?
3 ... fragen, was jemand gestern getan hat?
4 ... jemanden um Hilfe bitten?

Tip: Look again at pages 8–19.

SOUNDS

Anhand der Lautschrift kannst du erkennen, wie ein englisches Wort ausgesprochen wird.
Eine Übersicht der Zeichen findest du auf Seite 137 unter **Sounds**.
Manche Zeichen sehen wie vertraute Buchstaben aus, andere sind besondere Zeichen.

1 Nenne je zwei englische Wörter, die mit diesen Lauten anfangen.

1 [b] *book, ...* **2** [k] *car, ...* **3** [j] *yellow, ...* **4** [v] **5** [p] **6** [s]

1 15

2 Zischen [s] oder Summen [z]?
Was trifft zu?

1 zoo, Sue, six, zero, sit, Sam, sign
2 yes, his, this; cars, cats, days, rooms, clocks; makes, rides, comes, runs, brings, looks

WORKING WITH A DICTIONARY

Wenn du in einem Wörterbuch die Vergangenheitsform eines Verbs nachschlägst, wird meist auf die Grundform *(infinitive)* verwiesen:

Beispiele: went → **go** saw → **see** caught → **catch** left → **leave**

1 What's the infinitive? Check in a dictionary. What are the verbs in German?
Wie lautet der Infinitiv? Überprüfe deine Lösung im Wörterbuch. Was bedeuten die Verben?

1 knew – *know (kennen)* **3** stood **5** wore **7** slept
2 made – **4** shone **6** told **8** thought

LEARNING SKILLS

Wie kannst du Vokabeln wiederholen? Ein guter Tipp: Lerne Wörter in Gruppen.
Ordne die Wörter nach Themen – zum Beispiel mithilfe eines Wortnetzes *(word web)*.

1 Copy this word web and put in more words.
Zeichne das Wortnetz ab und ergänze weitere Wörter.

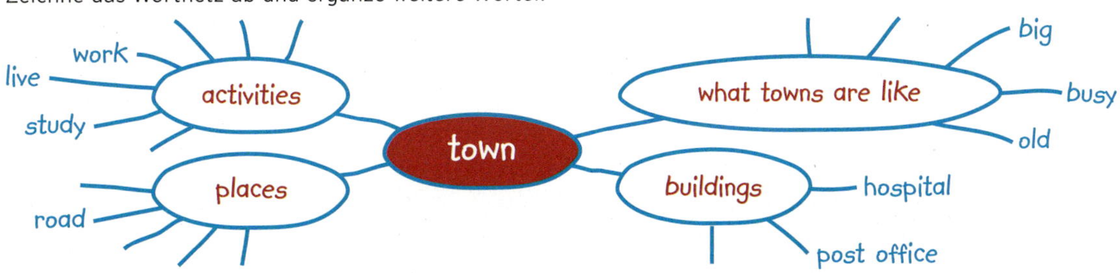

2 Make a word web. Here are some ideas.

→ home • school • free time • time • ...

STRUCTURES

1 Faye's class visited London Zoo last week. What happened on the visit?

Look at their programme.

1 They travelled by tube to ...
2 They ...
3 ...

1 Travel by tube to Camden Town.
2 Finish the journey by boat.
3 Learn about animals and birds.
4 Watch a video about sea animals.
5 Answer questions in a quiz.
6 Visit the zoo shop.

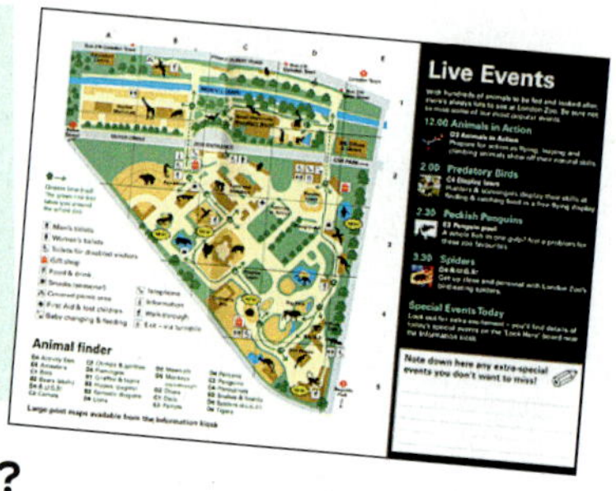

• 2 After the trip to the zoo: What did Mrs Weston ask Faye?

Stelle Fragen über Fayes Besuch in der letzten Woche.
Dabei musst du meist auch ein passendes Fragewort verwenden.

Tipp:
Lies die Antworten. Sie helfen dir bei der Auswahl des Fragewortes.

1 How much did the zoo cost? – £5.
2 How long ... you stay there? – Three hours.
3 ... you travel there? – By tube and boat.
4 ... you go? – At 10 o'clock.
5 ... you do first? – We saw the birds.
6 ... you buy that T-shirt? – In the shop.
7 ... you enjoy the trip to the zoo? – Yes, I did.
8 ... you see nice animals? – Yes, we did. And some terrible ones!

3 The Patel family had a day in central London.

a) Look at their souvenirs and answer the questions about their day.

→ Yes, they did. • No, they didn't.

1 Did they go to Tower Bridge?
2 Did they visit the Tower of London?
3 Did they ride on the London Eye?
4 Did they go to Madame Tussaud's?
5 Did they buy a book about London?
6 Did they go to the zoo?
7 Did they get a postcard of Big Ben?
8 Did they visit Buckingham Palace?

b) Where did the Patels go in London? Where didn't they go? Make two lists.

→ Tower Bridge • Madame Tussaud's • a museum • Covent Garden • the London Eye
the river • Buckingham Palace • Big Ben • Brixton • London Zoo

They went to *Tower Bridge*.
They went to ...

They didn't go to *a museum*.
They didn't go to ...

► W 13, 14

• **4 Find the right verb forms for the newspaper report: simple past or simple present.**

Tipp:
Schau dir die Zeitangaben genau an. Der Checkpoint hilft dir auch.

London carnival – a summer hit!

Thousands in Notting Hill streets again

Last weekend it (is/was) the Notting Hill carnival again. It first (starts/started) in 1964. But then, only a few people (go/went) to it. Now the carnival (is/was) Europe's biggest street party.

In the past most of the people (are/were) Londoners from Trinidad. Now the carnival (is/was) popular with all Londoners – black and white.
In 2004 more than a million people (enjoy/enjoyed) the carnival.

The carnival (happens/ happened) two days every August. It (is/was) always very noisy. Every year people (write/wrote) special songs and music for it.

Last weekend there (are/were) hundreds of stalls with food and souvenirs. Last Sunday (is/was) children's day. And last week the weather (is/was) sunny and everybody (has/had) a great day.

CHECKPOINT

Typische Zeitangaben:
simple present: now, always, often, every week, every weekend — I **go** to school every day.
simple past: yesterday, last year, last weekend, in 1999 — I **went** to school yesterday.

5 Faye Weston is talking about her family. Put in the right pronouns.

1 We live in Brixton. ... house is OK.
2 But our neighbours have a dog. ... dog is noisy.
3 My mum works in a hospital now. It's ... new job.
4 My dad drives underground trains. He likes ... job.
5 Brixton is OK. I like it. ... shops and markets are good.
6 Darris and I go to a youth club. We like ... club.
7 And you? What's ... town like?

CHECKPOINT

Besitzanzeigende Pronomen:
This is **my** dog.
Where's **your** bike?
Tom is with **his** dad.
Pat is with **her** friend.
The dog wants **its** ball.
Here's **our** house.
Are they **your** friends?
The cats want **their** food.

▸ W 15

• **6 Information about London: Can you put the sentences together?**

1 Tourists come to London	because it has so many sights.
2 Not many tourists visit Brixton	but now it has shops and cafés.
3 London has an underground	so that they can go skateboarding.
4 7 million people live in London	and a million more people work there.
5 Covent Garden was a market	because it has cheap food markets.
6 People like Brixton	because it doesn't have many famous sights.
7 Teenagers visit Stockwell Skate Park	and it has 275 stations.

simple past (Wiederholung)

Die *simple past*-Form kennst du schon.
Damit sagst du, was in der Vergangenheit geschah.

Aussagen

- **Regelmäßige Verben** enden auf *-ed*:

clean → clean**ed**
watch → watch**ed**
visit → visit**ed**

At the weekend we **visited** my grandma.
We **travelled** to the seaside on Sunday.
I **stayed** at home at the weekend.

I played football yesterday. Ich spielte gestern Fußball. / Ich habe gestern Fußball gespielt.
The train arrived late. Der Zug kam zu spät an. / Der Zug ist zu spät angekommen.

- **Unregelmäßige Verben** haben besondere Vergangenheitsformen:

see → **saw**
write → **wrote**
come → **came**

Tipp: Weitere Beispiele findest du auf S. 159.

We **were** in Munich for our holidays.
We **went** to the USA.
I **had** a holiday in Scotland.

Mr Hill went to the cinema. Herr Hill ging ins Kino. / Herr Hill ist ins Kino gegangen.
I saw Sue last week. Ich sah Sue letzte Woche. / Ich habe Sue letzte Woche gesehen.

Verneinung

- Mit *didn't* sagst du, was nicht geschah:

I was ill last week.
I **didn't go** to school.
I **didn't see** my friends.
I **didn't ride** my bike.

We didn't visit the zoo. Wir besuchten nicht den Zoo. / Wir haben den Zoo nicht besucht.
She didn't repair the car. Sie reparierte nicht das Auto. / Sie hat das Auto nicht repariert.

Fragen

- Fragen stellst du mit *did*:

Did you eat a hamburger yesterday? Hast du gestern einen Hamburger gegessen?
Did you work in the garden yesterday? Habt ihr gestern im Garten gearbeitet?

Gebrauch

- Mit der *simple past*-Form kannst du ausdrücken, was in der Vergangenheit zu einem bestimmten Zeitpunkt geschehen ist.
- Oft wird *simple past* in Berichten und Erzählungen verwendet.

Häufig findest du Wörter oder Wortgruppen mit Zeitangaben in der Vergangenheit dabei:

yesterday • last week • last month • last year • last summer • a year ago • in 2004

IN DIESER UNIT HAST DU GELERNT, WIE ...

... du im Fremdenverkehrsamt um Informationen bittest. ▸ *How can I get to the zoo, please?*
What's the nearest station?
What number bus goes there?
Can I have a brochure, please?

... nach Öffnungszeiten fragst. ▸ *When's the zoo open, please?*

DU HAST WIEDERHOLT, WIE ...

... du über Vergangenes sprichst. ▸ *I walked to the shops.*
I bought an ice cream.
We didn't go to Big Ben yesterday.
Did you go?

... du sagst, wem etwas gehört. ▸ *This is my dog. Their dog is noisy.*

DU KANNST AUCH VERSTEHEN, WIE ...

... gesagt wird, was jemand (nicht) tun soll. ▸ *You should see me!*
But you shouldn't forget the river.

▸ W Test yourself 1–3

A weekend in London: Saturday

1 16

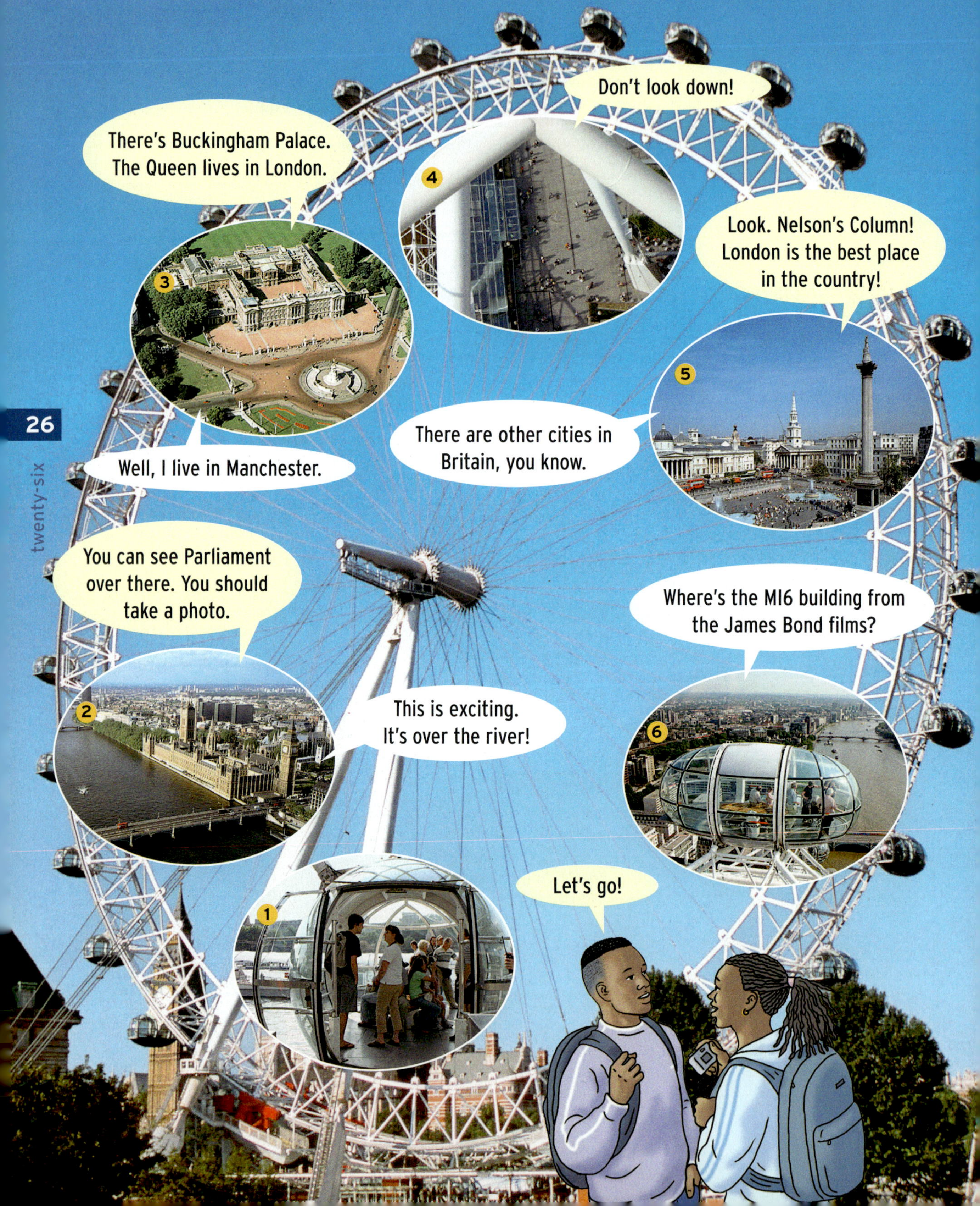

What activities can Grace and Darris do in Brixton?

A weekend in London: Sunday

1 17

Next day Grace and Darris stayed in Brixton. Their day began at Brixton library ...

"We can surf the Internet here. I'll show you a good website about activities: *Brixton for Cool Kids,*" Darris said. "Hey, Stockwell Skate Park looks cool," said Grace and clicked on it. There were terrific photos and a webcam.

They went back to the *Cool Kids* website. For the evening they found a teenage dance party at a church youth club. "We should go there. We have good clubs in Brixton," Darris said.

Darris and Grace walked to the park. Lots of boys liked the skate park, but not many girls went there. "We're great at skateboarding in Brixton. I hope you won't find it too difficult," Darris said. Grace said nothing. Grace took out her MP3 player.

But Darris said, "That isn't a good idea in this part of Brixton. You shouldn't do that! Somebody stole my mate's player near here."
"Is it so dangerous in Brixton?"
"Not really, but you should be careful. Be careful with your mobile too."

At Stockwell Park Darris showed Grace his best tricks. Grace watched. Then she stood on her board. Darris was surprised. She was terrific! "We have skateboarding in Manchester too," she laughed.

In the evening Grace and Darris went to the church youth club. First they bought a cola, sat down and listened. It was really great music – reggae, garage and hip hop.

"I know you can skate, but can you dance?" Darris shouted over the music.
Grace smiled. "OK, I'll show you how we dance in Manchester."

It was dark when Grace and Darris left the club. Lots of teenagers stood together and talked. Some looked at Darris and Grace. They said something.

Darris and Grace didn't answer. A boy shouted, "Hey, girl, come and talk to us!" Grace was frightened. Grace and Darris didn't wait. "Don't stop," Darris said.

They walked faster. But some boys ran after them. "You aren't very friendly," one said. "We want a word with you."
It was too late. The boys stood round them.

One boy took something out of his pocket. "We saw you at the skate park today," he told Grace. "You're a good boarder."
He gave her a leaflet. "There's a skateboarding competition next month."
"Cool," Grace said. "But ..."
"My cousin lives in Manchester," Darris said.

"Manchester! That's a pity," the boy said.
"They're great boarders in Manchester," Darris said. "There are other cities in Britain, you know. And I'm sure she'll come back."

▸ W 16–18

Unit 2

A good time

The Evans family is planning a day out.

1 18

WE KNOW ...

- **what people buy in shops:** They buy clothes. They ...
- **the names of some sports.**

KATIE EVANS (13) lives with her family in
1 19 South Wales. They live in Aberdare.
It's a small town in a valley near Cardiff.
The valleys near Cardiff were famous for their coal. But that industry finished.
A lot of people had no jobs.
Now there are new factories and offices.
Mrs Evans works in a call centre.
Mr Evans has a job at a TV factory.

KATIE

We're all crazy about sport in our family.
I like outdoor sports.
I have a mountain bike, and I ride it in the Welsh mountains.

My brother plays rugby.
Rugby is the Welsh national sport.
Dad often watches rugby on TV with him.
But we all sometimes go to watch Wales at the big Millennium Stadium in Cardiff.
Sport is good fun, isn't it?

▸ W1

PRESENTATION

A–C
1 20–22

A Katie is very excited.
Her class will be at a Welsh activity centre all next week.
It's in Pembroke.
She searched on the Internet and found its website.

▶ Home ▶ Schools ▶ Brochure ▶ Book ▶ Jobs ▶ Contact us

PC PEMBROKE CENTRE PC

The Activity Centre on the South Wales coast.

You're never bored at PC!

What sports do we do here? We ...

... sail. ... canoe. ... hike. ... mountain bike.

... abseil. ... play football. ... ride. ... climb.

What other things do we do? We ...

... dance. ... sing. ... make bubbles. ... make films. ... make music.

Ideal for school groups (Year 7 – 11)

Exercise 1: You can do lots of activities at PC.

a) What sports can you do?
You can sail. You can ...

b) What other activities can you do?
You can ...

▸ W 2

B The next day Katie is telling her friend about the Pembroke Centre website.

MEGAN What activities do they have?
KATIE There are lots of activities. They have sailing. They have …

sailing

canoeing

hiking

mountain biking

abseiling

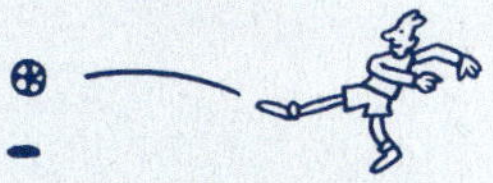
playing football

riding

climbing

AND YOU?

What do you think about the sports?

I think	sailing canoeing hiking …	is	good. boring. difficult. cool. terrible. dangerous.

▸ W 3

C

KATIE They're great activities, aren't they? I love playing sport.
MEGAN Ugh! I'm not so sure. I don't like playing sport. You know that.
KATIE Playing sport is fun! But they have other activities too.
MEGAN What other activities do they have? Is taking photos an activity at the centre?
KATIE No, it isn't. Sorry.

Exercise 2: What other activities do they have at PC? Look at page 32.
They have dancing. They have singing. They have making …

Exercise 3: You and a partner: Talk about other activities at PC.

YOU Is	camping • looking after pets making music • painting • reading singing • swimming • taking photos • …	an activity at the centre?	

A PARTNER Yes, it is. / No, it isn't.

AND YOU?

What activities would you like to try?
I'd like to try sailing/… • I wouldn't like to try sailing/…

▸ W 4

CHECKPOINT

Mit dieser *ing*-Form des Verbs kannst du über Aktivitäten oder Hobbys sprechen:

Swimming is fun.	**Playing football** is popular.	I love **sailing**.
Schwimmen macht Spaß.	Fußballspielen ist beliebt.	Ich liebe Segeln.

They have sailing. Playing sport is fun!

D–E
1 23, 24

D Katie is at the activity centre with her class. It's the first half of the week. There are some pupils from Brixton at the centre too.

KATIE What did you do today?
DARRIS We did abseiling. And you?
KATIE I did water sports – canoeing and sailing.
JAKE Abseiling is better than water sports. It's more exciting, isn't it?
MEGAN You mean it's more dangerous! I tried riding today. Riding was fun.
DARRIS Riding horses is always popular with girls.
KATIE I don't agree. Boys like riding too.
MEGAN Well, it's more interesting than abseiling down a cliff.

Exercise 4: Girls' activities and boys' activities: What do you think? Talk to a partner.

YOU I think	riding cooking playing football reading magazines listening to boy bands swimming playing sport playing computer games	is popular with boys and girls. is more popular with boys. is more popular with girls.

A PARTNER I agree. / I don't agree. I think ...

Exercise 5: What do you think about the activities at the centre?

abseiling • canoeing • climbing
dancing • hiking • making bubbles
making cards • making films
making music • playing football
mountain biking • riding • sailing
singing

I think ... is	nicer better easier cooler more dangerous more interesting more difficult more exciting more boring	than ...

CHECKPOINT

Die Steigerungsform bei einigen mehrsilbigen Adjektiven bildest du mit *more* ...:
Abseiling is **more dangerous** than swimming.
The DVD is **more expensive** than the CD.
TV is **more popular** than homework.
This DVD is **more exciting** than that DVD.

▸ W 5

more exciting

E

DARRIS
Abseiling down the cliffs is the most exciting activity here. And you see beautiful beaches. Wales has the most beautiful beaches in Britain.

KATIE
Sailing, mountain biking and canoeing are the best activities for me. The most difficult activity is sailing.

JAKE
I was really bad at abseiling. It was the most difficult activity for me. Playing football is fun. Making films is the most interesting activity.

MEGAN
I go riding every day here. We went to the beaches on the most interesting day. Football is the most boring thing here.

Exercise 6: What do the teenagers think about the activities at the centre?

→ most beautiful • most boring • most difficult (2x) • most exciting • most interesting

1. Darris thinks abseiling is the ... activity.
2. He says Wales has the ... British beaches.
3. Katie thinks sailing is the ... activity.
4. Jake says abseiling is the ... activity.
5. Making films is the ... activity.
6. Megan thinks football is the ... activity.

CHECKPOINT

Beachte die Steigerungsform bei einigen mehrsilbigen Adjektiven mit *most* ...:
What's the **most dangerous** road in your town?
This is the band's **most popular** song.
This is the **most expensive** bike in the shop.
Which is the **most exciting** DVD?

SONG* – Sailing

1 ◉ 25

1 I am sailing, I am sailing
Home again 'cross the sea.
I am sailing stormy waters
To be near you, to be free.

2 I am flying, I am flying
Like a bird 'cross the sky.
I am flying, passing high clouds,
To be with you, to be free.

3 Can you hear me, can you hear me
Through the dark night far away?
I am dying, forever crying,
To be with you, who can say. (2x)

4 We are sailing, we are sailing
Home again 'cross the sea.
We are sailing stormy waters
To be near you, to be free.

most beautiful

LISTENING – Phoning home

1 ◉ 26

Tipp: Schon der Titel verrät dir, worum es im Hörtext geht.

1 Before you listen: Look at the title.

1 What's Katie doing?
2 They talk about a *swimsuit* in the dialogue. What do you think it is in German?

2 Read the two questions. Then listen to the dialogue and answer them.

1 Who's talking? **a)** Katie and Megan. **b)** Katie and her mum.
2 Where's Katie now? **a)** At a post office. **b)** At an activity centre.

3 Can you find the right pictures? Read the sentences. Listen to the dialogue again.

1 Mrs Evans is here.
2 Katie forgot this.
3 The other school comes from here.
4 One of Katie's activities.
5 Mrs Evans must look in this.
6 Mrs Evans would like this.

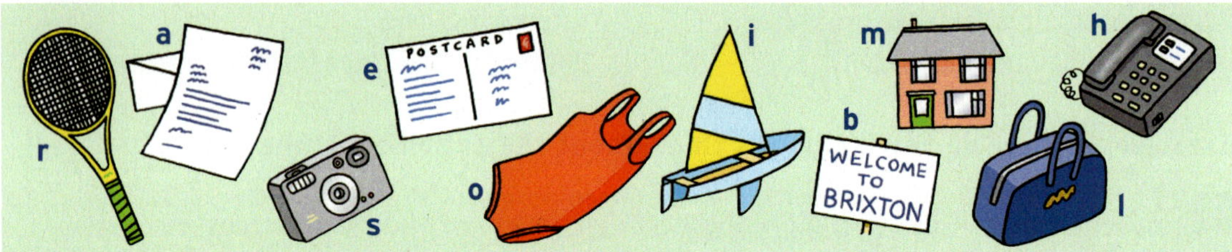

The six letters of the pictures make a word for an important thing in the dialogue. What's the word?

► W 6, 7

READING – From a magazine

Look at page 37. Is it a test for teachers or teenagers?

Tipp: Ein erster Blick sagt dir oft, worum es sich bei einem Lesetext im Allgemeinen handelt.

1 Basic reading

1 How many questions does the quiz have: four, eight or ten?
2 Is the quiz about school, free time or food?

2 Reading for details

1 Which question is about video games?
2 Find a word in the quiz for: a boy or girl between 13 and 19; an activity in the water; CD.

3 Find the English sentences.

1 Was möchtest du zum Geburtstag?
2 Ich bin Experte/Expertin.
3 Was ist deine Meinung?
4 Ich sehe keine Serien im Fernsehen.

4 Language tasks

1 Find the English words: Gutschein, an der Spitze, Meinung, Reifenpanne.
2 Find four adjectives in the quiz with *-est*, and four adjectives with *most* …
3 Find opposites for these words in the quiz: cloudy, cheapest, boring.

► W 8

Tip: New words on page 37 are in the dictionary (page 118–136).

teen! mag

Just for fun

Personality test

What kind of a teenager are you?

List your answers (A – D) to our eight questions.

1 What's your ideal activity for a sunny summer evening?
- **A** Watching an exciting film.
- **B** Meeting friends at the park.
- **C** Swimming.
- **D** Shopping for the best summer clothes.

2 What would you like for your birthday?
- **A** A games console.
- **B** Tickets for you and a friend for your favourite football team.
- **C** A season ticket for a swimming pool.
- **D** A voucher for the coolest clothes shop in town.

3 Which do you think is most important?
- **A** Having the most expensive electronic gadgets.
- **B** Having fun with good friends.
- **C** Being good at sports.
- **D** Looking good in the latest fashions.

4 Do you know the album at the top of the music charts this week?
- **A** Yes. I bought it last week.
- **B** No, but my friends will know.
- **C** I'm too busy with sports activities.
- **D** I always know the most popular songs.

5 How good are you at your favourite video game?
- **A** I'm an expert.
- **B** Not very. My friends are better.
- **C** I only play sports, not video games.
- **D** Not good. But I play the newest ones.

6 What's your opinion? Which is the best for you?
- **A** Watching TV is my favourite activity.
- **B** Watching TV with friends is often fun.
- **C** Watching TV is more boring than playing sport.
- **D** I only like the latest cool programmes for teenagers.

7 What's truest for you?
- **A** I never miss the most interesting soaps on the box.
- **B** My friends like soaps more than I do.
- **C** I don't watch TV soaps.
- **D** You need to know what happens in the most popular TV soaps.

8 Your bike has a puncture. What will you do?
- **A** I don't ride a bike.
- **B** Ask a friend to repair it for me.
- **C** Repair it because I often need my bike.
- **D** Forget it – a bike isn't very cool.

teen! mag 89

Check your answers on page 160.

ACTIONS – At a B&B or a youth hostel

1 27

At a B&B (Bed and Breakfast):
How many nights will Tom stay?

TOM Do you have a room free, please?
WOMAN Yes, we do. It's for one night, isn't it?
TOM Yes. I'd like one night, please. How much is the room, please?
WOMAN It's £34 a night. That's with full English breakfast.
TOM Can I see the room, please? Is it quiet?
WOMAN Of course. Come with me, please.

At a youth hostel:
What meal would the girls like?

TINA Hello, we have a booking for tonight. We booked two beds online.
MAN Can I have your youth hostel cards, please?
TINA Here you are.
MAN Thanks. Would you like an evening meal and breakfast?
TINA We'd like breakfast, please. What time will breakfast be?

1 Look again.

1 Wie fragst du nach einem Zimmer?
2 Wie fragst du nach dem Zimmerpreis?
3 Wie sagst du, dass ihr eine Reservierung für heute Nacht habt?
4 Wie fragst du nach der Frühstückszeit?

2 What are these people saying at a youth hostel?

beds • booking • cards • meal • night • phone

1 Can we eat? Do you have an evening ...?
2 We phoned earlier and have a ...
3 We'd like to stay for one ...
4 Here are our youth hostel ...
5 Does the hostel have a ..., please?
6 Do you have two ... for tonight?

3 Ask for these things at the youth hostel shop with *I'd like a ..., please.*

1

2

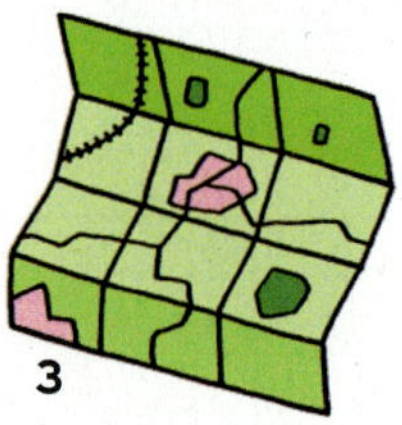
3

4

5

► W 9, 10

SPEAKING

1 28

1 Intonation: Listen and say

1 Can I see the room, please? Can I ..., please?

→ have a key • buy a postcard • use the phone • have breakfast • put my bike here

2 Would you like an evening meal? Would you like ...?

→ a map • a snack • a brochure • a room • a room with a TV • a meal

2 You and a partner: Make dialogues at a youth hostel.

- Can I | stay at this youth hostel, / book a bed for tonight, / have an evening meal, / buy a map/postcard/..., | please?
- How much does it cost?
- Do you have information about the town/village/museum/..., please?

- Yes, of course. / Sorry.
  Do you have your card, please? / We have no beds tonight.
  The meal is at ... o'clock.
  The maps/... are over there. / We don't have maps/...
- It costs £ ...
- Yes, of course. Here you are. / There are some brochures over there.

▸ W 11

• 3 Make a dialogue at a B&B.

Begrüße den Gast.

⇩

Erwidere die Begrüßung. Frage, ob ein Zimmer frei ist.

⇩

Sage ja. Du hast ein ruhiges Zimmer.

⇩

Frage, wie teuer das Zimmer ist.

⇩

Nenne einen Preis.

Sage, das ist OK. | Sage, das ist zu teuer. Verabschiede dich.

PRACTICE AND REVISION

WORDPOWER

1 Favourite things: What are Anne's questions and Emily's answers?

ANNE

What's your favourite

hobby?
colour?
book?
magazine?
sport?
drink?

EMILY

– I like painting best.
– I like ... best.

AND YOU?

My favourite hobby is ...

2 What are the *-ing* forms of the verbs? Careful with the spellings!

Achte auf die Schreibweise!

a) ride, skate, write, hike, dance, take

b) swim, travel, run, stop, sit, win

ride → **riding**
skate → ...

swim → **swimming**
travel → ...

3 Find the sports activities.

a) Make a list of them.

b) Find two more sports activities.

4 Terrible jokes: And one word is missing!

In jedem Witz fehlt ein Wort: Aber welches?

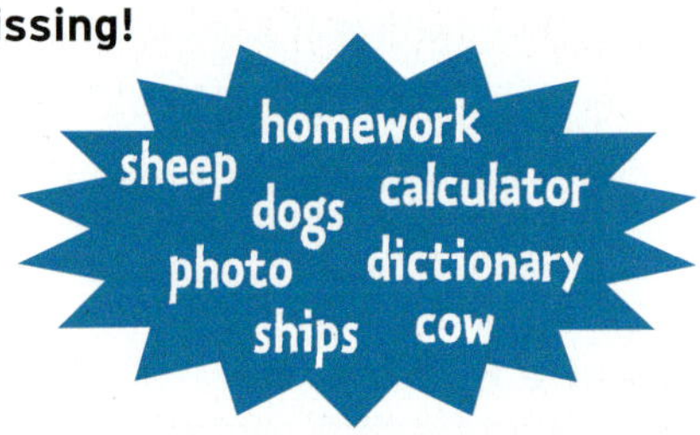

1 In a shop: Buy this ... today. It'll do half of your work for you. – Good. I'll take two!
2 Where does an American ... live? – Moo York!
3 What do sea monsters eat? – Fish and ...!
4 When does August come before February? – In the ...!
5 What looks like a cat, but isn't a cat? – A ... of a cat!
6 Your teacher was angry because you didn't do something? – Yes, my ...!
7 What meals do cats hate? – Hot ...!
8 Doctor, doctor, I think I'm a ...! – That's baaaaaad!

► W 12, 13

SITUATIONS

Wie kannst du auf Englisch ...

1 ... sagen, dass du gern Sport treibst?
2 ... sagen, dass du nicht so sicher bist?
3 ... sagen, dass Schwimmen Spaß macht?
4 ... fragen, ob ein Zimmer frei ist?
5 ... fragen, ob du dir das Zimmer ansehen darfst?
6 ... sagen, dass ihr Frühstück möchtet?

Tip: Look again at pages 30–39.

► W 14

SOUNDS

Wörter, die unterschiedlich geschrieben werden, können ähnlich klingen.

Beispiele: **hear** [hɪə] = hören **half** [hɑːf] = halb
here [hɪə] = hier **laugh** [lɑːf] = lachen

1◉ 29

1 Welches Wort reimt sich nicht mit den anderen?

1 [uː] you, do, zoo, through, love, blue
2 [ʊ] good, should, wood, could, food
3 [eɪ] date, great, eight, sight, wait, hate
4 [iː] key, we, me, see, sea, tea, idea

2 Suche zu jedem Wort einen Partner, der sich damit reimt.

1 near – ...
2 late – ...
3 opposite – ...
4 bread – ...
5 ways – ...
6 know – ...

eight • maize • said • no • sit • here

WORKING WITH A DICTIONARY

Viele Wörter können mehr als eine Bedeutung haben. So findest du oft mehrere Möglichkeiten im Wörterbuch. Die Bedeutung eines Wortes hängt vom Zusammenhang ab.

1 Welche Bedeutungen haben diese Wörter im *Dictionary* (S. 118)? Schlage nach.

1 book 2 ride 3 light 4 ticket 5 student 6 holiday

2 Was bedeutet das farbig hervorgehobene Wort?

1 Let's **book** a holiday.
2 Can you **ride** a horse?
3 Will it be **light** at 6 a.m.?
4 I must buy a **ticket** at the cinema.
5 **Students** in year 8 are 13 years old.
6 Christmas Day is always a **holiday**.

LEARNING SKILLS

Auch durch ein Gedächtnisspiel kannst du Wörter lernen. Schreibe Wortpaare auf kleine Karten (1. Karte: englisches Wort; 2. Karte: deutsche Übersetzung). Lege alle Wortkarten verdeckt auf den Tisch. Nacheinander werden immer zwei Karten umgedreht. Jedes richtig gefundene Wortpaar wird entfernt, bis keine Karten mehr übrig bleiben.

1 Stelle dir ein Gedächtnisspiel mit zehn neuen Wörtern aus Unit 2 her. Verwende dabei die Wortschatzliste auf den Seiten 109/110.

PRACTICE AND REVISION

STRUCTURES

1 People do lots of activities. Write about different activities.

→ buying clothes • eating sweets • going to the cinema • fishing
listening to music • playing sport • reading • riding a bike • skateboarding
swimming • talking to friends on a mobile • watching ... on TV

a) Can you finish the sentences?

1 ... is a popular activity.
2 ... is a healthy activity.
3 ... isn't easy.
4 ... isn't very healthy.
5 ... doesn't cost much money.

b) And your ideas about activities?

1 I think ... is fun.
2 I think ... is boring.
3 I think ... is a cool activity.
4 I think ... is a terrific activity at weekends.
5 I think ... is better than ...

Going to the cinema is a popular activity.

I think watching football on TV is fun.

▸ W 15

2 Pembroke Centre: What activities was Katie good at? (✔ = good at, ✘ = not good at)

1 ✔

2 ✘

3 ✔

4 ✘

5 ✔

6 ✘
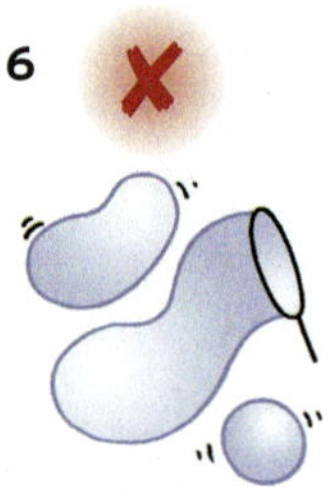

1 She was good at canoeing. 2 She wasn't good at making ...

• 3 Their favourite activities

1 Sam likes skateboarding.
He's good at skateboarding.
2 Mrs Hill likes driving her car.
She's good at ...
3 Tamsin likes ...

1 Sam

2 Mrs Hill

3 Tamsin

4 Amy

5 Jenny

6 Jake

4 What's the right form?

1 ➔ popular • more popular • the most popular

Fun is ... song this week. – It's number one.
Summer is a ... song than *My idea*.
But all these songs are very ...

This week's Top Ten CDs
1. Fun *The Boys* (1)
2. Summer *Barry Gates* (8)
3. My idea *Samantha* (9)

2 ➔ expensive • more expensive
the most expensive

B&Bs aren't very ...
But a B&B is ... than camping.
Hotels are ...

3 ➔ difficult • more difficult • the most difficult

Question 3 is ... question.
All the questions are ...
And question 3 is ... than question 2.

MATHS TEST
1. $4(3 - 2) + 2(4 + 2) =$
2. $2x + 4x = 3(2 + 3)$
3. $6x + 2x - 3x^2 = 4x^2 - 2$

▸ W 16, 17

5 At an activity centre: *will* or *won't*?

1 It's near the sea. Sailing ... be good there.
2 I hope the activities ... be fun.
3 I don't like bikes. I ... do mountain biking.
4 I hope the centre ... have good activities.
5 When ... you phone home?
6 The shop ... be open because it's 9 p.m.
7 I'm not good at running. I ... win the race.
8 I hope the other students ... be friendly.

CHECKPOINT

***will*-Futur:**
Damit kannst du sagen, was in der Zukunft geschehen wird.
I'm sure Kate **will** be at the party.
Will it rain tomorrow?

Die verneinte Form ist *won't* (= *will not*).
I **won't** be at school tomorrow.
You **won't** enjoy the film.

6 What do you say?

Welche Erwiderung passt am besten zur Aussage?

1 I'm so thirsty.
2 I can't repair my bike.
3 I can't buy a ticket in German.
4 I'm going to the shopping centre too.
5 We're really tired and hungry.

I'll buy one for you.
We'll repair it for you.
We'll take you in our car.
I'll make a snack for you.
I'll buy a drink for you.

CHECKPOINT

Mit der *will*-Form kannst du auch anbieten, etwas zu tun.
I'**ll** (= I will) help you with your jobs.
We'**ll** (= We will) help you.

▸ W 18–20

SUMMARY

ing-Form

Mit der *ing*-Form kannst du eine Tätigkeit benennen.
Damit kannst du beispielsweise über Interessen oder Hobbys sprechen.

Singing is fun. Singen macht Spaß.
Juggling isn't easy. Jonglieren ist nicht einfach.
Dancing is popular. Tanzen ist beliebt.

Um die *ing*-Form zu bilden, wird *-ing* an den Infinitiv eines Verbs angehängt:

sing → sing**ing** read → read**ing** draw → draw**ing**

! Beachte die Schreibweise:

dance → dancing | swim → swimming
skate → skating | run → running
make → making | sit → sitting

Manchmal ist die *ing*-Form Teil eines längeren Ausdrucks.

Waiting for a bus isn't very nice. Es ist nicht sehr schön, auf einen Bus zu warten.
I enjoy **watching football** on TV. Ich sehe mir gerne Fußball im Fernsehen an.

Gebrauch

- Die *ing*-Form kann am Satzanfang stehen:

Skating is Tom's hobby.

Swimming costs £2 here.

- Die *ing*-Form folgt oft auf bestimmte Verben:

enjoy • hate • like • love
start • stop • try

Emma enjoys **writing**.

She likes **painting** too.

- Du gebrauchst die *ing*-Form auch nach diesen Ausdrücken:

bad at • good at
interested in

Sam is good at **skiing**.

Tim is interested in **reading**.

Vergleiche mit *more …, most …*

Manchmal willst du Personen oder Sachen miteinander vergleichen.

- Diese Steigerungsformen mit *-er* oder *-est* kennst du schon:

Sally is young.
Kylie is young**er** than Sally.
Daisy is the young**est**.

- Bei mehrsilbigen Adjektiven werden Steigerungsformen mit *more …, most …* benutzt:

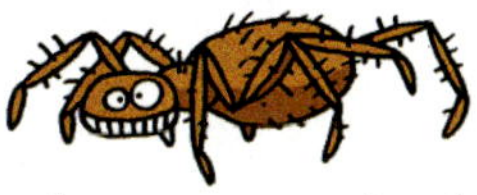

a dangerous animal

… a **more** dangerous animal

… the **most** dangerous animal!

You must be more careful. Du musst vorsichtiger sein.
What's the most popular hobby? Was ist das beliebteste Hobby?
It's the most expensive meal. Es ist das teuerste Essen.

Folgende Adjektive, die mit *more …, most …* gesteigert werden, kennst du schon:

boring • difficult • expensive • famous • frightened • interesting • modern • popular

IN DIESER UNIT HAST DU GELERNT, WIE …

… du über Hobbys, Gewohnheiten und andere Tätigkeiten sprichst.	▶ *Hiking is fun. My favourite sport is swimming.*
… du über Vorlieben oder Abneigungen sprichst.	▶ *My dad likes cooking. I don't like playing sport.*
… du sagst, was jemand (nicht) gut kann.	▶ *Tom is/isn't good at sailing.*
… du weitere Vergleiche machst.	▶ *TV is more boring than a good book. This is my most expensive T-shirt.*
… du nach einer Unterkunft fragen kannst.	▶ *Do you have a room free? How much is the room? We have a booking for tonight.*

DU HAST WIEDERHOLT, WIE …

… du über die Zukunft sprichst. ▶ *I'll see you in the café.*

DU KANNST AUCH VERSTEHEN, WIE …

… jemand Zustimmung sucht (vgl. … *nicht wahr / gell?*). ▶ *Sport is good fun, isn't it? They're great activities, aren't they?*

▶ W Test yourself 1–3

STORY (2)

What can the kids do on their free afternoon?

Chilling out at the sea

1 30, 31

At the activity centre

MEGAN What a week!
It's always so busy here, isn't it?
JAKE Yes, doing activities is hard work.
DARRIS At last – a free afternoon!
KATIE So what can we do?
MEGAN Do? Nothing. Let's chill out!
JAKE Let's go to the beach.
Let's have a quiet afternoon.
MEGAN We can lie on the sand.
KATIE The beaches here are the most fantastic in Wales.
JAKE And we can swim too, can't we?
DARRIS When we did abseiling, I saw a sandy beach.
MEGAN There's a bus to the cliffs.
DARRIS Then we can walk to the beach.
MEGAN We should tell the warden.
You must always say where you go.
JAKE It's a silly rule. Sitting on a beach isn't dangerous!
KATIE The bus is in five minutes.
DARRIS Come on! I have my mobile.
We can call later, can't we?
KATIE Let's get our swimsuits.
MEGAN Yes, let's go!

On Skerry Beach

The kids walked on the path down the cliffs.
The sandy beach was an hour away.
They forgot the phone call to the warden.
First they sat on the sand. Then they walked to some rocks near the sea.
They jumped off the rocks into the water.
They played with a ball in the sea and the swimming was fantastic.

After an hour Megan said, “Perhaps we should go back now.”
Katie turned – but the rocks weren’t there!
The rocks were almost under water!
“The sea is coming in,” shouted Megan.
The wind was stronger too.
The kids ran to their clothes. They got their clothes and ran along the beach. The sea came nearer and nearer. It looked more dangerous than before.
And they were so far from the path.
They were very frightened.
But Darris had his mobile.
He had an idea. He called 999.

“Help, we’re on Skerry Beach and the sea is coming in. We’re very frightened. We ...”
Then the mobile fell into the sea!
“Run – run for your life!” shouted Jake.
But running through the water was more difficult now.
Darris got to the path first. He turned and pulled the others up. They were safe!

Sitting at the top, they felt better.
“We were lucky,” said Megan.
“We won’t tell the warden what happened.”
But then the kids heard a loud noise – a helicopter.
“Oh, no!” said Darris. “We phoned 999!
I forgot. Now there will be trouble!”

► W 21–24

Unit 3

Welcome to Scotland!

An American family is in Scotland for the first time.

1 32

Edinburgh and Scotland tours

All our tours start in Edinburgh.

Edinburgh open top bus tour

From £8.

See the famous sights of Edinburgh: Get on, get off service.

Scottish Highlands and islands

From £199.

A three-day-tour to beautiful places.

Loch Ness and the Highlands

From £33.

Perhaps you'll see Nessie, the Loch Ness monster!

Edinburgh and Glasgow

From £156.

Scotland's two big cities, with a night in a hotel.

WE KNOW ...

- **how people can travel:** They can travel by bus. ...
- **the names of some countries.**

GRAHAM MURRAY (13) and his family
1 33 are Scottish. They live in Edinburgh. Edinburgh is the capital of Scotland. Scotland became part of the United Kingdom about 300 years ago, but it has its own long history.

GRAHAM

I'm very proud to be Scottish.
I feel more Scottish than British.
I like music and I play in a band.
My brother Andy is 11.
He likes terrible music.
I'm glad that I have my own MP3 player!

Most Scottish people live near the big cities of Glasgow and Edinburgh – not in the Highlands. We have an oil industry, and a computer industry too.

Tourists like our traditions, our bagpipes and castles. And they like our Highlands and islands. But Scotland is more than a country for tourists.

Some things are special in Scotland. Hogmanay – New Year – is big in Scotland. We celebrate with a big street party in Edinburgh. People come here from all over the world.

▶ W1

PRESENTATION

A–E
1 34–38

A

Erin and John are new students in Graham's class.
They're from the USA. Their family has moved to Scotland for a year.
Last week Erin and John visited the old town.
Later they planned to meet Graham at Edinburgh Castle.

B

At first Erin and John had lots of fun.
Edinburgh has lots of old streets.

The city has a lot of hills too.
So the streets are on lots of different levels.

And they have a lot of strange names.
Erin and John spent a lot of time with the map ...

CHECKPOINT

Die Mengenangaben *lots of* und *a lot of* verwendest du, wenn etwas in großer Anzahl vorhanden ist:

Anne gets **a lot of** pocket money.
Don't run! We have **lots of** time.
You have **a lot of** DVDs.
Lots of people have mobile phones.

Exercise 1: What things did Erin and John do?

1 saw – places – interesting – a lot of – They
2 Edinburgh – lots of – took – photos – They – in
3 their map – a lot of – spent – They – time – with
4 They – hills – lots of – walked on
5 fun – the old town – in – They – had – lots of

C It was 1 o'clock. Graham waited at the castle. But Erin and John weren't there. He phoned them.

GRAHAM Erin! Hi! Is there a problem?
ERIN I'm sorry, Graham, but we're lost.
We've walked around the old town.
There are lots of old streets with funny names here.
But now we can't find the way to the castle.
It's easier in Denver. – Lots of our streets have numbers!
GRAHAM Where are you now?
ERIN It's an old street. We're at a statue of a dog.
GRAHAM A dog? Oh, Greyfriars Bobby!
I know where you are.
Stay there. I'll be with you in ten minutes.

D Graham walked around the town with Erin and John. Then they went to a café.

JOHN I like this Irn-Bru drink.
ERIN Tea is better. It's cold in Edinburgh.
GRAHAM Well, it's January, isn't it?
ERIN How much snow do you have in Edinburgh?
GRAHAM Only a little.
JOHN I expected a lot of snow here.
GRAHAM What ideas do people in America have about Scotland?
ERIN They think all the men wear kilts.
GRAHAM We only wear kilts on special days.
JOHN How many special days do you have?
GRAHAM Only a few.

Exercise 2: Make some of Erin and John's other questions.

→ How many • How much

1 ... people live in Edinburgh?
2 ... rain is there in Edinburgh in summer?
3 ... students go to our school?
4 ... homework do we get in year 8?
5 ... pocket money do you get?
6 ... men have kilts in Scotland?

CHECKPOINT

How many ...?
How many boys are in your class?
How many tickets do we need?

How much ...?
How much money do you have?
How much milk should I buy?

Exercise 3: What does Graham say about Scotland?

→ a few • a little

1 I only wear my kilt on ... special days.
2 Edinburgh has only ... snow.
3 Only ... people can play the bagpipes.
4 People say that we spend only ... money.
5 We have ... fun with Loch Ness monster stories.
6 Only ... Scottish people live in the Highlands.

CHECKPOINT

a few
I have **a few** sweets. Would you like one?
We only had **a few** sunny days on holiday.

a little
Would you like **a little** milk in your tea?
I only have **a little** money with me.

E

► W 2

F–G
1 39, 40

F Robert Burns was a famous Scottish poet.
His birthday was on January 25th.
Scottish people all over the world celebrate his birthday.

They eat with some friends.
They hear some speeches.
They have some poems.
They tell some jokes.
They have some songs.

They enjoy some Scottish food.
They eat some haggis.
They have some music.
They have some dancing.
– And they drink some whisky!

CHECKPOINT

some **= einige**
I have **some** magazines.
Here are **some** apples.

some **= etwas**
We have **some** cheese.
Would you like **some** water?

G Year 8 has a Burns Night meal every year.

There are some bagpipes.	There aren't any singers.
Most people eat some haggis.	A few people don't eat any haggis.
They drink some Irn-Bru.	They don't have any whisky.
There are some short poems.	There aren't any long poems.

Year 8
Burns Night Meal
Welcome music
The grace
Arrival of the star – the haggis!
Poem to the haggis
Meal
Speeches
Scottish songs and poems
Song: Auld Lang Syne

some poems, some music; (not) any

Exercise 4: The Burns Night meal at Graham's school:

a) What they had ...

1 They had some soup.
2 ... some haggis.
3 ... potatoes.
4 ... speeches.
5 ... songs.
6 ... Irn-Bru.

b) What they didn't have ...

1 They didn't have any fish.
2 ... any sausages.
3 ... broccoli.
4 ... stories.
5 ... games.
6 ... whisky.

CHECKPOINT

Bei Verneinungen verwendest du *any*:
There are some comics.
– There are**n't any** books.
I have some juice.
– But I do**n't** have **any** cola.

▸ W 3

Exercise 5: Write about your family. What special day does your family celebrate?

Christmas

Eid

New Year

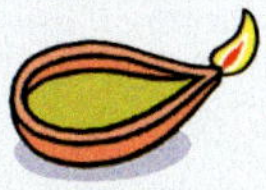
Diwali

Easter

Halloween

birthdays

Mother's Day

→
- We celebrate Christmas / Eid / New Year / Diwali / Easter / Halloween / birthdays / Mother's Day / ...
- We celebrate with the family / with friends / with all our relatives.
- We eat some special food. We eat ... / We don't eat any special food.
- We wear some special clothes. / We don't wear any special clothes.
- We stay at home. / We go to church / the mosque / a restaurant / ...
- We get some presents. / We don't get any presents.
- We send some cards. / We don't send any cards.
- We have a tree/fireworks/...

▸ W 4

TRUE STORY* – Greyfriars Bobby: A famous Edinburgh dog

1 ⦿ 41

In the early years of the nineteenth century John Gray, a poor gardener, went to Edinburgh for work. There weren't any jobs for gardeners. But they needed a man to look after the city at night. John Gray became a kind of policeman. He got a small Highland dog. The dog's name was Bobby.

Every night they walked around Edinburgh. They were soon both very popular with the people. But one day John Gray became ill. In 1858 he died.

Next day Bobby went to the grave in Greyfriars Church. A few people sent him away but he came back. The dog stayed there. He left for food at 1 o'clock, when he heard the big gun at the castle. But he always returned. There were lots of stories about Bobby.

He stayed at the grave for 14 years and became very famous. Later, people put up a statue of Bobby. There is a film about his life too. – You can see it on DVD.

LISTENING – Alan is calling for train information

1 42

1 Before you listen: Look at the title. How does Alan want to travel?

> **Tipp:** Der Titel verrät dir schon, wer zu hören ist und worum es gehen wird.

2 Read the two questions. Then listen to the dialogue and answer them.

1 What country is Alan in?
2 Does Alan need information about train times or ticket prices?

3 Read the four sentences. Then listen to the dialogue. Are they right or wrong?

1 Alan wants to visit Aberdeen.
2 Alan's mother has a brochure.
3 Alan doesn't have a junior railcard.
4 Alan thinks the telephone service is very good.

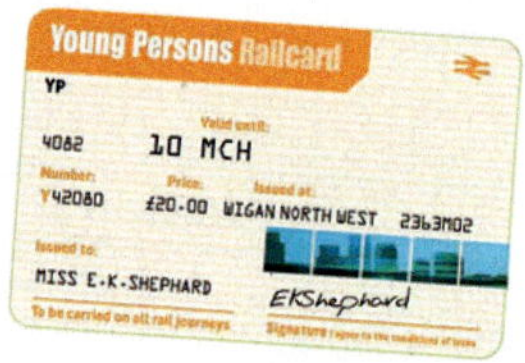

4 Note taking: Find out this information. Listen again and write notes.

1 The price of a junior railcard.
2 The phone number of Scotland Trains.
3 The number for railcard information.

▸ W 5

READING – From a handbook

> **Tipp:** Nicht immer musst du alles auf einmal lesen: Bei einer Gebrauchsanweisung sucht man oft nur bestimmte Informationen. Zur Orientierung helfen die Überschriften.

Look at page 55. You want to put a new battery in your phone. Will this page help you?

1 Basic reading

1 What's the name of the phone company?
2 Can you use the phone in other countries?
3 Does the company have a website?

2 Reading for details

1 How much are text messages in the UK?
2 Where can you buy more talk time?
3 Do you pay when you get calls in other countries?

3 Find the English sentences.

1 Wie viel Sprechzeit hast du?
2 Brauchst du mehr Sprechzeit?
3 Vergiss nicht!

4 Language tasks

1 Find the English words: Handy, wählen, aufstocken, Vorwahl, Klingelton.
2 Find a phrase for: an SMS with a photo; typical shops.

▸ W 6

Tip: New words on page 55 are in the dictionary (page 118–136).

So you have a great new **STAR** mobile?

Using your new STAR mobile

What you pay

STAR to other mobiles	35p*
STAR to STAR or landlines	35p*
text messages	10p
picture messages	30p
video messages	50p

* per minute

Check your talk time

How much talk time do you have?
Just dial 345 and hear your balance.

Topping-up your phone

Do you need more talk time? There are two options:

1 STAR top-up card

Buy more talk time at lots of High Street shops. Show your card. That's all!

2 bank card

Do you have a bank card? You can buy talk time at a hole in the wall. Check our website for a list of cash machines and banks.

Phoning on holiday

You can use your mobile in other countries.

	Europe	USA	Rest of the world
Calling the UK*	£1.30	£1.40	£1.50
Getting calls from the UK*	60p	70p	90p
Sending text messages	30p	40p	50p

* per minute

Holidays: Don't forget!
- The dialling code for the UK is +44 without the first 0. Example: 0179-987396 is +44-179-987396
- Top-up your talk time before you go!

And great STAR extras too!

Ringtones, pictures, games ...
Just check out our website.

ACTIONS – On the telephone

1 43

What's Sally happy about?

SALLY Hello, Jamie. How are things?
JAMIE Fine. And your football match?
SALLY I got a goal.
JAMIE Well done! Congratulations!
SALLY But the Glasgow girls won.
JAMIE Never mind! Better luck next time.

Alan is phoning home.
Why will he be late?

MUM Hello. 8776054.
ALAN Hello, Mum. It's me.
MUM Hello, Alan. Are you on the train?
ALAN Yes, I am.
MUM I'll meet you at the station.
ALAN Thanks. But my train is running late.
MUM When will it arrive?
ALAN I don't know. I'll call again later.
MUM Good idea! Bye. Thanks for calling.

1 Look again.

1 Wie fragst du eine Freundin / einen Freund, wie es ihr/ihm geht?
2 Wie kannst du jemandem gratulieren?
3 Wie kannst du jemanden trösten?
4 Wie kannst du viel Glück für das nächste Mal wünschen?
5 Wie kannst du dich melden, wenn du ein Familienmitglied anrufst?
6 Wie bietest du an, jemanden am Bahnhof abzuholen?
7 Wie sagst du, dass dein Zug Verspätung hat?
8 Wie sagst du, dass du später noch mal anrufst?

▸ W 7, 8

• 2 Can you say these phone numbers?

1 452379, 649782, 938176
2 608213, 804940, 302417
3 886349, 453558, 294677
4 9046337, 6306641, 55428004
5 0779-793591
6 01875-7893418

CHECKPOINT

How you say telephone numbers:
In Dreiergruppen sprechen:
873241 = eight seven three – two four one
Null aussprechen:
6034521 = six oh three – four five two – one
Doppelte Zahlen aussprechen:
288416 = two double eight – four one six
Vorwahl (dialling code) getrennt nennen:
0128 ... = oh one two eight ...

SPEAKING

1 44

1 Intonation: Listen and say

1 Hello, Jamie. Hello, ...

→ Mum • Dave • Sally • Mrs Hall • Jenny • Mohammed • Mr Green

2 Well done! Congratulations!

→ Never mind! • Good idea! • Welcome! • Happy Birthday!

2 Act a phone call with a partner.

Begrüßung	Hello. Hi, Pat/... Hello, this is ...	⇨	Hello. Hello, this is ...
Hauptteil	How are things? I'm on the bus/train/... I'm in ... / at ... I'm ill/late/... I have two tickets for the cinema/football/... Let's meet at ... / go to ... / play / ...	⇨	Fine. / OK. / Not so good. I'm sorry. / Never mind. Good idea! / Great! OK. Let's meet at ... Sorry, I can't come. I'm busy.
Schluss	OK. See you later. Never mind. Bye.	⇨	Bye. Thanks for calling.

► W 9

• 3 Act the dialogue with a partner: A girl/boy (Partner A) is visiting an English friend (Partner B).

PARTNER A	PARTNER B
Rufe deine englische Freundin / deinen englischen Freund mit deinem Handy an.	Melde dich am Telefon.
Sage, wer du bist. Sage, du sitzt im Zug. Der Zug hat aber Verspätung.	Sage, es tut dir leid. Frage, wann der Zug ankommen wird. Sage, du willst sie/ihn vom Bahnhof abholen.
Sage, du weißt nicht, wann der Zug ankommen wird. Du wirst später noch einmal anrufen.	Verabschiede dich. Bedanke dich für den Anruf.

WORDPOWER

1 Letter or telephone? Put the words and phrases in the right group.

Tip: There are five words and five phrases in both groups.

mobile • pen • read
speak • battery • write
address • listen • Sorry?
stamp

Dear John, • Thanks for calling. • It's me.
I'll write again soon. • I'll call later again.
This is 547232. • I must buy a stamp for this now.
Best wishes, Dave. • This is Anne. • Love, Jake.

letter words and phrases:
pen, ...
Dear John, ...

telephone words and phrases:
mobile, ...
Thanks for calling. ...

2 What things can you buy ...

a) ... in a carton?

milk,
...

b) ... in a tin?

soup,
...

c) ... in a bottle?

lemonade,
...

d) ... in a bag?

crisps,
...

3 *At, on* or *in*? Make the right time phrases.

my birthday
Monday
the weekend
9.15
the afternoon
summer

holiday
April
2006
October 4th
Friday evening
2 o'clock

1 *on* holiday 2 ... April

CHECKPOINT

Zeitausdrücke: *at, on* oder *in*?
at bei Uhrzeiten
on vor Tagen
in bei Monaten, Jahren, Jahreszeiten

Besondere Ausdrücke:
at Christmas, on holiday, in the week,
in the evening/morning/afternoon,
at the weekend

► W 10–12

SITUATIONS

Wie kannst du auf Englisch ...

1 ... sagen, dass ihr viel Zeit habt?
2 ... fragen, wie viel Geld jemand bei sich hat?
3 ... anbieten, für die Getränke zu zahlen?
4 ... sagen, dass ihr mit der Familie feiert?
5 ... fragen, ob jemand im Zug ist?
6 ... dich für den Anruf bedanken?

Tip: Look again at pages 48–57.

SOUNDS

Die Laute [b]/[p] klingen ähnlich. Der Laut [p] ist jedoch stimmlos. Der Laut [b] ist stimmhaft.
Beispiele: **pig** [pɪg] **big** [bɪg] **pen** [pen] **Ben** [ben]

Die Lautpaare [t]/[d], [k]/[g] sind ebenfalls stimmlos bzw. stimmhaft.
Beispiele: **wrote** [rəʊt] **road** [rəʊd] **class** [klɑːs] **glass** [glɑːs]

1 45

1 Welcher der beiden Laute ist im Wort enthalten?

1 [p] – [b] job, club, above, poor, apple, rubber, shop
2 [t] – [d] showed, want, and, red, cold, walked, laughed, wood
3 [k] – [g] flag, go, come, book, big, speak, bag, talk

2 Nur ein Laut ist anders. Suche den jeweiligen Partner.

1 dog – ...	3 back	5 came	7 good
2 try – ...	4 ride	6 bored	8 Paul

→ bag • ball • bought • could • dock • dry • game • right

▸ W 16

WORKING WITH A DICTIONARY

Im Wörterbuch findest du für ein deutsches Wort oft mehrere englische Wörter. Welches du auswählst, hängt vom Zusammenhang ab. Achte daher auf Beispielsätze und Erklärungen!

1 Welches englische Wort wäre hier richtig? Prüfe in einem Wörterbuch nach.

1 **Essen** food; meal
- a) Tom hat für uns ein tolles **Essen** zubereitet.
- b) Gesundes **Essen** ist für mich sehr wichtig.

2 **hören** hear; listen (to)
- a) Wir **hören** oft Musik.
- b) Es ist hier so laut. Ich kann dich nicht **hören**.

3 **über** above; about
- a) Erzähl mir **über** deine Ferien.
- b) Die Familie wohnt **über** einem Geschäft.

4 **Karte** card; ticket; map
- a) Das Dorf ist auf der **Karte**.
- b) Ich habe eine **Karte** für das Konzert.
- c) Hast du meine **Karte** zum Geburtstag bekommen?

LEARNING SKILLS

Note taking: Wenn du dir Informationen merken willst, die du gehört oder gelesen hast, schreibe am besten nur Stichworte auf.

1 Was bedeuten diese Notizen?

a)
- leave London 9.15
- arrive Edinburgh 15.10
- £65

b)
- Sat. 20th, 7.30 p.m.
- Howe Road Youth Club
- bring CDs!!!

PRACTICE AND REVISION

STRUCTURES

1 Graham has a lot of things in his bag. But he can't find three things.

a few • a little • no

1 He has *a few* books.
2 He has *a little* chocolate.
3 He has *no* MP3 player.
4 He has ... pencils.
5 He has ... photos.
6 ... money
7 ... stamps.
8 ... headphones.
9 ... string.
10 ... mobile phone.

AND YOU?

What's in your bag? Look and write about three things.
I have a few ... • I have a little ... • I have no ...

▸ W 13

2 Graham went to a café with John and Erin.

a) What did Graham have?
Graham had some orange juice.
He had some ...

b) What didn't he have?
Graham didn't have any coffee.
He didn't have any ...

c) What things would you like?
What wouldn't you like?
I'd like some ...
I wouldn't like any ...

3 Erin wrote a letter to her cousin. Put in the right words. Use *some/any*.

January 26th

Dear Belle,
Yesterday I went to Burns Night meal.
I tried ... Irn-Bru – it's Scottish lemonade. It was OK.
I had ... vegetables and I didn't know what they were!
But I didn't try ... haggis.
A man played ... music on the bagpipes.
There were ... poems and ... songs too.
I didn't understand ... Scottish words.
After that we had ... dancing.
At the end they sang "Auld Lang Syne", but I didn't know ... of the words.
It was a great party. How is life in Denver?
Love, Erin

▸ W 14, 15

4 A teenage magazine has tested some MP3 players.

This month our teenage team tests ...

MP3 players

MP3 players are one of the most popular gadgets.
Our team looks at four of the latest models.

?

What's the best?

	How much? (£)	How big? (cm)	memory	How easy to use?	Battery (hours)	Headphones	Popular with our team?
Eplay	230	8 x 5 x 2	60 GB	★★★	15	★★★★	★★★
Coolplay	95	4 x 2 x 1	20 GB	★★	8	★	★★
Esong	115	9 x 6 x 3	2 GB	★★★★	23	★★★	★★★★
Toni	80	6 x 4 x 2	8 GB	★	6	★★	★★

★★★★ = very good ★★★ = good ★★ = OK ★ = poor

a) Look at the article. Find the answers to the questions.

1 Which was the cheapest player?
– *The Toni.*
2 Which was the most expensive player?
3 Which was the smallest player?
4 Which player had the best battery?
5 Which player was the easiest to use?
6 Which player was the most popular one with the team?

**b) The teenage team looked at four different players.
Help with the report. Write eight sentences.**

The *Eplay* *Coolplay* *Esong* *Toni*	was	cheaper smaller bigger easier to use more difficult to use more popular	than the *Eplay*. *Coolplay*. *Esong*. *Toni*.
	had	more memory a better battery better headphones	

Example:
The *Esong* was bigger than the *Coolplay*.
The *Eplay* had a better battery than the ...

• c) Which MP3 player is the best one? What do you think? Why?
I think the ... is the best player.
It's the ...est / most ... player. It's ...
It has the ...est / best / most ...

▸ W 17, 18

How much ...? – How many ...?

How much music do you have on it?

How much milk is in the fridge?
Wie viel Milch ist im Kühlschrank?

How much? gebrauchst du in Fragen bei nicht zählbaren Nomen, z. B. *water, fruit.*

How many CDs did you buy?

How many apples do we have?
Wie viele Äpfel haben wir?

How many? gebrauchst du in Fragen bei zählbaren Nomen, z. B. *books, biscuits.*

a little – a few – a lot of – no

How many comics do you have?

A few comics.

A lot of comics.

No comics.

How much cheese do you have?

A little cheese.

A lot of cheese.

No cheese.

I have **a few** rolls in my bag. Ich habe einige Semmeln in meiner Tasche.
You have **a lot of** CDs. Du hast viele CDs.
I got **no** cards last Christmas. Ich habe letzte Weihnachten keine Karten bekommen.

I have **a little** money for the holidays. Ich habe ein bisschen Geld für die Ferien.
You have **a lot of** ice cream. Du hast viel Eiskrem.
We have **no** time. Wir haben keine Zeit.

some – (not) any

Das Wort *some* bedeutet „etwas“ *(some cheese)* oder „einige“ *(some books)*.

We have **some** ice cream.

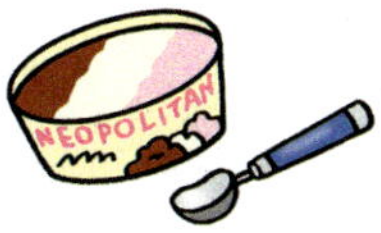

Would you like some ice cream?
Möchtest du etwas Eiskrem haben?

Here are **some** CDs.

Can I have some sweets, please?
Kann ich bitte ein paar Süßigkeiten haben?

Statt *some* steht in einem verneinten Satz *any*.

There is**n't any** water in the bottle.
Es ist kein Wasser in der Flasche.

I do**n't** have **any** T-shirts in my cupboard.
Ich habe keine T-Shirts in meinem Schrank.

I don't have any American stamps. Ich habe keine amerikanischen Briefmarken.
We don't need any milk today. Wir brauchen heute keine Milch.

IN DIESER UNIT HAST DU GELERNT, WIE ...

... du nach Mengen fragst. ▸ *How much money do you have?*
How many boys are in your class?

... du über Mengen sprichst. ▸ *I have a few books, a lot of comics, but no games.*
I have a little milk, a lot of lemonade, but no cola.

... du sagst, was vorhanden ist. ▸ *The shop has some new T-shirts.*
There's some great music on the radio.

... du sagst, was nicht vorhanden ist. ▸ *There aren't any cars in the road.*
There isn't any juice in the glass.

... du telefonieren kannst. ▸ *Hello, Mum. It's me.*
I'll call again later.

DU HAST WIEDERHOLT, WIE ...

... Dinge verglichen werden. ▸ *It was cheaper. It was more popular than the other player.*

DU KANNST AUCH VERSTEHEN, WIE ...

... gesagt wird, was jemand gerade getan hat. ▸ *We've walked around the old town.*

▸ W Test yourself 1–3

What can you see and do at Loch Ness?

Loch Ness – a good place for a holiday?

1 ⊙ 46

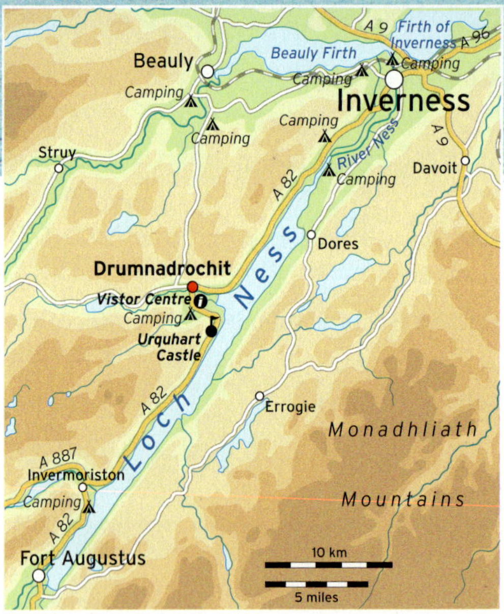

Loch Ness is a big lake in the north of Scotland. It's 35 km long and deeper than the North Sea. It's a beautiful place, and it has become very popular with tourists. It has also become very famous …

People first said they saw a monster in the lake hundreds of years ago. And there are many stories about it. There are some photos too. But they aren't very good.

People called the monster Nessie. There is now a big Nessie industry with shops, a cinema and a centre for visitors. Nessie has a website, and a webcam too.

A lot of people love Nessie – true or not!

NESSIE JOKE

I saw Nessie in the road outside our swimming pool. She was too mean to go in and buy a ticket!

Will Graham enjoy a holiday at Loch Ness?

Loch Ness – a good place for a holiday?

1 ◉ 47

The Murrays always had camping holidays in Scotland. Graham's parents love walking in the Highlands. But Graham wasn't so sure. "I like Scotland – but Loch Ness again! I'd like a holiday with some sun. And there aren't any young people in the Highlands." But here they were again. It was August and they were at Loch Ness ...

"This is the place for the tents," Mr Murray said. "Can you put your own tent up, Graham?" "I've put it up before – it's easy!" "OK. Well, we don't have any food so your mum and I will buy a few things. See you in an hour."

The campsite was OK, but very quiet and boring. There were only a few tents. Graham noticed a little rain. He took his tent.

Then another tent opened and a girl looked out. Graham smiled and said, "Hi." The girl said "Hi", but she didn't look very friendly. And then Graham saw her shirt – an England football shirt! The rain and the wind became stronger. The girl watched Graham. Putting up the tent wasn't easy. – And it was more difficult when somebody watched. Suddenly the wind hit the tent hard – and it all fell down. Graham looked around. He wasn't sure, but he thought there was a smile on the girl's face. Graham was angry. "Typical English girl", he thought, "they're always unfriendly."

Graham didn't see the girl the next day. But in the afternoon he was in the village shop. He saw the newspaper.

It said *"Italy 3, England 2!"* on the first page. He smiled.

When Graham came out of the shop, he saw four older boys in the road.

Three had kilts – and all had beer.

Then Graham saw the girl from the campsite too.

She had her England football shirt again.

The four boys shouted: "3:2! Your team is no good. England lost again. England lost again."

They drank some beer.

Then they shouted again.

The girl looked frightened.

The laughing and shouting was very loud now.

Graham felt sorry for her. He went towards her

"Hi again," he said.

"Oh, nice to see you," she said. And this time she smiled at him.

"I think we should go," Graham said.

They walked away from the shop and down to Loch Ness.

"My name's Graham. What's yours?"

"Julie. I didn't like those boys. I'm not sure Loch Ness is a good place for a holiday."

"An England shirt isn't very popular here," Graham said.

"But England's match was against Italy, not Scotland."

"Well, Julie, Scotland and England ... – It's a long story. I'll try to explain ..."

▸ W 19–21

Unit 4

Idols

Nick is phoning Belle.

2 2

WE KNOW ...

- **some music words:** singer, listen to, play, ...
- **other words for *good* and *bad*:** nice, ...

BELLE WALKER (14) lives in Denver, Colorado. Her family has a house in the suburbs.
She has a lot of relatives in Denver. But her cousins, Erin and John, are living in Edinburgh, Scotland this year.

2 ◉ 3

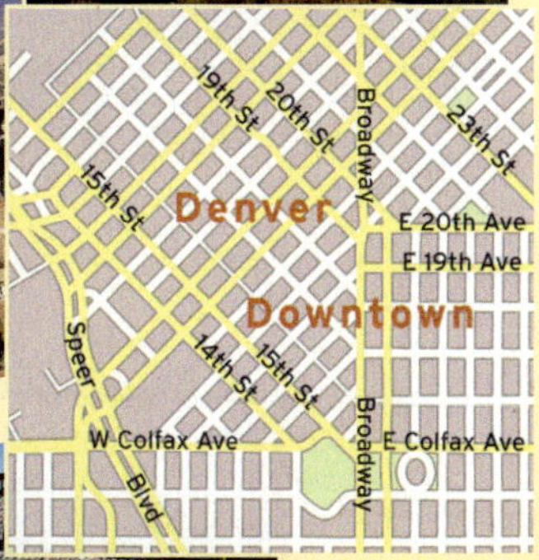

BELLE
Denver is a great place. We have more than 300 sunny days a year. It's hot in the summer, and winters aren't very cold, with some warm days too. Snow doesn't stay long in downtown Denver.
Denver is very flat, but it's near the Rocky Mountains. You can see the Rockies from almost every street here. And the city is already high up. It's about a mile up, so everybody calls it *Mile High City*.

Local people – and tourists – love the outdoor activities. Lots of people ride bikes. And in the mountains there's mountain biking and hiking in the summer. In the winter there's skiing and snowboarding. We have some important sports teams. Baseball, football and soccer are really big here.

... But I'm not mad about sport.
I ride a bike of course.
But I love music.
I'm in our middle school's marching band.

► W1

A–E
2 4-8

A Belle plays the flute in the marching band at her school.
She can practise it at school or in her room.
But she doesn't like playing the flute.
She wants to be a drummer in a rock band.
She can't practise the flute and the drums. There isn't enough time ...

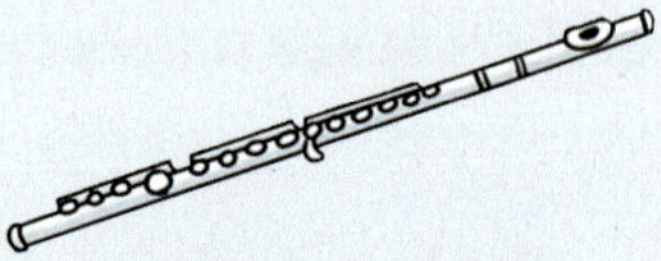

So Belle has to leave the school band.
She has to practise the drums every day.
She has to play at home.
She has to play in the garage. – The drums are so loud!

B A few weeks later, Belle is practising the drums in the garage ...

DAD The neighbours phoned again. They phoned once last week, and at the weekend too. That's three times! They say you're very loud.
BELLE But I have to learn a new solo. And I have to play in the garage.
DAD I have a good idea! We can carry your drums to the basement. You can play there.
BELLE But the basement is full of junk.
DAD Sure. You have to clear everything first. – That's why I think it's a really good idea!

C Belle is looking at a poster at school. It's about the *Middle School Idol* competition.

Exercise 1: Some students are interested in the competition. They have to do a few things.
They have to get the form.
They have to choose ...

Exercise 2: Belle is interested in the competition too.
She has to get the form.
She has to ...

► W 2

CHECKPOINT

Mit *has to / have to* sagst du, was jemand tun muss:
Belle **has to** practise every day.
Belle **has to** clear the basement.
The neighbours **have to** listen to the drums every day.
Students in the school band **have to** practise often.

D How do you become the *Middle School Idol*?

You have to go to your school competition.

– You don't have to win. You have to be one of the best three.

You have to go to the state competition. It's on local TV.

– You don't have to win. You have to be one of the best two.

You have to go to the national competition. It's on national TV.

– But you have to win that!

E

Belle would like to play the drums in a band.
Some older girls at her school are making a new band – *Sistas*.
But she doesn't know many songs. And they say she's too young.
They're very good but they seem a bit arrogant.
Belle is fed up. The school competition is next week.

But later Belle has an idea ...
She doesn't have to play with other people.
She doesn't have to be in a band.
She doesn't have to learn a new piece of music for the competition.
She can just play her favourite solo!

Exercise 3: Before the competition: Belle has to do some things. But she doesn't have to do some other things.

→ has to • doesn't have to

1 Belle wants to win the competition. So she ... practise.
2 Belle can play an instrument alone. She ... find a band.
3 She has a favourite solo. She ... learn a new piece of music.
4 But she can't practise in the garage. She ... clear the basement.
5 Her father is helping her. She ... clear the basement alone.
6 The school has some drums. So she ... take her drums to school for the competition.

▸ W 3

CHECKPOINT

Mit *don't/doesn't have to* sagst du, was jemand nicht tun muss:

Belle **doesn't have to** find new music.
She **doesn't have to** be in a band.
Students **don't have to** win the first competition.
Students **don't have to** pay for the competition.

F–I
2 9–12

F The first part of the music competition is always at school.

The students go to school on a Saturday.
They do their acts in the gym. The students in the competition sing, dance, play music or rap.
There's a programme for the competition.

There's a competition jury: the principal, two music teachers and three students. And worse: there are other students in the gym too – hundreds!

After an act the people on the jury give their points – and their opinions!
That's a bad part of the competition – but the worst thing is waiting for the result at the end!

Exercise 4: Talk about the competition at school.

Students have to	go	to the jury's opinions.
	check	their act in the gym.
	do	for the result.
	stand	in front of a jury.
	listen	to school on Saturday.
	wait	the competition programme.

G **MOM** It's the competition tomorrow.
Do we have to take your drums to school in the car?
BELLE No, we don't. There are drums at school.
MOM Can your dad and I come and listen?
BELLE Do you really have to come? I'll be so nervous.
DAD OK. But the best students have to go on a big TV show.
It's a very popular show. We can watch you then!

Exercise 5: Partner game: What's the popular German TV competition?

Gelingt es dir mit nur drei Fragen, eine Fernsehshow deiner Partnerin / deines Partners zu erraten? Was muss man in der Show machen?

PARTNER A Do you have to ...?
PARTNER B Yes, you do. / No, you don't. ...

PARTNER A I think it's ...
PARTNER B Yes, it is. / No, it isn't.

Do you have to ...?
answer questions • sing • cook • dance
wear silly clothes • live in a special house
make things • do silly things
be in a team • live with a family

CHECKPOINT

So kannst du fragen, was jemand tun muss:
Do you **have to** help at home?
Do I **have to** do my homework now?
Does Tom **have to** clean his room?
Does your mum **have to** go to work by bus?

H It's the competition. Belle is looking at the programme with Mrs Bates, a music teacher.

Exercise 6: The people on the jury are talking about Belle's act. They don't agree. Finish their questions.

→ Do • Does

BETH ... you have to play alone? I think a drummer should be in a band. – Six points.
MRS BATES ... a drummer have to be in a band? I don't agree. I liked Belle. – Eight points.
MR GREEN ... you have to look so angry when you play? Smile more! – Five points.
MR GALE ... she have to play so long? It was a very long solo. – Six points.
JILL ... she have to play drums? Other instruments are better. – Four points.
KATE ... you have to be so difficult, Jill? Drums are a great instrument. – Eight points.

How many points did Belle get?

I

The competition was long.
The first act was at 9 a.m. – The last one was at 12.15.
Lots of bands were good. – The best ones were rock bands.
The singers weren't so good. – The worst ones were very bad.
And the winners?
The first winner was a band – *Sistas*.
The next one was a singer.
And the third one was – Belle!

▸ W 4

CHECKPOINT

Mit *one/ones* sprichst du über etwas, was schon erwähnt wurde:
Were there two singers? – Yes. The first **one** was a girl. The other **one** was a boy.
I'd like some apples, please. – Fine. The green **ones** or the red **ones**?

LISTENING – The Rick Miles radio show, Denver

2 13

Tipp:
Der Titel sagt dir schon, um welche Art von Tonaufnahme es sich handelt und woher sie stammt.

1 Before you listen: Look at the title.

1 What do you think you will hear?
2 What country is the programme from?

2 Read the two questions. Then listen to the show and answer them.

1 What was Deutschendorf's famous name?
2 What state did the singer love?

3 Read the four questions. Then listen to the show again and answer them.

1 Was John born in Denver?
2 What was John's first big hit?
3 Did he die in a plane, car or train?
4 Which song is about being homesick?

4 Note taking: Find four facts about the singer. Listen again and write notes.

▸ W 5

READING – A blog

Where do you see texts like the one on page 75?
Who are the people in the text?

Tipp:
Auch das Aussehen eines Textes vermittelt dir oft auf Anhieb einige Informationen über den Inhalt.

1 Basic reading

1 What country do the teenagers live in?
2 Where did they make a video?

2 Find the date when ...

1 ... they played at a school.
2 ... the band made a video.
3 ... they didn't play.
4 ... they were late for a show.

3 Find the English sentences.

1 Wir haben keine Zeit.
2 Wir müssen mehr spielen.
3 Wir haben die Show verpasst.
4 Wir haben vielleicht eines Tages einen Hit.

4 Language tasks

1 Find the English words: Auftritt, beliebt, Fernsehsender, Teil, berühmt.
2 Find a phrase for: newest songs; not only; on Saturdays and Sundays.

▸ W 6

Tip: New words on page 75 are in the dictionary (page 118–136).

Welcome to

THE ROCKIES BLOG

Life with your local band

May 24th Hi Rockies fans! We had a cool gig last night. A school dance again. It was as good as the other ones! The kids were great. And our latest numbers were popular. We've had lots of emails. Not just kids from Colorado read our blog.

May 14th Have you listened to The Music Show? It's a cool new podcast from Colorado for rock fans. We'd like to do a podcast for you, but we don't have time.

May 3rd We made a video today! Hope you like the photos. The ones in this blog are in John's basement.

April 29th We couldn't play today. We have to play more together – but when? We all have school – and weekend jobs. Music is sometimes really hard work.

March 14th A big chance today – and nothing went right! We were on the way to our local TV station for a competition. We were already late. (We often are!) And then our van had a flat. We missed the show …

March 2nd We saw this information about the music industry. It's a big industry, and lots of people work in it. A band is only one part of it. You have to sell a lot of albums to live off music! Perhaps we'll have a hit one day! But most bands aren't famous of course. They get nothing. They just play music for no money. And we love doing that – famous or not.

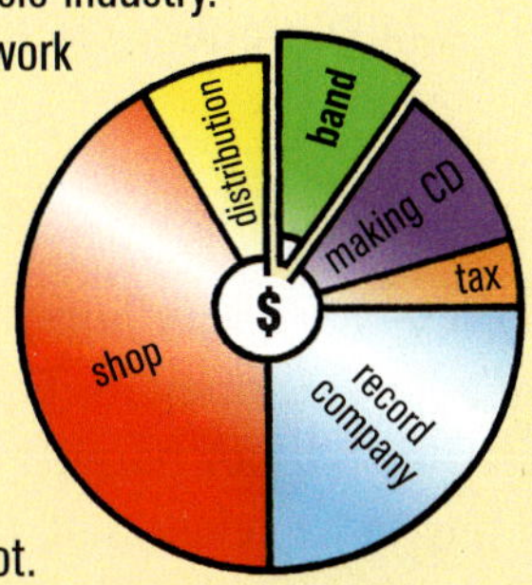

next page >>>

contact us

listen to us

our favourite things

music links

Rockies info

other cool stuff

ACTIONS – Talking about people

2 14

Who does Grace like?

JOE What are you downloading?
GRACE The latest Dave Blue album. It's new today. I have to buy it!
JOE What do you think of him?
GRACE He's so nice ... and friendly ... and funny. And so good-looking.
JOE He's only a singer! He isn't better than the other ones.
GRACE I don't agree. He's important and rich and famous. – He's a star. I admire him. He's my idol.

Who will Cindy and Eve talk to?

CINDY Hi. Can I walk to school with you?
EVE Sure. Nobody is as friendly as you. Some girls don't like me.
CINDY I know. They're stupid.
EVE They follow me after school every day. They're so unfriendly.
CINDY The teachers will be helpful. Let's talk to one.
EVE I'm not sure ...
CINDY I'm not frightened of those girls. I'll go with you.
EVE Really? You're a star!

1 Look again.

1 Wie fragst du nach einer Meinung über jemanden?
2 Wie sagst du, dass du jemanden bewunderst?
3 Wie kannst du sagen, dass du unsicher bist?
4 Wie sagst du, dass du keine Angst hast?
5 Wie kannst du jemandem sagen, dass du sie/ihn sehr schätzt?

2 Finde elf Wörter in den Dialogen, die Menschen beschreiben können.

nice, ...

3 What's the right word?

Tipp:
Alle diese Adjektive beschreiben Menschen und sind in den Dialogen enthalten.

1 Dave tells lots of jokes. – He's very *funny*.
2 Some pop stars have a lot of money. – They are very ...
3 Jill cooked and washed up for her parents yesterday. – She was very ...
4 Pat went to the new boy in her class and said hello. – She was very ...
5 Some big, noisy dogs ran next to Jake's bike. – He was very ...

▸ W 7, 8

SPEAKING

2 15

1 Intonation: Listen and say

1 What are you downloading? What are you ...

→ playing? • making? • doing? • watching? • painting? • singing?

2 They're so unfriendly. They're so ...

→ funny. • lucky. • famous. • excited. • grumpy. • tired. • helpful.

2 Who do you like? Who don't you like? Talk to a partner about some people.

a film star · a singer · a famous person · an idol · a friend · a person on TV

DIALOGUE A

Sage, wen du magst.
I like ...

↓

Frage, warum.
Why do you like her/him?

↓

Sage, was du an ihr/ihm magst.
I think she's/he's so
nice • funny • friendly • good-looking
helpful • brave • clever • interesting • ...

DIALOGUE B

Sage, wen du nicht magst.
I don't like ...

↓

Frage, warum nicht.
Why don't you like her/him?

↓

Sage, was du an ihr/ihm nicht magst.
I think she's/he's so
silly • unfriendly • boring • noisy
quiet • arrogant • stupid • ...

↓

Sage, dass du diese Meinung teilst / nicht teilst.
I agree. / I don't agree.
She's/He's very ...

▸ W 9

WORDPOWER

1 Belle is writing an email to her cousin Erin in Edinburgh.

a) Her computer has checked the spelling and found some problems. Write the email again for her.

Tip: All the words are verbs in the simple past.

We hda the Middle School Idol competition yesterday.
It aws at school. I palyed the drums in it of course.
Before the competition I tierd my act in the basement.
At the competition all the students erew very nervous.
A jury lstenide to us of course.
But hundreds of other students edwtach the acts too.
A band nwo the competition with 43 points.
But I gto 37 points and I cmae in third place.

b) Now can you finish the email for Belle?

A lot of the acts were terrific – really ...
So I felt very ... about third place. It's the state competition next!
I feel very ... about it! But I have to be very ... – and learn a new solo!
Love, Belle xx

brave
good
happy
nervous

2 Almost the same! What are these German words in English?

1 BANANE
2 WORT
3 FISCH
4 IDEE
5 FOTO
6 HALB
7 MUSIK
8 OKTOBER
9 TEE
10 TOMATE

3 What's the right word?

nearest • next

a) 1 Excuse me. Where's the ... post office?
2 When's the ... bus to Denver?
3 Where will you be for the ... few weeks?
4 After the accident they took me to the ... hospital.

last • latest

b) 1 Listen. Madonna's ... album is on the radio.
2 Do you have the ... information about the accident?
3 Would you like the ... biscuit in the tin?

CHECKPOINT

Leicht zu verwechseln (1):
nearest nächst(gelegener)
Where's the nearest bank?
next nächst(folgender)
When's the next bus?

CHECKPOINT

Leicht zu verwechseln (2):
latest neueste
Is that the latest *Teenmag*?
last (aller)letzte
The last bus was at 8 p.m.

▸ W 10–12

SITUATIONS

Wie kannst du auf Englisch fragen, ...

1 ... ob jemand interessiert ist?
2 ... ob jemand wirklich mitkommen muss?
3 ... was los ist?
4 ... was jemand gerade herunterlädt?

Tip: Look again at pages 68–77.

SOUNDS

Beim flüssigen Sprechen werden im Englischen einzelne Wörter oft miteinander verbunden.

Beispiele: Our‿other bikes are‿in the garage.
The‿information is in the‿email.
Do you have an‿office?
My‿aunt‿Ella would like‿ice cream.
The‿other car in the‿accident was red.
Are you an‿American?

16, 17

1 Can you say these phrases?

1 to‿England, no‿apples, for‿Alan, her‿album, three‿oranges
2 the‿angry dog, the‿evening, the‿other table, the‿uncles
3 an‿old man, an‿underground, an‿accident, an‿address, an‿office

2 Can you say these phrases and sentences?

1 an‿orange, no‿apples, for‿us:
➔ I have an orange but no apples for us.

2 the‿early morning, the‿afternoon, the‿evening:
➔ Come in the early morning, the afternoon or the evening, please.

3 to‿our house, by‿underground, your‿old bike:
➔ Did you come to our house by underground or on your old bike?

WORKING WITH A DICTIONARY

Im Wörterbuch kannst du die Aussprache eines Wortes nachschlagen.
Bei mehrsilbigen Wörtern erfährst du auch, welche Silbe am stärksten betont wird. Das Zeichen ['] zeigt die Hauptbetonung.
Es steht vor der betonten Silbe.

Beispiele: **April** ['eɪprəl] **officer** ['ɒfɪsə] **arrive** [ə'raɪv] **forget** [fə'get]

1 Welche Wörter werden auf der ersten Silbe betont? Prüfe im Wörterbuch nach.

1 hello, accent, perhaps, nineteen, ninety, surprise, nervous, cousin
2 restaurant, magazine, information, expensive, afternoon

LEARNING SKILLS

Do you like listening to English and American pop music?
So kannst du auch trainieren, die englische Sprache besser zu verstehen!

Zunächst versuchst du, einzelne Wörter zu erkennen.

Beim wiederholten Zuhören versuche, genauer zuzuhören – so wirst du allmählich einige Zeilen im Lied verstehen.

Und danach vielleicht ein wenig mitsingen?
– Englisch lernen durch Karaoke!

PRACTICE AND REVISION

STRUCTURES

1 Belle isn't happy. She has too little free time!
What jobs does she have to do?

1 Belle has to help at home.
2 She ... clean her room.
3 She has to ...
4 She has to ...

1 
... help at home.

2 

... clean her room.

3 

... do homework.

4 
... feed the cats.

5 
... do babysitting.

6 

... wash the car.

7 
... go shopping.

8 
... help in the garden.

AND YOU?

Do you have to do those jobs?

I have to I don't have to	help at home. clean my room. do homework. feed the cats. ...

What other things do you have to do? Write three sentences.
I have to go ...
I have to ...

2 Ask for things in shops: Use *one/ones*.

Which MP3 player would you like?
– I'd like the small one, please.

Which apples would you like?
– I'd like the green ones, please.

1 Which T-shirt would you like? (red)
– I'd like the red one, please.
2 Which bike would you like? (cheaper)
3 Which album would you like? (latest)
4 Which headphones would you like? (small)
– I'd like the small ones, please.
5 Which socks would you like? (blue)
6 Which jeans would you like? (black)

► W 13–15

3 On a *Middle School Idol* jury:

a) The people on the jury don't like the acts. What do they say?

Karen Lang was a bad singer.
She was worse than the other singers.
She was the worst singer in the competition.

Denver City was a bad band.
They were ... than the other bands.
They were the ... band in the competition.

Jody Cool was a bad rapper.
He was ... than the other rappers.
He was the ... rapper in the competition.

CHECKPOINT

Vergleichsformen von *bad*:
bad – worse – worst
Tom is a bad singer.
He's worse than you.
He's the worst in the class.

b) But you're on the jury too. You don't agree ...

YOU Karen Lang was a good singer.
She was better than the other singers.
She was the best singer in the competition.

Denver City ...
Jody Cool ...

CHECKPOINT

Vergleichsformen von *good*:
good – better – best
That's a good bike.
It's better than the other bikes.
It's the best bike in the shop.

4 After the competition, a student took a photo of *Sistas* and Belle for the school newspaper. But he doesn't know their names.

Cindy and Haley are wearing red T-shirts.
Haley is carrying an instrument.
Sue is drinking cola.
Jo is carrying a black bag.
Cindy is carrying a blue bag.
Sue and Jo are wearing blue jeans.

a) What are the names of the *Sistas* from left to right?

1 The first girl is ...
2 The second girl is ...
3 The third girl is ...
4 The fourth girl is ...

b) Write information about Belle for the student.

1 Belle is wearing ...
2 She's drinking ...
3 She's listening to ...

c) Can you answer these questions about the photo?

1 Who's reading a text message?
2 Who's carrying an instrument?
3 Who's wearing a black T-shirt?
4 What's Jo wearing?
5 Who's talking on her phone?
6 Which girls have mobiles?

► W 16–18

have to

Mit *have to* / *has to* sagst du, was jemand tun muss.

You **have to** take the dog for a walk.

John **has to** help his parents in their shop.

Aussagen

I You We You They	**have to** make a meal.
He She It	**has to** make a meal.

All children have to go to school.
Alle Kinder müssen zur Schule gehen.
Sally has to work today.
Sally muss heute arbeiten.

Verneinung

I You We You They	**don't have to** go home.
He She It	**doesn't have to** go home.

You don't have to cook today.
Heute musst du nicht kochen.
My sister doesn't have to help today.
Meine Schwester muss heute nicht helfen.

Fragen und Kurzantworten

Do	I you we you they	**have to** go to the shops?
Does	he she it	**have to** go to the shops?

Do you have to get up early? – Yes, I do.

Do pupils have to learn French? – No, they don't.

Does Tom have to go to school? – Yes, he does.

Does he have to help at home? – No, he doesn't.

one/ones

Mit *one* (Mehrzahl *ones*) kannst du Wortwiederholungen vermeiden.

Which bike do you like? The red bike or the blue bike?
– The red bike.
Which bike do you like? The red **one** or the blue **one**?
– The red **one**.

The yellow bags are cheaper than the black bags.
The yellow bags are cheaper than the black **ones**.

The new skateboard is better than the old one.
Das neue Skateboard ist besser als das alte.
Which T-shirt would you like? This one or that one?
Welches T-Shirt möchten Sie? Dieses oder jenes?
The mobiles over there are the most expensive ones.
Die Handys da drüben sind die teuersten.

IN DIESER UNIT HAST DU GELERNT, WIE ...

... du sagst, was jemand tun muss. ▸ *We have to tidy the basement.*
Belle has to clean her room.

... du sagst, was jemand nicht tun muss. ▸ *I don't have to go to school today.*
My brother doesn't have to help at home.

... du Wortwiederholungen vermeiden kannst, z. B. bei Vergleichen. ▸ *This game is better than that one.*
The blue socks are nicer than the red ones.

... du Wortwiederholungen vermeiden kannst, z. B. beim Auswählen. ▸ *Which shirt do you like? This one or that one?*
I'd like some apples. – Which ones?

DU HAST WIEDERHOLT, WIE ...

... gesagt wird, was jemand gerade macht. ▸ *Ann is carrying a bottle of water.*
She's writing a text message.

DU KANNST AUCH VERSTEHEN, WIE ...

... über jemanden, niemanden und alle gesprochen wird. ▸ *I'll listen to somebody on the radio first.*
Nobody is as friendly as you.
Everybody knows him.

... über etwas, nichts oder alles gesprochen wird. ▸ *Tell us something about John Denver.*
They get nothing.
You have to clear everything first.

▸ W Test yourself 1–3

STORY (4)

Who's the new Sistas drummer at the Middle School Idol competition?

9 Star dreams

2 ◉ 18

The state competition was at a TV station in Denver. Belle's parents took her.

Belle's favourite DJ was on the jury.

Belle played but she wasn't very good because she was so nervous.

The jury said some bad things about her.
Rick Miles was the worst.
Belle walked away.

Then she spoke to the *Sistas*. They had a big problem. They told Belle about it.

What was the problem?
What happened next?
What was the rest of the competition like?

Read Belle's letter to her cousin Erin, and find out!

2 ◉ 19

March 25th

Dear Erin,

I told you about the competition in my email. Now here's something from the newspaper. It's a nice report, but you know the REAL story of course!

I felt so bad after my act when I spoke to the Sistas. But when their lead singer answered her cellphone, she looked worse. She looked SICK when she heard the news about their drummer's accident! A broken arm was unlucky for their drummer, but her accident was lucky for me.

Suddenly the Sistas were very friendly. "Can you play with us, Belle? Do you know 'Star dreams'?" They were lucky – I know that one. But a few weeks ago the Sistas weren't so nice to me. I wasn't sure at first. And I felt bad after my act. But the Sistas really needed me! "Please, Belle. You have to help us." And it was a big chance for me, so I said yes. I played in the competition twice!

After my solo act Rick Miles said, "Girl drummers are all terrible." And he was so unfriendly too. But after "Star Dreams" he ate his words! Before the competition, I really liked him – now I know better! He's a star radio DJ, but isn't my idol!

I like playing in a band. We're really great together. Next month it's the competition in New York. But we have to practise together first!

Love, **Belle**

PS What about some photos of Edinburgh and that cool Scottish boy?

LOCAL GIRLS NEW IDOLS

Teenagers win state competition

There was great new music last night at a competition. First prize went to Sistas – an exciting young all-girl band. Th…

Their lead singer was cool, but the jury loved their drummer. They played "Star Dreams" and

► W 19–21

Unit 5

Going places

How can I go to school?

2 20

WE KNOW ...

- **some travelling words:** go to, holiday, train, ...
- **things you need when you travel.**

GARY INMAN (13) and his family live near Detroit. Their home is in a suburb. Gary has two sisters – Holly and Alice. Holly is 16. Alice is only 11.

2 ⊙ 21

Detroit is a big city with a lot of industry. The city is most famous for its car factories so people sometimes call it *Motor City* or *Motown*.

Gary's parents have two cars.
His father usually drives the SUV to work.
He works in a car factory in Detroit.
His mother works in a school.
She usually takes their other car.

GARY

I usually go to school by school bus.
I don't like getting up in the morning so I sometimes miss it.
Then I ride my bike.
It's sometimes as fast as the bus, because
the bus often stops for more students.
And a bike causes less air and noise pollution too!

Here's a photo of our motorhome.
We use it for weekend trips and vacations.
We leave the city and the suburbs.
We drive to the open highway.
We stay on campsites and sleep in the country.
It's great!

▸ W1, 2

PRESENTATION

A–D
2 22-25

A

Gary's class is doing a traffic project.
They want answers to some questions.

- *How do students go to school?*
- *How do they travel at weekends?*

B

Gary often goes to school by bus.
He sometimes goes to school by car.
He ... goes to school by bike.
He ... goes to school by train.
He ... walks to school.
At weekends Gary often travels by car.
He sometimes ... He doesn't often ...

Traffic Project Name: Gary Inman

How do you travel?
SCHOOL

	always	usually	often	sometimes	never
by bus			✔		
by car				✔	
by bike				✔	
by train					✔
walk					✔

WEEKENDS I often travel by car.
I sometimes ride my bike. I don't often walk.

Exercise 1: And his friend Abbie?

Abbie sometimes goes to school by bus.
She ... by car.
She ...

At weekends Abbie often ...
She ... by car. She doesn't ...

Traffic Project Name: Abbie Greenbaum

How do you travel?
SCHOOL

	always	usually	often	sometimes	never
by bus				✔	
by car					✔
by bike		✔			
by train					✔
walk				✔	

WEEKENDS I often ride my bike.
I sometimes travel by car. I don't travel by train.

AND YOU?

I ... go to school by bus.
I ... go to school by car.
I ... go to school by bike.
I ... go to school by train.
I ... walk to school.

At weekends I ...

▸ W 3

CHECKPOINT

Mit der Zeitform *simple present* kannst du über Gewohnheiten sprechen.
Oft sind auch Häufigkeitsangaben wie *always, usually, often, sometimes, never* dabei:

I usually **watch** TV in the evening.
Pat often **listens** to her MP3 player on the bus.
We always **play** football after school.
I **go** to bed at 9 o'clock.

goes/go; always, usually, often, sometimes, never (Wdh.)

C Here are the results of the traffic project at Gary's school:

35 % of students go to school only by car.
17 % use the school bus.
12 % walk.
3 % ride their bikes to school.
2 % go by local bus.
31 % use more than one way.

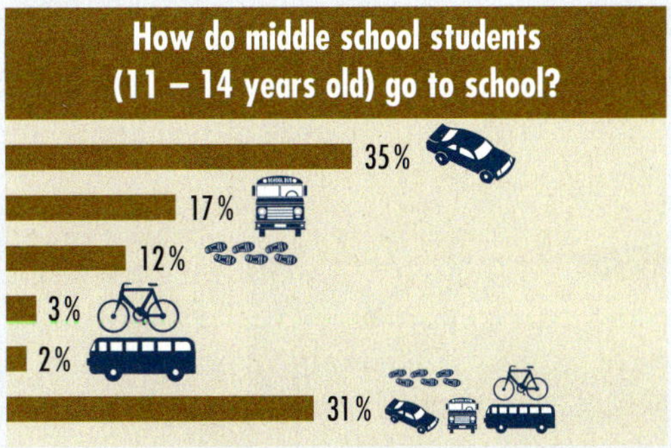

Exercise 2: Talk about the results of the traffic project.

1 Most students	takes 17 % of the students to school.
2 A lot of parents	use more than one way.
3 Some students	go to school by car.
4 A school bus	go to school by train.
5 Few students	ride their bikes to school.
6 No students	take students by car.

Exercise 3: What's Gary's problem? Choose the right form of the verb.

1 Gary and his sisters (live/lives) near Detroit.
2 Gary (go/goes) to a middle school.
3 Most students (go/goes) to school by car.
4 Gary usually (go/goes) by bus. The journey (take/takes) 20 minutes.
5 But Gary sometimes (get/gets) up late and he (miss/misses) the bus.
6 Then he (arrive/arrives) late. He (get/gets) a note from his teacher.
7 After two notes a student's parents (get/gets) a letter.
8 And after three notes the student (go/goes) to school on a Saturday!

CHECKPOINT

Verben im *simple present* haben eine *s*-Endung nach:

- **einzelnen Namen**
  Emily swim**s** every day.
  Eminem come**s** from Detroit.
- **he/she/it**
  She (= Emily) swim**s** here.
  It (= the pen) cost**s** $2.
- **Nomen im Singular**
  My dad love**s** ice cream.
  The bus leave**s** at 2 p.m.

▸W 4

D Gary's sister Holly works at a supermarket on Saturdays. Now she can buy a cheap car.

E–F
2 26, 27

E The USA is a big country. (It's 27 times bigger than Germany!)
Transport was very important in the history of the USA.
With better forms of transport, the USA became a big, successful country.

Native Americans travelled in boats or walked. The first Europeans arrived by ship.

At first the Europeans had horses and waggons. There were no roads of course. Travelling west was difficult.

Travelling became easier with trains. In 1869 a line went across the country. People travelled to the west and between new cities.

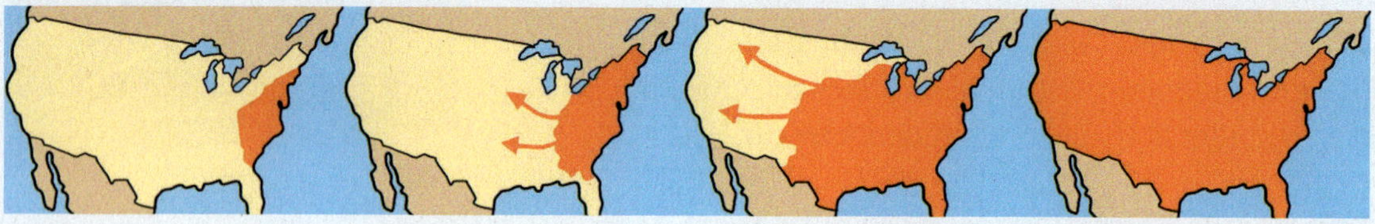

▸ W 5

F

Modern Americans choose the car for most journeys.
In the USA most people over 16 drive a car.
People use cars for local and long journeys.
People often travel by air for longer journeys, though some people travel between towns by bus or train.

Buses and trains aren't so popular as cars and planes.
But few people choose them now.

AND YOU?

What can you say about travelling in Germany?

People	use	cars	for local journeys.
People don't	choose	planes	for longer journeys.
Some people	like	trains	for holidays.
Few people		buses	between towns.
		bikes	for shopping.

CHECKPOINT

Mit dem *simple present* kannst du sagen, was normalerweise der Fall ist:

Most Americans **live** in cities.
Most young people **like** music.
Most people **travel** by car.
Tina **goes** to work by bus.

TRUE STORY – Henry Ford's big idea

2 ⦿ 28

Henry Ford (1863 – 1947)

As a child, Henry Ford lived on a farm in Michigan. He left school early. Because he was interested in machines he became an engineer. He was interested in all machines, though his great love was a new way of travelling – the car. In 1896 he made his first one.

He started a company in Detroit. In 1908 they made the first Model T. It made Henry Ford famous.

Why was it special? Before the Model T, cars were very expensive, and only rich people could buy them. They often cost $5000. The Model T was not so expensive as the other cars. It cost only $850. Henry Ford's great idea was a moving assembly line in the factory.

They made lots of cars with the same parts. At first all the cars were the same: "You can have any colour, as long as it's black." His workers earned more than at other factories. Soon half the cars in America were Model Ts. In 1925 they made a car every ten seconds. And in 1925 the car cost only $360. They sold 15 million Model Ts, and made the last one in 1926.

Now millions of people drive cars in the USA. Ford and the Model T changed the way people travel.

He changed the way we make things in factories. And he changed America too.

SONG* – On the road again

2 ⦿ 29

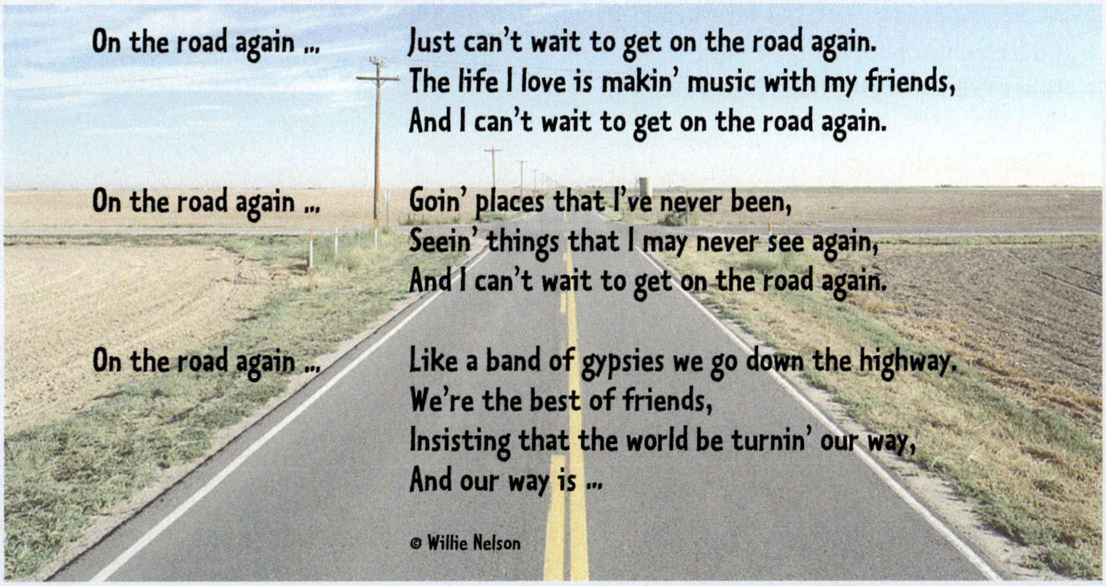

On the road again ...

Just can't wait to get on the road again.
The life I love is makin' music with my friends,
And I can't wait to get on the road again.

On the road again ...

Goin' places that I've never been,
Seein' things that I may never see again,
And I can't wait to get on the road again.

On the road again ...

Like a band of gypsies we go down the highway.
We're the best of friends,
Insisting that the world be turnin' our way,
And our way is ...

LISTENING AND READING

LISTENING – Loudspeaker information

2 ⦿ 30

1 Listen to the three scenes. Find the right photo for each scene. One photo doesn't belong here.

SCENE 1 Photo ... **SCENE 2** Photo ... **SCENE 3** Photo ...

> **Tipp:**
> Du musst das erste Mal nicht alles verstehen. Die Aufnahmen hörst du mehrmals. Die Fotos zeigen dir, wo die jeweilige Aussage zu hören ist.

A

B

C

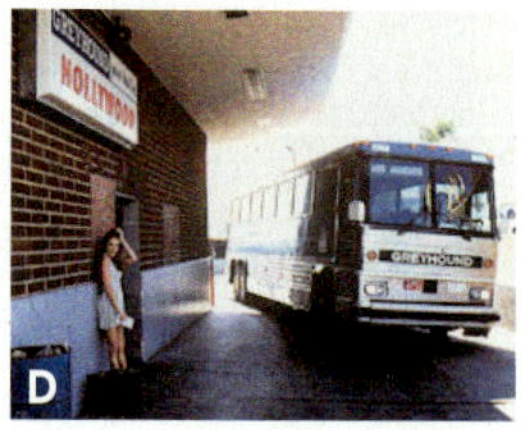
D

2 Listen to number 1 again. Which is the right sign for the plane?

A NORTH EAST AIR 876 / MIAMI GATE 69

B AMERICAN AIR 876 / MIAMI GATE 66

C NORTH EAST AIR 876 / DETROIT GATE 69

3 Listen to number 2 again. Where will the bus <u>not</u> go?

A Battle Creek **B** Detroit
C Ann Arbor **D** Denver

4 Read a question. Then listen to number 3 again and find the answer.

1 What's the train number?
2 What's the last town the train will go to?
3 Can people smoke on the train?

► W 6

READING – A poster

Look at the poster on page 93. When's the special week?

> **Tipp:**
> Auf den ersten Blick kannst du wichtige Informationen, z. B. über die Zeit, herausfinden.

1 Basic reading

1 Is the special week only in the USA?
2 What should people do in the week?
3 Where can you get more information?

2 Does the poster tell you ...

1 ... how often the week happens?
2 ... why the week is a good idea?
3 ... who has more information?
5 ... a teacher's phone number?

3 Find the English words and phrases.

1 einmal im Jahr
2 weltweit
3 weniger Autos
4 in der Nähe von Schulen
5 Fang an!

4 Language tasks

Make a list of English words about traffic. How many can you find in the text?

► W 7

Tip: New words on page 93 are in the dictionary (p. 118–136).

iwalk

International Walk to School

October 3-7

Join children and adults around the world for a week of walking!

why walk?

International Walk to School Week happens once a year. It is an event to raise awareness world wide of walking issues.

Walking week ...

- is healthy.
- teaches safe walking to younger children.
- shows how walkable a district is.
- reminds people about the environment.
- helps towards cleaner air.
- means fewer cars and traffic jams.
- makes roads near schools safer.
- brings people together and is fun!

get started at:

www.iwalktoschool.org

and contact your local coordinator: Mrs Fernandez

ACTIONS – Asking about journeys

2 31

Where's the campsite for tents?

JILL Do you have a campsite for tents?
MAN Sorry. Only motorhomes stay here. Hikers go to Sundale.
JILL How far is it?
MAN About an hour.
JILL How do I get there?
MAN Just drive along the road. Then left and go along the river to Sundale.
JILL Pardon? Can you say that again, please?
MAN I'll show you a map.

How often do buses go to Chicago?

WOMAN Hi. How can I help you?
BOB How do I get to Springfield?
WOMAN Take a bus to Chicago. Then take another bus to Springfield from there.
BOB How long is the journey?
WOMAN About 12 hours.
BOB How often do the buses go?
WOMAN Buses to Chicago leave every hour.

1 Look again.

1 Wie fragst du, wie weit etwas entfernt ist?
2 Wie fragst du nach dem Weg?
3 Wie fragst du, wenn du jemanden nicht verstanden hast?
4 Wie bittest du jemanden, etwas zu wiederholen?
5 Wie fragst du nach der Reisedauer?
6 Wie fragst du, wie oft die Busse verkehren?

2 Finde vier Verben in den Dialogen, die mit Fortbewegung zu tun haben.

go, …

3 What's the right word?

1 The trains take between 50 and 70 minutes – That's … an hour.
2 Is the station on the right or on the …?
3 I don't know the way. I think I'll buy a … of the town.
4 The bus leaves at 1 p.m. and arrives at 2 p.m. The … takes one hour.
5 When's the next bus from here … Detroit?
6 How … is it from New York to Chicago?

Tipp: Alle Wörter sind in den Dialogen enthalten.

▶ W 8

SPEAKING

2 ⊙ 32

1 Intonation: Listen and say

1 Just drive along the road. Just drive to the ...

→ supermarket. • museum. • bridge. • car park. • church. • town.

2 How do I get to Springfield? How do I get to ...

→ the station? • the campsite? • Dean Road? • the park? • the hotel?

2 Make a dialogue at a tourist office. Get information about a campsite.

Frage, wie du behilflich sein kannst.	⇨	Frage, wie du zum Campingplatz kommst.
Sage, der Campingplatz ist in Greenbridge.	⇨	Frage, wie weit es mit dem Rad ist.
Sage, die Fahrt dauert etwa eine Stunde.	⇨	Frage, wie du dorthin kommst.
Biete an, dass du den Weg auf einer Landkarte zeigst.	⇨	Bedanke dich.

▸ W 9

PROJECT* – How our class comes to school

1. Make groups. Each student in your group asks about a different way of coming to school.

   → by bike • by bus • by car • by train • by tram • on foot

2. Each student makes a list. (Don't forget yourself on the list!)

   Now ask all the other students in your group:
   How often do you come to school by bus?
   Tick (✔) the right box.

bus	Tom	Alina	Jenny	Anne	me
usually		✔	✔		
sometimes				✔	
never					

3. Report back to the class.
   I asked about coming by bus: Two students usually ...

4. Write the information on the board.
   Or you can make a poster of all the information from your class.

5. Discuss the information.
   15 students come by ...
   ... students always come to school on foot. More students come by ... than by ...

PRACTICE AND REVISION

WORDPOWER

1 People do lots of things with computers.

a) Can you find ten different things?

1 You can listen to music.
2 You can ...

b) You can't do everything with a computer! Can you find one more thing?

You can't download food!

2 The motorhome: Put the sentences together and make one new sentence.

→ and • because • but • so • though

1 Gary's parents have two cars. They have a motorhome too.
2 They bought a motorhome. They like camping.
3 They like camping. They don't have long holidays.
4 They don't work at weekends. They often drive to the country.
5 They always find a place. The campsites are often full.
6 Grandma Inman lives in St Louis. They can't often see her.
7 It's a long journey. They often take the motorhome.
8 They visit grandma. They always watch their favourite team too!

CHECKPOINT

Konjunktionen verbinden Sätze:
and = und
but = aber
so = daher, also
because = weil
though = obwohl

3 Which words can finish the sentence? Only three are OK.

1 Please answer the ... phone. • letter. • dog. • question.
2 Let's book a ... holiday. • table. • ticket. • lake.
3 I must open the ... gate. • letter. • birthday. • door.
4 I'll wear my new ... curtains. • swimsuit. • jeans. • uniform.
5 Can you play ... this game? • this book? • football? • an instrument?
6 Put the book in your ... map. • cupboard. • bag. • pocket.

► W 10, 11

SITUATIONS

Wie kannst du auf Englisch fragen, ...

1 ... wie jemand fährt/reist?
2 ... ob dich jemand mitnimmt?
3 ... wie die Zugnummer ist?
4 ... wie du helfen kannst?

Tip: Look again at pages 86–95.

SOUNDS

Das Buchstabenpaar *th* hat zwei Aussprachevarianten.
Die phonetische Umschrift gibt den Laut mit den Zeichen [ð] bzw. [θ] wieder.
[ð] ist stimmhaft: **mother, brother, the, with**
[θ] ist stimmlos: **think, month, thank, three**

33, 34

1 Can you say these words?

1 [ð] father, other, then, clothes, with, together, weather
2 [θ] bathroom, thirsty, month, teeth, thousand, through, nothing, north

• 2 Can you say these word pairs?

1 ten – then, wetter – weather; Dan – than, day – they; sat – that, say – they
2 part – path, tree – three, tent – tenth; sing – thing, use – youth ▸ W 15

WORKING WITH A DICTIONARY

Wörterbücher verwenden oft Abkürzungen für zusätzliche Informationen über ein Wort.

Beispiele: **pink** [pɪŋk] *adj.* rosa (= Das Wort *pink* ist ein Adjektiv)
write sth. down etwas aufschreiben *(sth. = something)*

1 Wofür stehen diese häufigen Abkürzungen aus Wörterbüchern?

1 Deutsch: ugs., usw., jd., jdm., bzw., Adj.
2 English: sb., AE, BE, pl., e.g.

LEARNING SKILLS

Do you like using a computer?
You can learn English words with it.
Schreibe die neuen Wörter (z. B. im *Vocabulary*) mit der deutschen Übersetzung in Spalten ab. Diese Liste kannst du auch ausdrucken. Decke eine Spalte zu und teste dich.
Wenn du ein Wort gelernt hast, kannst du es durchstreichen bzw. in einer neuen Fassung im Computer löschen. So bleiben immer nur die Wörter übrig, die du noch zu lernen hast.

Do you often use your mobile phone?
Auch auf deinem Handy kannst du Wörterlisten anlegen.
Gib das englische Wort und die deutsche Übersetzung ein.
Oder du legst dir eine Liste mit den unregelmäßigen Verben, den Vergangenheitsformen und der Übersetzung an.
Wenn du auf deine Freunde oder den Bus wartest, kannst du gut diese englischen Vokabeln lernen.

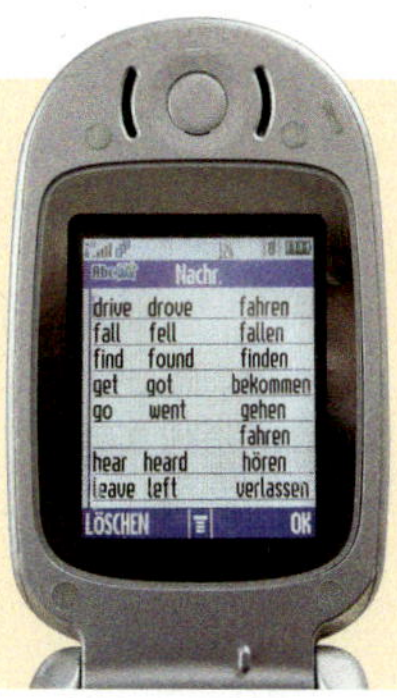

PRACTICE AND REVISION

STRUCTURES

1 The *coolphone*

a) What do the people do with it?

They make phone calls.
They send text messages.
They play ...
They ...

**b) Gary has a *coolphone*.
What things does he do with it?**

1 He makes phone calls with it.
2 He ... text messages with it.
3 He ... games with it.
4 He ... the time with it.

c) What things doesn't Gary do with it?

1 He doesn't read emails with it.
2 He ... music with it.
3 He ... videos with it.
4 He ... the Web with it.

new · new · new · new · new · new

coolphone

- Make phone calls.
- Send text messages.
- Play games.
- Check the time.
- Read emails.
- Listen to music.
- Watch videos.
- Surf the Web.

coolphone – for active people

CHECKPOINT

Beachte im *simple present* bei *he/she/it*:
- **die *s*-Endung:**
He make**s** phone calls with his *coolphone*.
- **die verneinte Form mit *doesn't*:**
He **doesn't read** emails with it.

AND YOU?

I have a mobile phone.
I ... with my mobile phone.
I don't ... with my mobile phone.

I don't have a mobile phone.
I like / don't like mobile phones.
I want / don't want a mobile phone.

2 Holly has a *coolphone* too. How does she use it?

phone calls • emails
text messages • videos

Holly makes phone calls with it.
She ... with it. She ...

games • the time
music • the Web

She doesn't play games with it.
She doesn't ...

3 Can you say two things about different ways of travelling?

What are your ideas?

1 Local buses
They don't take you on long journeys.
They take you to your local shops.
2 Planes
3 Bikes
4 Cars
5 Trains

You (don't) wait for them.
You (don't) stay dry when it rains.
They (don't) take you to your local shops.
They (don't) take you on long journeys.
They (don't) carry a lot of things for you.
They (don't) cause pollution.
They (don't) go everywhere.

▸ W 12, 13

4 Alice is doing a project about cars and bikes. Help her with facts about bikes. Use *don't*.

1 Cars need big car parks in cities. — Bikes don't need big car parks in cities.
2 Cars cause traffic problems. — Bikes don't ...
3 Cars make noise pollution. — Bikes ...
4 Cars cause air pollution. — Bikes ...
5 Cars kill lots of people. — Bikes ...
6 Cars need big roads. — Bikes ...

5 Gary is visiting you in Germany.

a) What are his questions?

1 I live in a suburb.
– Do you live in a suburb?
2 I go to a middle school. – Do you go ...?
3 I go to school by bus. – Do you ...?
4 I sometimes arrive late for school. ...?
5 I have two sisters. ...?
6 We spend weekends in the country. ...?
7 We use a motorhome for vacations. ...?
8 I love baseball. ...?

b) Ask him four questions.

Do you	like	Germany?
	eat	football • ...
	play	Bavarian sausages?
	watch	an MP3 player?
	have	Munich • ... (your town/village)?
	listen to	... (a singer / a band)?

Example: Do you like Wasserburg?

6 How do older American students get to school? Look at the information.

a) Answer the questions.

→ Yes, they do. • No, they don't.

1 Do most students go to school by bus?
2 Do some students drive their own car?
3 Do a lot of students go with their parents?
4 Do more students go by bike than by car?
5 Do some students go to school by train?

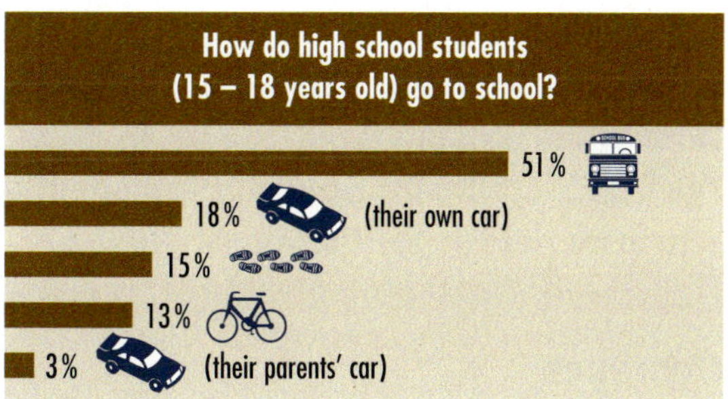

● **b) Write a report about the American high school students.**

... % of students	ride	their bikes to school.
Most students	go	their own car.
Only a few	walk	to school by car/train/bus.
No students	drive	to high school.
Some students		

Going to an American high school

This is a report about some American high school students. The students are between 15 and 18 years old.
Most students go to school by ...

► W 14, 16

simple present (Wiederholung)

In Unit 5 hast du die Gegenwartsform *simple present* wiederholt.

John and Frank cook lunch every Sunday.
But they don't cook lunch in the week.

Bildung

We live in Bavaria.

- **Aussagen** sehen so aus:

I eat fish. Ich esse Fisch.
We live in Bavaria. Wir leben in Bayern.
They drive a French car. Sie fahren ein französisches Auto.

! Nach *he, she, it* hat das Verb die Endung *-s*.
She work**s** in a shop. Sie arbeitet in einem Geschäft.
Tom sleep**s** in this bedroom. Tom schläft in diesem Schlafzimmer.

- Bei **Verneinungen** steht *don't/doesn't* vor dem Verb:

We **don't** have a dog. Wir haben keinen Hund.
I **don't** play tennis. Tennis spiele ich nicht.
Alan **doesn't** swim. Alan schwimmt nicht.
Julia **doesn't** eat fish. Julia isst keinen Fisch.

She doesn't eat fish.

- **Fragen** werden mit *do/does* gestellt:

Do you like animals? Magst du Tiere?
Do the boys play in a band? Spielen die Jungen in einer Band?
Does Darris come from Brixton? Kommt Darris aus Brixton?
Where **do** you live? Wo wohnst du?

Do you like animals?

Gebrauch

- Was immer wieder geschieht:

School starts at 9 o'clock. Die Schule fängt um 9 Uhr an.

- Was jemand immer wieder tut:

I ride my bike every day. Ich fahre jeden Tag Rad.

- Was immer der Fall ist:

Cars need roads. Autos brauchen Straßen.

- Was du magst (oder nicht magst):

I like animals. Ich mag Tiere.

Zeitangaben

Beim *simple present* zeigen meist Zeitangaben, wie oft eine Handlung geschieht:

on Wednesday • at weekends

every day • every week
every month • every year

On Sundays we go to church.
Sonntags gehen wir in die Kirche.

always • often • never
sometimes • usually

My sister often goes to the cinema.
Meine Schwester geht oft ins Kino.

IN DIESER UNIT HAST DU GELERNT, WIE ...

... du um Auskunft bittest. ▸ *How far is it?*
How often do the buses go?

... du bei Unsicherheit nachfragen kannst. ▸ *Pardon? Can you say that again, please?*

DU HAST WIEDERHOLT, WIE ...

... du über Gewohnheiten berichtest. ▸ *I go to school by bike.*
Tom gets up at 7 o'clock.

... du sagst, was immer der Fall ist. ▸ *Most people travel by car.*
Most Americans live in cities.

... du nach Gewohnheiten fragst. ▸ *Do you often watch TV?*
Does Jill play tennis?

DU KANNST AUCH VERSTEHEN, WIE ...

... Sachen verglichen werden. ▸ *A bus is as fast as a car.*
Buses aren't so popular as cars.

▸ W Test yourself 1–3

STORY (5)

How do the Inmans travel on their weekend trips?

9 On the road again

2 35

I like the weekend trips in our motorhome.
We often drive to places in Michigan and
stay at a campsite in the country.
There are lakes, rivers and forests.
There are wild animals in the forests too.

Before we go ...

2 36

Before we leave we always run around a lot.
We take so much: everything except
the kitchen sink – that's already in
the motorhome!
For dad, the trip starts with the same
Willie Nelson song.
Like last weekend ...

On the road ...

2 37

But at last everything goes in the motorhome.
We start our journey, though we always leave late.

2 38

Then we arrive ...

We always arrive at the campsite in the evening.
But the quiet life doesn't start then.
Dad cooks the evening meal. I fix the hook-ups.
Then I have to help mom with the table and chairs.
We like eating outside.

► W 17–19

Schlüssel zu den Einträgen

Tipp
Jede Unit beginnt mit einem Lerntipp.

Seitenzahl
Das neue Wort kommt auf dieser Seite in der Unit vor.

Wortschatz
Die **fett** gedruckten Wörter sollst du verstehen und benutzen können.

Wortschatz
Schräg gedruckte Wörter kommen in Liedern, Reimen, Projekten usw. vor.

Wortschatz
Normal gedruckte Wörter sollst du verstehen.

Pfeile
verweisen auf die Kästen.

Die Lautschrift
zeigt dir die richtige Aussprache.

Unit 1

Unit 1

TIPP Freunde und Bekannte

Wahre Freunde sind Wörter, die auf Englisch und Deutsch gleich sind.
Beispiele: *camping, hotel, computer, poster …*
Aber Vorsicht bei der Aussprache!
Denke auch an die Schreibweise: Auf Englisch werden nur das Personalpronomen „I" und Namen groß geschrieben.

Gute Bekannte sind Wörter, die auf Englisch und Deutsch ähnlich sind. Der Zusammenhang im Satz hilft dir bei der Bedeutung. Beispiele: *banana, December, family, garden …*

In Unit 2 werden wir auch noch **falschen Freunden** begegnen.

In London

p. 8	**for business** [fə ˈbɪznəs]	geschäftlich	→ She goes to London for business.
	study [ˈstʌdi]	lernen, studieren	
	learn [lɜːn]	lernen	→ Learn five new English words every day.
p. 9	**traffic** [ˈtræfɪk]	Verkehr	
	crime [kraɪm]	Verbrechen, Kriminalität	
	proud [praʊd]	stolz	→ He's proud!
	Londoner [ˈlʌndənə]	Londoner/Londonerin	
	should [ʃʊd]	sollte/solltest/sollten/solltet	
	background [ˈbækgraʊnd]	Hintergrund, Herkunft	
	language [ˈlæŋgwɪdʒ]	Sprache	
	sight [saɪt]	Sehenswürdigkeit →	
	act [ækt]	darstellen, vorspielen	

→ *Beachte!*
gh wird nicht ausgesprochen: sight, right, light

Sights of London

p. 10	waxworks [ˈwækswɜːks]	Wachsfiguren(kabinett)	
	column [ˈkɒləm]	Säule	
	admiral [ˈædmərəl]	Admiral	
	experiment [ɪkˈsperɪmənt]	Experiment, Versuch	→ We did an experiment in the lesson.
	dinosaur [ˈdaɪnəsɔː]	Dinosaurier	
	queen [kwiːn]	Königin	→ Elizabeth II is the Queen of England.
	home [həʊm]	Zuhause, Heim, Heimat	
p. 11	**juggler** [ˈdʒʌglə]	Jongleur, Gaukler/Gauklerin	
	dancer [ˈdɑːnsə]	Tänzer/Tänzerin	
	about [əˈbaʊt]	ungefähr	→ There are about 950 pupils in my school.
	bell [bel]	Glocke	
	bridge [brɪdʒ]	Brücke	

Presentation

p. 12	**sightseeing** [ˈsaɪtsiːɪŋ]	Besichtigung, Besichtigung von Sehenswürdigkeiten	
	guide book [ˈgaɪd bʊk]	Reiseführer	
	central [ˈsentrəl]	zentral, Zentral-	
	underground [ˈʌndəgraʊnd]	U-Bahn →	
	stop [stɒp]	anhalten	
p. 14	**go skateboarding** [gəʊ ˈskeɪtbɔːdɪŋ]	zum Skateboarden gehen	
p. 15	**terrific** [təˈrɪfɪk]	wunderbar, hervorragend	→ This computer game is terrific!

→ Underground
London has the oldest and longest underground in the world.

ʌ study, London   dʒ juggler, bridge

107 a hundred and seven

Die rechte Spalte
enthält **Anwendungsbeispiele** sowie **Kästen** mit weiterführenden Informationen.

Rot = Schwerpunkt: Grammatik
Blau = Schwerpunkt: Sprache
Gelb = Schwerpunkt: Kulturelle Besonderheiten

Unit 1

TIPP **Freunde und Bekannte**

Wahre Freunde sind Wörter, die auf Englisch und Deutsch gleich sind.
Beispiele: *camping, hotel, computer, poster ...*
Aber Vorsicht bei der Aussprache!
Denke auch an die Schreibweise: Auf Englisch werden nur das Personalpronomen „I" und Namen groß geschrieben.

Gute Bekannte sind Wörter, die auf Englisch und Deutsch ähnlich sind. Der Zusammenhang im Satz hilft dir bei der Bedeutung. Beispiele: *banana, December, family, garden ...*

In Unit 2 werden wir auch noch **falschen Freunden** begegnen.

In London

p. 8	**for business** [fə 'bɪznəs]	geschäftlich	→ She goes to London for business.
	study ['stʌdi]	lernen, studieren	
	learn [lɜːn]	lernen	→ Learn five new English words every day.
p. 9	**traffic** ['træfɪk]	Verkehr	
	crime [kraɪm]	Verbrechen, Kriminalität	
	proud [praʊd]	stolz	→ He's proud!
	Londoner ['lʌndənə]	Londoner/Londonerin	
	should [ʃʊd]	sollte/solltest/sollten/solltet	
	background ['bækgraʊnd]	Hintergrund, Herkunft	
	language ['læŋgwɪdʒ]	Sprache	
	sight [saɪt]	Sehenswürdigkeit →	
	act [ækt]	darstellen, vorspielen	

→ *Beachte!*
gh wird nicht ausgesprochen:
sight, right, light

Sights of London

p. 10	waxworks ['wækswɜːks]	Wachsfiguren(kabinett)	
	column ['kɒləm]	Säule	
	admiral ['ædmɪrəl]	Admiral	
	experiment [ɪk'sperɪmənt]	Experiment, Versuch	→ We did an experiment in the lesson.
	dinosaur ['daɪnəsɔː]	Dinosaurier	
	queen [kwiːn]	Königin	→ Elizabeth II is the Queen of England.
	home [həʊm]	Zuhause, Heim, Heimat	
p. 11	**juggler** ['dʒʌglə]	Jongleur, Gaukler/Gauklerin	
	dancer ['dɑːnsə]	Tänzer/Tänzerin	
	about [ə'baʊt]	ungefähr	→ There are about 950 pupils in my school.
	bell [bel]	Glocke	
	bridge [brɪdʒ]	Brücke	

Presentation

p. 12	**sightseeing** ['saɪtsiːɪŋ]	Besichtigung, Besichtigung von Sehenswürdigkeiten	
	guide book ['gaɪd bʊk]	Reiseführer	
	central ['sentrəl]	zentral, Zentral-	
	underground ['ʌndəgraʊnd]	U-Bahn →	
	stop [stɒp]	anhalten	
p. 14	**go skateboarding** [gəʊ 'skeɪtbɔːdɪŋ]	zum Skateboarden gehen	
p. 15	**terrific** [tə'rɪfɪk]	wunderbar, hervorragend	→ This computer game is terrific!

→ Underground
London has the oldest and longest underground in the world.

ʌ **stu**dy, L**o**ndon   dʒ **j**u**gg**ler, bri**dg**e

economy flyer [ɪ'kɒnəmi flaɪə]	*hier:* Überflieger	
fly by [flaɪ 'baɪ]	vorbei-/vorüberfliegen	
get busy [get 'bɪzi]	sich mit etwas beschäftigen	
sky [skaɪ]	Himmel	→ He studies the sky.
he will take to the air [hi wɪl teɪk tə ði 'eə]	er wird an der Luft Gefallen finden, er wird sich an die Luft gewöhnen	
stare [steə]	(an)starren	
move [mu:v]	(sich) bewegen	
every now and then [everi naʊ ənd 'ðen]	ab und zu, hin und wieder	
climb [klaɪm]	klettern	
rap rhymes [ræp 'raɪmz]	Reime „rappen"	
scene [si:n]	Szene, Ort	
quick [kwɪk]	schnell, flott	
keen [ki:n]	eifrig, kühn, verwegen	
cannot ['kænɒt]	kann/kannst/können/könnt nicht →	
conceal [kən'si:l]	verbergen, verheimlichen	
feel [fi:l]	(sich) fühlen, sich anfühlen	
speed [spi:d]	rasen, schnell fahren	
retire [rɪ'taɪə]	sich zurückziehen, zurücktreten	
get higher and higher [get haɪər ənd 'haɪə]	immer höher aufsteigen	
defy [dɪ'faɪ]	trotzen, sich widersetzen	
gravity ['grævɪti]	Schwerkraft	
quite [kwaɪt]	recht, ziemlich	
heavenly ['hevənli]	himmlisch, göttlich	
poet [pəʊɪt]	Dichter/Dichterin	

→ ***cannot* und *can't***
Beim Sprechen wird *cannot* mit der Kurzform *can't* ersetzt:
I can't play football today.

Listening and Reading

p. 16	**... the story is about ...** [ðə 'stɔ:ri ɪz ə'baʊt]	... die Geschichte handelt von ...	→ What's this book about? 
	brochure ['brəʊʃə]	Broschüre, Prospekt	
	tourist ['tʊərɪst]	Tourist/Touristin	
	basic reading [beɪsɪk 'ri:dɪŋ]	Basiswissen: Lesen	
	detail ['di:teɪl]	Detail, Einzelheit	
	task [tɑ:sk]	Aufgabe	→ This is a difficult task.
	way [weɪ]	Art, Weise, Möglichkeit	→ What's the best way to learn English?

Active English

p. 18	**a.m.** [eɪ'em]	vormittags, morgens	
p. 19	**act** [ækt]	darstellen, vorspielen	

Practice and Revision

p. 21	**copy** ['kɒpi]	kopieren, abschreiben	→ Sarah is copying the picture. 
p. 23	**carnival** ['kɑ:nɪvəl]	Karneval	
	first [fɜ:st]	zuerst, zum ersten Mal	→ First have a drink. Then let's talk.
	put together [pʊt tə'geðə]	zusammensetzen	

Story (1) – A weekend in London

p. 27	**surf the Internet** [sɜ:f ði 'ɪntənet]	im Internet surfen	

ɜ: first, church   i: reading, detail

	church [tʃɜːtʃ]	Kirche	
	great at ['greɪt ət]	super/großartig in	→ She is great at all sports.
	nothing ['nʌθɪŋ]	nichts	
	somebody stole → steal [sʌmbədi 'stəʊl]	jemand stahl, jemand hat gestohlen	
	steal [stiːl]	stehlen	
	mate [meɪt]	Freund, Kumpel *(ugs.)*	
	not really [nɒt 'rɪːəli]	eigentlich nicht	
	mobile ['məʊbaɪl]	Handy, Mobiltelefon	
p. 28	**trick** [trɪk]	Trick, Kunststück	
	she stood → stand [ʃi 'stʊd]	sie stand, sie hat gestanden	
	skate [skeɪt]	„skaten", Skateboard fahren	
	dance [dɑːns]	tanzen	
	shout [ʃaʊt]	rufen, schreien	
	want a word [wɒnt ə 'wɜːd]	sich unterhalten wollen, ein Wort wechseln wollen	
p. 29	**pocket** ['pɒkɪt]	Tasche	
	he gave → give [hi 'geɪv]	er gab, er hat gegeben	→ Anna gave Tim a birthday present.
	give [gɪv]	geben	
	leaflet ['liːflet]	Flugblatt, Werbeprospekt, Handzettel	
	competition [kɒmpə'tɪʃn]	Wettbewerb	→ There's a school swimming competition.
	That's a pity. [ðæts ə 'pɪti]	Das ist schade.	
	prize [praɪz]	Preis, Gewinn	

Unregelmäßige Verben
Der Pfeil → weist auf die Grundform (Infinitiv) des Verbs hin.

Vorsicht!
Handy (deutsch) – *mobile* (englisch)

Leicht zu verwechseln:
price [s] - *prize* [z]

Unit 2

TIPP Falsche Freunde

Vorsicht bei **falschen Freunden**!
Das sind englische Wörter, die wie deutsche Wörter aussehen, es aber nicht sind.
Beispiele: *Our art teacher is very nice.* (*art* = Kunst)
Spring is here. (*spring* = Frühling)
Am besten zeichnest du hinter diese Wörter beim Abschreiben ein Warndreieck.

A good time

p. 30	**day out** [deɪ 'aʊt]	(Tages-)Ausflug	→ Kate's class had a day out at the zoo.
p. 31	**valley** ['væli]	Tal	
	coal [kəʊl]	Kohle	
	office ['ɒfɪs]	Büro, Amt	→ Mrs Davies has a desk in her office.
	crazy about sport ['kreɪzi əbaʊt 'spɔːt]	verrückt nach Sport	→ Ben is crazy about sport!
	outdoor ['aʊtdɔː]	im Freien, draußen	
	national ['næʃənl]	national, National-, Landes-	→ a national game in Britain

Presentation

p. 32	**search** [sɜːtʃ]	(durch)suchen	
	coast [kəʊst]	Küste	→ It's very hot today. Let's go to the coast.
	you're bored [jɔː 'bɔːd]	du langweilst dich, dir ist langweilig	
	sail [seɪl]	segeln	
	canoe [kə'nuː]	Kanu fahren	

Leicht zu verwechseln!
I'm bored. = Ich langweile mich.
I'm boring. = Ich bin langweilig!

ɪ trick, give   ʃ **sh**e, **sh**out

	hike [haɪk]	wandern	
	mountain bike ['maʊntən baɪk]	Mountainbike fahren	
	abseil ['æbseɪl]	abseilen	
	ride [raɪd]	reiten →	
	climb [klaɪm]	klettern	
	bubble ['bʌbl]	Blase	
	card [kɑːd]	(Spiel-, Gruß-)Karte	
	ideal [aɪ'dɪəl]	ideal	
	I wouldn't like [aɪ 'wʊdnt laɪk]	ich würde nicht gern	
p. 34	**half** (*pl.*: **halves**) [hɑːf, hɑːvz]	Hälfte →	
	water sports ['wɔːtə spɔːts]	Wassersport	
	popular with ['pɒpjələ wɪð]	beliebt bei	
	agree [ə'griː]	übereinstimmen, zustimmen	
	cliff [klɪf]	Klippe	
p. 35	**beautiful** ['bjuːtɪfəl]	(wunder)schön	
	bad at ['bæd ət]	schlecht in	→ Jill is bad at singing.
	'cross (= across) [krɒs (ə'krɒs)]	(quer) über, durch; hinüber, herüber	
	stormy ['stɔːmi]	stürmisch	
	to be near you [tə biː 'nɪə juː]	um dir nahe zu sein, um in deiner Nähe zu sein	Tom is good at singing.
	fly [flaɪ]	fliegen	
	sky [skaɪ]	Himmel	
	pass [pɑːs]	vorbeigehen, -fahren, -ziehen	
	cloud [klaʊd]	Wolke	
	far away [fɑːr ə'weɪ]	weit weg	→ America is far away.
	I'm forever crying [aɪm fərevə 'kraɪɪŋ]	ich werde ewig weinen	

→ *ride, drive*
***ride** a horse oder a bike*
Aber: ***drive** a car*

→ Unregelmäßige Pluralformen:
Aus *-f(e)* wird *-ves (half → halves).*
Was ist der Plural von *leaf* und *life*?
Erinnerst du dich?

Listening and Reading

p. 36	**title** ['taɪtl]	Titel, Überschrift	→ What's the title of your favourite book?
	swimsuit ['swɪmsuːt]	Badeanzug, Badehose	

Active English

p. 38	**B&B (Bed & Breakfast)** [bed ənd 'brekfəst]	Frühstückspension, Zimmer mit Frühstück →	
	youth hostel ['juːθ hɒstl]	Jugendherberge	
	booking ['bʊkɪŋ]	Buchung, Reservierung	

→ Bed and Breakfast
Schilder mit *B&B* findet man überall in Großbritanien. Dort gibt es gute, preiswerte Unterkünfte.

Practice and Revision

p. 40	**spelling** ['spelɪŋ]	(Recht-)Schreibung, Schreibweise →	
	one word is missing [wʌn wɜːd ɪz 'mɪsɪŋ]	ein Wort fehlt	

→ Achtung: *spelling*
Manche Wörter hören sich ähnlich an, werden aber unterschiedlich geschrieben, z.B.: *straight – late*.

Story (2) – Chilling out at the sea

p. 46	**at last** [ət 'lɑːst]	endlich	→ No school! It's holidays at last!
	sand [sænd]	Sand	
	sandy ['sændi]	sandig, Sand-	
	warden ['wɔːdən]	Aufsicht, Aufseher/Aufseherin	
	silly ['sɪli]	blöd, albern	

eɪ **day**, cr**a**zy   aɪ h**i**ke, cl**i**mb

	rule [ru:l]	Regel, Vorschrift	→ "No talking on Tuesdays." — That's a silly rule!
	call [kɔ:l]	anrufen	
	later ['leɪtə]	später	
	path [pɑ:θ]	Weg, Pfad	
	down [daʊn]	herunter, hinunter	
	(phone) call [('fəʊn) kɔ:l]	(Telefon-)Anruf, (An-)Ruf	→ There's a call for you. It's your father.
	they forgot → forget [ðeɪ fə'gɒt]	sie vergaßen, sie haben vergessen	
	they sat → sit [ðeɪ 'sæt]	sie saßen, sie haben gesessen	
	rock [rɒk]	Fels, Stein	
	jump off [dʒʌmp 'ɒf]	herunter-, hinunterspringen von	 → She is jumping off the rocks.
p. 47	**turn** [tɜ:n]	(sich) umdrehen, wenden	
	wind [wɪnd]	Wind	
	strong [strɒŋ]	stark	→ strong – stronger – strongest 
	along [ə'lɒŋ]	entlang	
	it fell → fall [ɪt 'fel]	es fiel, es ist gefallen	
	fall [fɔ:l]	fallen, stürzen	
	Run for your life! [rʌn fə jɔ: 'laɪf]	Renn/t um dein/euer Leben!	
	pull up [pʊl 'ʌp]	hochziehen	
	safe [seɪf]	sicher	→ It isn't safe to go swimming at night.
	at the top [æt ðə 'tɒp]	oben, an der Spitze	→ The café is at the top of the building.
	they felt → feel [ðeɪ 'felt]	sie fühlten (sich), sie haben (sich) gefühlt	
	feel [fi:l]	(sich) fühlen, sich anfühlen	→ It feels funny!
	we were lucky [wi: wə 'lʌki]	wir hatten Glück	→ The English test was easy. I was lucky!
	loud [laʊd]	laut	→ The music was very loud. 
	helicopter ['helɪkɒptə]	Hubschrauber	
	trouble ['trʌbl]	Ärger, Schwierigkeiten	

Unit 3

TIPP Unregelmäßige Verben

Die unregelmäßigen Verben und ihre besonderen Vergangenheitsformen findest du auf S. 159. Diese Verben musst du dir jedoch gut merken, z.B. *buy → bought*. Schreibe sie immer zu den Grundformen. Nimm dabei für Buchstaben, die in der Grundform **nicht** vorkommen, eine andere Farbe.

Welcome to Scotland

p. 48	open top bus [əʊpən tɒp 'bʌs]	Bus mit offenem Dach
	get on, get off service [get 'ɒn get 'ɒf sɜ:vɪs]	Bus-Service zum Zu- und Aussteigen
	Scottish ['skɒtɪʃ] 	schottisch →
	island ['aɪlənd]	Insel →
p. 49	**capital** ['kæpɪtl]	Hauptstadt
	it became → become [bɪ'keɪm]	es wurde →
	become [bɪ'kʌm]	werden
	part [pɑ:t]	Teil
	own [əʊn]	eigene
	glad [glæd]	froh
	oil [ɔɪl]	Öl
	tradition [trə'dɪʃn]	Tradition

→ Scottish island
Es gibt viele Inseln an der Westküste Schottlands, aber gar keine an der Ostküste.

→ Beachte!
island: ***s*** wird nicht ausgesprochen.

→ Verwechslungsgefahr!
get* und *become
*He **got** a Lotto ticket as a present.*
*He won the Lotto and **became** rich.*

ə **and, at**   ŋ **spelling, strong**

	bagpipes ['bægpaɪps]	Dudelsack	
	celebrate ['selɪbreɪt]	feiern	

Presentation

p. 50	**their family has moved** [ðeə 'fæmɪli həz 'mu:vd]	ihre Familie ist umgezogen	
	move [mu:v]	(um)ziehen *(Wohnort)*	
	at first [ət 'fɜ:st]	zuerst	→ At first it was sunny, then it rained.
	level ['levl]	Ebene, Höhe	
	strange [streɪndʒ]	seltsam, sonderbar	→ a strange noise
	they spent → spend [ðeɪ 'spent]	sie verbrachten, sie haben verbracht	→ The family spent three weeks in Scotland
	spend (time/money) [spend]	verbringen (Zeit), ausgeben (Geld)	– and they spent a lot of money, too.
	we've (= we have) walked [wi:v 'wɔ:kt]	wir sind gegangen, wir gingen	
	around [ə'raʊnd]	umher, herum	
	statue ['stætʃu:]	Statue	
p. 51	Irn-Bru [ɜ:n 'bru:]	schottisches Limonadengetränk	
	snow [snəʊ]	Schnee	
	expect [ɪk'spekt]	erwarten, annehmen, vermuten	→ It's late. I expect you are hungry.
	kilt [kɪlt]	Schottenrock	
	they say [ðeɪ 'seɪ]	man sagt	
	mean [mi:n]	geizig, kleinlich	
	true [tru:]	wahr	→ Is it true that there is a monster in Loch Ness?
	The drinks are on me. [ðə drɪnks ɑ:r ɒn 'mi:]	Die Getränke gehen auf mich., Ich bezahle die Getränke.	
p. 52	**poet** ['pəʊɪt]	Dichter/Dichterin	
	speech [spi:tʃ]	Rede, Ansprache	→ a long speech
	haggis ['hægɪs]	schottisches Gericht aus Schafsinnereien	
	not any [nɒt 'eni]	kein/e	
	singer ['sɪŋə]	Sänger/Sängerin	
	short [ʃɔ:t]	kurz	→ a short speech
	grace [greɪs]	Gnade; Tischgebet	
	arrival [ə'raɪvl]	Ankunft	
p. 53	Easter ['i:stə]	Ostern	
	Mother's Day ['mʌðəz deɪ]	Muttertag	
	relative ['relətɪv]	Verwandte/Verwandter	→ He works in Scotland but his relatives all live in England.
	mosque [mɒsk]	Moschee	
	tree [tri:]	Baum	
	century ['sentʃʊri]	Jahrhundert	
	gardener ['gɑ:dənə]	Gärtner/Gärtnerin	
	for work/food/... [fə 'wɜ:k 'fu:d]	um Arbeit/Essen/... zu suchen	
	kind [kaɪnd]	Art	
	policeman [pɒ'li:smən]	Polizist	
	both [bəʊθ]	beide	
	he died → die [hi 'daɪd]	er starb	
	grave [greɪv]	Grab	
	gun [gʌn]	Kanone	
	return [rɪ'tɜ:n]	zurückkehren	
	put up [pʊt 'ʌp]	aufstellen, errichten	

ð **th**e, mo**th**er θ bo**th**, **th**ings

Listening and Reading

p. 54	junior railcard [dʒuːnjə ˈreɪlkɑːd]	„Bahncard" für Jugendliche	
	handbook [ˈhændbʊk]	Gebrauchsanweisung	

Active English

p. 56	**How are things?** [həʊ ə ˈθɪŋz]	Wie geht's?, Wie läuft's? *(ugs.)*	
	goal [gəʊl]	Tor	
	Congratulations! [kɒngrætʃʊˈleɪʃnz]	Herzlichen Glückwunsch!	
	they won → win [ðeɪ ˈwɒn]	sie gewannen, sie haben gewonnen	
	good luck [gʊd ˈlʌk]	(viel) Glück	→ Better luck next time!
	he is late [hiːz ˈleɪt]	er kommt zu spät, er verspätet sich	
	it's me [ɪts ˈmiː]	ich bin's	
	on the train/bus/... [ɒn ðə ˈtreɪn ˈbʌs]	im Zug/Bus/...	
	I'll meet you at the station. [aɪl ˈmiːt juː ət ðə ˈsteɪʃn]	Ich hole dich vom Bahnhof ab.	
	run late [rʌn ˈleɪt]	sich verspäten, Verspätung haben →	
	double [ˈdʌbl]	doppelt, Doppel-	
	dialling code [ˈdaɪəlɪŋ kəʊd]	Vorwahl →	

→ ***Running late***
Wenn ein Zug oder Bus seinen Fahrplan nicht einhält, sagen wir *it's running* (= fährt) *late*.

→ ***London dialling codes***
London ist so groß, dass es zwei *dialling codes* hat: 0207 und 0208.

Practice and Revision

p. 60	**have** [hæv]	essen, trinken	→ Can we have pasta for lunch?
	coffee [ˈkɒfi]	Kaffee	
p. 61	**latest** [ˈleɪtəst]	neueste(r, s)	→ the latest car
	memory [ˈmeməri]	Speicher; Gedächtnis, Erinnerung	
	poor [pɔː]	schwach, dürftig	

Story (3) – Loch Ness – a good place for a holiday?

p. 64	**kilometer** [ˈkɪləmiːtə]	Kilometer	
	deep [diːp]	tief	→ This fish lives deep in the sea.
p. 65	**visitor** [ˈvɪzɪtə]	Besucher/Besucherin	
p. 66	**before** [bɪˈfɔː]	schon einmal	
	notice [ˈnəʊtɪs]	bemerken	
	another [əˈnʌðə]	ein/e andere(r, s), ein/e weitere(r, s)	→ Have another cake!
	it hit → hit [ɪt ˈhɪt]	schlug, stieß, traf →	
	hit [hɪt]	treffen, schlagen, stoßen	
	smile [smaɪl]	Lächeln	
	face [feɪs]	Gesicht	
p. 67	beer [bɪə]	Bier	
	Your team is no good. [jɔː ˈtiːm ɪz nəʊ ˈgʊd]	Dein Team /Deine Mannschaft taugt nichts.	
	it lost → lose [ɪt ˈlɒst]	verlor, hat verloren	
	lose [luːz]	verlieren	→ Sally lost her hat yesterday!
	they drank → drink [dræŋk]	sie tranken	
	feel sorry for somebody (sb.) [fiːl ˈsɒri fə sʌmbədi]	jemanden (jdn.) bedauern, Mitleid mit jemandem (jdm.) haben →	

→ ***hit – hit***
Bei diesem unregelmäßigen Verb sind *simple present* und *simple past* identisch!

→ **Merke!**
Somebody wird oft *sb.* abgekürzt.

ɒ won, lost ɔː before, your

towards [tə'wɔːdz]	entgegen, in Richtung auf, auf ... zu	
smile at somebody (sb.) ['smaɪl ət sʌmbədi]	jemanden (jdn.) anlächeln, jemandem (jdm.) zulächeln	
those [ðəʊz]	die (da), jene (dort)	
explain [ɪk'spleɪn]	erklären	→ I don't understand this word. Can you explain it to me?

Unit 4

TIPP Präpositionen

Diese kleinen Wörter *(at, in, on, to, ...)* haben oft mehrere Bedeutungen. Die Präposition *at* bedeutet z.B. „in" *(at school)*, „um" *(at 10 o'clock)*, und „zu" *(at home)*. Du kennst auch schon feste Verbindungen mit *at* wie *at the moment, at the weekend, at breakfast*.

Auch Verben haben feste Verbindungen: *look **at**, smile **at**, listen **to**, talk **to***. Aber manche Verben bekommen eine ganz andere Bedeutung, wenn eine bestimmte Präposition dabei ist, z.B. *look **after*** (sich kümmern um) oder *look **for*** (suchen).

Idols

p. 69	**downtown** *(AE)* ['daʊntaʊn]	Innenstadt, Stadtzentrum →
	flat [flæt]	flach, eben
	already [ɔːl'redi]	schon, bereits
	mile [maɪl]	Meile →
	a mile up [ə maɪl 'ʌp]	eine Meile hoch
	call [kɔːl]	nennen
	skiing ['skiːɪŋ]	(das) Skilaufen, Skisport
	snowboarding ['snəʊbɔːdɪŋ]	Snowboard fahren, snowboarden
	soccer ['sɒkə]	Fußball →
	middle school ['mɪdl skuːl]	Schule für 11- bis 14-Jährige
	marching band ['mɑːtʃɪŋ bænd]	(Blas-)Kapelle

→ **American English *(AE)***
Wörter mit dieser Abkürzung werden eher im amerikanischen Englisch verwendet.

→ **1 mile = 1.6 km**
In den USA und Großbritannien werden Entfernungen in *miles* gemessen.

→ ***Soccer* und *football***
Die Amerikaner nennen unser Fußballspiel *soccer*. *American football* ist ein ganz anderes Spiel.

Presentation

p. 70	**flute** [fluːt]	(Quer-)Flöte	
	practise ['præktɪs]	üben	
	drummer ['drʌmə]	Schlagzeuger/Schlagzeugerin	
	drums *(pl.)* [drʌmz]	Schlagzeug	
	enough [ɪ'nʌf]	genug	→ Do you have enough money?
	so [səʊ]	daher, deshalb	
	once [wʌns]	einmal	→ You have breakfast once a day.
	carry ['kæri]	tragen	
	basement ['beɪsmənt]	Keller	
	junk [dʒʌŋk]	Gerümpel, altes Zeug, Müll	
	clear [klɪə]	aufräumen, ausräumen	
	that's why ['ðæts waɪ]	deshalb, daher	
	get [get]	holen	→ Please get me a drink.
	form [fɔːm]	Formular	
	choose [tʃuːz]	(aus)wählen	

dʒ **j**unk, **g**ym æ fl**a**t, th**a**t

	state [steɪt]	(Bundes-)Staat, ➔ (Bundes-)Land	 ➔ Jeder der 50 *stars* auf der amerikanischen Flagge steht für einen Bundesstaat.
p. 71	**seem** [siːm]	scheinen	
	arrogant ['ærəgənt]	arrogant	
	piece [piːs]	Stück	
p. 72	**act** [ækt]	Aufführung, Auftritt	
	gym [dʒɪm]	Turnhalle, Sporthalle	
	jury ['dʒʊəri]	Jury	
	principal *(AE)* ['prɪnsɪpl]	Schulleiter/Schulleiterin, Direktor/Direktorin	
	worse [wɜːs]	schlimmer, schlechter ➔	➔ **Beachte!** Wenn du Sachen vergleichst, sind diese Adjektive unregelmäßig: good – **better** – **the best**; bad – **worse** – **the worst**
	point [pɔɪnt]	Punkt	
	opinion [ə'pɪniən]	Meinung	
	the worst [ðə 'wɜːst]	der/die/das schlimmste, der/die/das schlechteste	
	result [rɪ'zʌlt]	Ergebnis	
	mom *(AE)* [mɒm]	Mutti, Mama	
	really ['rɪəli]	wirklich	→ –17°C! That's really cold.
	nervous ['nɜːvəs]	nervös, aufgeregt	
p. 73	**What's the matter?** [wɒts ðə 'mætə]	Was ist denn (los)?	
	brave [breɪv]	tapfer, mutig	→ He's brave! 

Listening and Reading

p. 74	**fact** [fækt]	Fakt, Tatsache	→ Cars have four wheels. That's a fact.

Active English

p. 76	**good-looking** [gʊd'lʊkɪŋ]	gut aussehend, attraktiv	 → He's a really good-looking singer.
	admire [əd'maɪə]	bewundern, verehren	
	nobody ['nəʊbədi]	niemand, keiner	→ Nobody answered the phone.
	as friendly as [əz 'frendli əz]	(genau)so freundlich wie	
	helpful ['helpfəl]	hilfreich, behilflich	→ She's nice and always very helpful.
	You're a star! [jɔːr ə 'stɑː]	Du bist ein Schatz! *(ugs.)*	

Story (4) – Star dreams

p. 84	**dream** [driːm]	Traum	
	TV station [tiː'viː 'steɪʃn]	Fernsehsender	
	take [teɪk]	hinfahren, bringen	→ I'm ill. Can you take me to the doctor?
	she spoke → **speak** [ʃi 'spəʊk]	sie sprach	
	rest [rest]	Rest	
p. 85	**cellphone** *(AE)* ['selfəʊn]	Handy	
	sick [sɪk]	deprimiert, betroffen; krank, übel	
	broken ['brəʊkn]	gebrochen, zerbrochen ➔	➔ *a broken leg* *a broken instrument*
	chance [tʃɑːns]	Chance, Gelegenheit	
	twice [twaɪs]	zweimal ➔	➔ **Aufzählungen:** ***once*** – ***twice*** – *three times* – *four times* – *five ...* usw.
	he ate → **eat** [hi 'eɪt]	er aß	
	he ate his words [hi 'eɪt hɪz wɜːdz]	er änderte seine Meinung	
	together [tə'geðə]	zusammen, gemeinsam	→ They go on holiday together.

s **star**, **speak**   z **as**, **words**

Unit 5

write – an exercise
– a test
– a poem
– a postcard
– a letter

cook – lunch
– breakfast
– a meal
– spaghetti
– chips

TIPP Wortverbindungen

Versuche Wörter möglichst nicht isoliert zu lernen, sondern immer mit anderen Wörtern zusammen. Um dich selbst zu testen und zu sehen, wie viel du schon kannst, nimm ein bekanntes Verb (*wear, cook, write, make, forget* usw.) und schreibe auf, wie viele Verbindungen dir einfallen.

Going Places

p. 87	**only** ['əʊnli]	erst
	motor ['məʊtə]	Motor
	SUV (= sports utility vehicle) [esju:'vi:]	Geländewagen
	work [wɜ:k]	Arbeit →
	fast [fɑ:st]	schnell
	cause [kɔ:z]	verursachen
	less [les]	weniger
	air [eə]	Luft
	pollution [pə'lu:ʃn]	(Umwelt-)Verschmutzung
	motorhome ['məʊtəhəʊm]	Wohnmobil
	vacation *(AE)* [və'keɪʃn]	Ferien, Urlaub

→ Do you have to go? It's only 6 o'clock.

Beachte! Gleiche Form, aber eine unterschiedliche Wortart:
work = arbeiten, die Arbeit
snow = schneien, der Schnee

expensive less expensive

Presentation

p. 88	**project** ['prɒdʒekt]	Projekt
p. 89	**per cent (%)** [pə 'sent]	Prozent
	few [fju:]	wenige →
	take [teɪk]	*hier:* dauern, brauchen →
p. 90	**transport** ['trænspɔ:t]	Transport, Verkehr, Beförderung
	successful [sə'ksesfl]	erfolgreich
	Native Americans ['neɪtɪv ə'merɪkənz]	amerikanischer Ureinwohner →
	European [jʊərə'pi:ən]	Europäer/Europäerin
	waggon ['wægən]	(Pferde-)Wagen
	line [laɪn]	Linie, Strecke
	across [ə'krɒs]	(quer) über →
	west [west]	Westen
	between [bɪ'twi:n]	zwischen
	though [ðəʊ]	jedoch, aber; obwohl
	not so popular as ... [nɒt səʊ 'pɒpjʊlə æz]	nicht so beliebt wie ...
p. 91	**as** [æz]	als
	engineer [endʒɪ'nɪə]	Ingenieur/Ingenieurin, Techniker/Technikerin
	great [greɪt]	groß, großartig
	love [lʌv]	Liebe
	they cost → **cost** [ðeɪ 'kɒst]	sie kosteten
	assembly line [ə'sembli laɪn]	Fließband
	any ['eni]	irgendein/e, jede/s, irgendwelche
	as long as [æz 'lɒŋ əz]	solange
	worker ['wɜ:kə]	Arbeiter/Arbeiterin

Vergleiche:
***Few** students walk to school.*
(= wenige)
***A few** students walk to school.*
(= einige)

Take kommt in verschiedenen Verbindungen vor:
*It **takes** 20 minutes.*
***take** photos*
***take** the dog for a walk*

Die Bevölkerung der USA
Es gibt 295 Millionen Amerikaner; davon sind 1% *Native Americans.*

Reisen in den USA
It takes five hours to fly across the USA, but three days to drive across it.

e any, less j few, popular

	earn [ɜːn]	verdienen	→ He earns some pocket money at the weekends.
	second ['sekənd]	Sekunde	
	change [tʃeɪndʒ]	verändern, wechseln	→ Trees change in summer and winter.
	can't wait [kɑːnt 'weɪt]	nicht abwarten können, es nicht erwarten können	
	I've never been [aɪv nevə 'biːn]	ich war (noch) nie, ich bin (noch) nie gewesen	
	may [meɪ]	vielleicht werden; können, dürfen	→ It may rain.
	gypsy ['dʒɪpsi]	Zigeuner/Zigeunerin	
	the best of friends [ðə 'best əv 'frendz]	die besten Freunde	
	insist [ɪn'sɪst]	bestehen auf, beharren auf	
	our way [aʊə 'weɪ]	in unsere Richtung, zu uns her	

Listening and Reading

p. 92	**loudspeaker** ['laʊdspiːkə]	Lautsprecher	
	scene [siːn]	Szene	
	each [iːtʃ]	jede(r, s)	→ Each ticket costs £10.

Active English

p. 94	**hiker** ['haɪkə]	Wanderer	
	far [fɑː]	weit	→ Chicago is far away.
	Pardon? ['pɑːdən]	Wie bitte? →	
p. 95	*on foot* [ɒn 'fʊt]	zu Fuß	
	yourself [jɔː'self]	du/dir/dich (selbst)	
	tick [tɪk]	ab-/anhaken	
	report [rɪ'pɔːt]	berichten	
	discuss [dɪ'skʌs]	diskutieren, besprechen	

→ **Immer höflich sein:**
I'm sorry. I didn't see you. (Es tut mir leid.)
Excuse me. Can you ask you ... (Entschuldigen Sie.)
Pardon? Can you say that again?

Practice and Revision

p. 97	**pair** [peə]	Paar	
p. 99	**Bavarian** [bə'veəriən]	bayerisch; Bayer/Bayerin	
	high school ['haɪ skuːl]	(US) Gesamtschule für 13- bis 18-Jährige	

Story (5) – On the road again

p. 102	**forest** ['fɒrəst]	Wald	
	wild [waɪld]	wild	
p. 103	**except** [ɪ'ksept]	außer	
	sink [sɪŋk]	Spül-/Waschbecken	
	puppy ['pʌpi]	Welpe, Hundejunges	
	behave [bɪ'heɪv]	sich benehmen	
	look forward to sth. [lʊk 'fɔːwəd tə sʌmθɪŋ]	sich auf etwas freuen	→ She's looking forward to her birthday.
	fresh [freʃ]	frisch	→ fresh air
	egg [eg]	Ei	
p. 104	**smell** [smel]	riechen	
	break [breɪk]	Pause	
	Gee! *(AE)* [dʒiː]	Mensch!, Mann!	
	err... [ɜː]	äh...	
p. 105	fix the hook-ups [fɪks ðə 'hʊkʌps]	das Verbingungskabel anschließen	
	skunk [skʌŋk]	Stinktier	

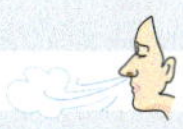

ʊ **look, tool** ɑː **far, pardon**

Alphabetische Liste der Wörter aus Band 1, 2 und 3 (Englisch-Deutsch)
Die Angaben nach den Einträgen verweisen auf das Vorkommen der Wörter:
U = Unit; Intro = Introduction; Fundstellen aus Band 1 und 2 sind mit **1 >** bzw. **2 >** gekennzeichnet.
Verwendete Abkürzungen:

AE = American English	sb. = somebody	sth. = something
jdn. = jemanden	jdm. = jemandem	ugs. = umgangssprachlich
pl. = Plural	no pl. = kein Plural	

Die Auszeichnungen (**fett**, normal, *kursiv*) verweisen auf den Lernstatus eines Wortes:
U5: 90 = produktives Wort in Unit 5 auf Seite 90,
U3: 49 = rezeptives Wort in Unit 3 auf Seite 49,
U2: 37 = fakultatives Wort in Unit 2 auf Seite 37.

A

a [ə] ein/eine **1 > Intro:** 10; **an** ein/eine **1 > U2:** 38; **a (day)** pro (Tag) **2 > U1:** 14
a.m. [eɪ'em] vormittags, morgens **U1:** 18
about [ə'baʊt] über **1 > U2:** 49; ungefähr **U1:** 11; **talk about** sprechen über **2 > U4:** 60; **mad about** verrückt nach **2 > U2:** 29; **ask a partner about** eine(n) Partner/in fragen über/nach **2 > U2:** 31; **... the story is about ...** ... die Geschichte handelt von ... **U1:** 16; **What about ...?** Wie wäre es mit ...? **1 > U3:** 54; **at about** gegen; (um) zirka **2 > U1:** 15
above [ə'bʌv] über **1 > Intro:** 18
abseil ['æbseɪl] abseilen **U2:** 32
accent ['æksent] Akzent **2 > U1:** 18
accident ['æksɪdənt] Unfall **2 > U2:** 30
across [ə'krɒs] (quer) über **U5:** 90
act [ækt] Aufführung, Auftritt **U4:** 72; darstellen, vorspielen **U1:** 19
action ['ækʃn] Action; Handlung, Aktion, Aktivität **2 > U2:** 28
active ['æktɪv] aktiv U2: 49
activity [æk'tɪvəti] Aktivität **1 > U4:** 69
addict ['ædɪkt] *Abhängige/r, Süchtige/r U2: 37*
address [ə'dres] Adresse, Anschrift **2 > U5:** 85
admiral ['ædmɪrəl] Admiral U1: 10
admire [əd'maɪə] bewundern, verehren **U4:** 76
adult ['ædʌlt] Erwachsene/r **2 > U1:** 18
advert ['ædvɜːt] Anzeige **2 > U6:** 93
after ['ɑːftə] nach (zeitlich) **1 > U3:** 59
afternoon: Good afternoon. [gʊd ɑːftə'nuːn] Guten Tag. (nachmittags) **1 > U1:** 28
again [ə'gen] wieder; noch einmal **2 > U1:** 18
against [ə'geɪnst] gegen **1 > U5:** 92; **race against** um die Wette laufen **1 > U5:** 92
ago [ə'gəʊ] vor **2 > U3:** 48
agree [ə'griː] übereinstimmen, zustimmen **U2:** 34
air [eə] Luft **U5:** 87; **air-conditioning** Klimatisierung, Klimaanlage **2 > U6:** 94
alarm clock [ə'lɑːm klɒk] Wecker **2 > U1:** 15
album ['ælbəm] Album **U2:** 37
alien ['eɪliən] Außerirdischer **2 > U2:** 37
all [ɔːl] der/die/das ganze; alle **2 > Intro:** 7; **all over** überall **2 > U3:** 48
almost ['ɔːlməʊst] fast, beinahe **2 > U1:** 18
alone [ə'ləʊn] allein **1 > U6:** 107
along [ə'lɒŋ] entlang **U2:** 47; **go along** entlanggehen **2 > U3:** 52
alphabetical order [ælfə'betɪkl 'ɔːdə] alphabetische Reihenfolge **2 > U1:** 23
already [ɔːl'redi] schon, bereits **U4:** 69
also ['ɔːlsəʊ] auch **2 > U4:** 62
always ['ɔːlweɪz] immer **1 > U2:** 40
America [ə'merɪkə] Amerika **1 > U5:** 96
American [ə'merɪkən] amerikanisch; Amerikaner/in **2 > U5:** 81; **Native Americans** amerikanische Ureinwohner **U5:** 90
and [ænd] und **1 > Intro:** 10
angry ['æŋgri] böse, wütend **1 > U3:** 57
animal ['ænɪml] Tier **1 > U4:** 72
another [ə'nʌðə] ein/e andere(r, s), ein/e weitere(r, s) **U3:** 66
answer ['ɑːnsə] Antwort **2 > U1:** 16; antworten; beantworten **2 > U3:** 50
any ['eni] irgendein/e, jede/s, irgendwelche **U5:** 91; **not any** kein/e **U3:** 52
Anything else? [eniθɪŋ 'els] Sonst noch etwas? **1 > U4:** 75
apart from [ə'pɑːt frəm] außer, abgesehen von **2 > U3:** 47
apple ['æpl] Apfel **1 > U3:** 53
April ['eɪprəl] April **1 > U5:** 98
are: Are they ...? [ɑː ðeɪ] Sind sie ...? **1 > U1:** 24; **aren't (= are not)** sind nicht **1 > U2:** 39
around [ə'raʊnd] umher, herum **U3:** 50
arrival [ə'raɪvl] Ankunft U3: 52
arrive [ə'raɪv] ankommen, eintreffen **2 > U1:** 15
arrogant ['ærəgənt] arrogant **U4:** 71
Art [ɑːt] Kunst **2 > U1:** 20
as [æz] als **U5:** 91; **the same as** genauso wie; dasselbe wie **1 > U4:** 75; **not so popular as ...** nicht so beliebt wie ... **U5:** 90; **as friendly as** (genau)so freundlich wie **U4:** 76; *as good as* (genau)so gut wie *U4: 75*; **as long as** solange **U5:** 91

[iː] he	[ɑː] car	[ɔː] or	[uː] too	[ɜː] girl	[i] sorry	[u] July	[ɪ] big	[e] yes	[æ] cat	[ʌ] bus	[ɒ] dog

ask [a:sk] fragen **1 > U3:** 58; **ask a partner about** eine(n) Partner/in fragen über/nach **2 > U2:** 31; **asked** fragte/fragten **1 > U3:** 58; **she's asking about** sie fragt nach **1 > U2:** 41
assembly line [ə'sembli laɪn] Fließband U5: 91
at [æt] an, in; bei **1 > Intro:** 19; **at ... house** bei ... zu Hause **1 > U2:** 42; **at last** endlich **U2:** 46; **at school** in der Schule **1 > Intro:** 10; **at the seaside** am Meer **1 > U5:** 86
ate → eat [eɪt] *simple past* von **eat U4:** 85; **he ate his words** er änderte seine Meinung U4: 85
August ['ɔ:gəst] August **1 > U5:** 98
aunt [ɑ:nt] Tante **1 > U3:** 60
Austria ['ɒstriə] Österreich **2 > Intro:** 11
autumn ['ɔ:təm] Herbst **1 > U5:** 99
awareness [ə'weənəs] Aufmerksamkeit, Bewusstsein *U5: 93*
away [ə'weɪ] verreist; weg **2 > Intro:** 7; *far away* weit weg *U2: 35*

B

B&B (Bed & Breakfast) [bed ənd 'brekfəst] Frühstückspension, Zimmer mit Frühstück **U2:** 38
back [bæk] zurück **1 > U6:** 109; **get back** zurückkommen/-finden **1 > U5:** 91
background ['bækgraʊnd] Hintergrund, Herkunft **U1:** 9
bad: not bad [nɒt 'bæd] nicht schlecht (es geht/ging so) **2 > Intro:** 11; **bad at** schlecht in **U2:** 35
badge [bædʒ] Abzeichen, Button **1 > U1:** 23
bag [bæg] (Schul-)Tasche **1 > Intro:** 11; Beutel, Tüte, Sack **2 > U4:** 63
bagpipes ['bægpaɪps] Dudelsack U3: 49
baked beans [beɪkt 'bi:nz] gebackene Bohnen (in Tomatensoße) **2 > U5:** 82; **baked potato** gebackene Kartoffel **2 > U4:** 62
balance ['bæləns] Kontostand *U3: 55*
ball [bɔ:l] Ball **2 > U2:** 29
banana [bə'nɑ:nə] Banane **1 > U3:** 53
band [bænd] Band, (Musik-)Gruppe **2 > U1:** 17; **marching band** (Blas-)Kapelle U4: 69; **rock band** Rockband **U4:** 70
bank [bæŋk] Bank, Sparkasse **2 > U3:** 52
barbecue ['bɑ:bɪkju:] Grillparty **2 > U6:** 97
baseball ['beɪsbɔ:l] Baseball **U4:** 69
basement *(AE)* ['beɪsmənt] Keller **U4:** 70
basic reading [beɪsɪk 'ri:dɪŋ] Basiswissen: Lesen **U1:** 16
basketball ['bɑ:skɪtbɔ:l] Basketball **1 > U6:** 105
bathroom ['bɑ:θru:m] Badezimmer **1 > U2:** 37
battery (*pl.* **-ies**) ['bætərɪ] Batterie, Batterien **1 > U5:** 96
Bavaria [bə'veəriə] Bayern **1 > U2:** 49; **Bavarian** bayerisch; Bayer/Bayerin **U5:** 99
BBC [bi: bi: 'si:] British Broadcasting Corporation (öffentlich-rechtliche Rundfunk- und Fernsehanstalt Großbritanniens) **1 > U4:** 74
be [bi] sein **1 > Intro:** 17
be fed up die Nase voll haben **1 > U6:** 108
be frightened verängstigt sein; Angst haben **2 > U5:** 82
beach [bi:tʃ] Strand **2 > U5:** 78
bean [bi:n] Bohne **1 > U3:** 53; **baked beans** gebackene Bohnen (in Tomatensoße) **2 > U5:** 82
bear: teddy bear ['tedi beə] Teddybär **1 > U4:** 73
beautiful ['bju:tɪfəl] (wunder)schön **U2:** 35
became → become [bɪ'keɪm] *simple past* von **become U3:** 49
because [bɪ'kɒz] weil **1 > U5:** 85
become [bɪ'kʌm] werden **U5:** 49
bed [bed] Bett **1 > U3:** 62; **Bed & Breakfast (B&B)** Frühstückspension, Zimmer mit Frühstück **U2:** 38
bedroom ['bedru:m] Schlafzimmer **1 > U2:** 37
been: I've never been [aɪv nevə 'bi:n] ich war (noch) nie, ich bin (noch) nie gewesen *U5: 91*
beer [bɪə] Bier U3: 67
before [bɪ'fɔ:] vor, bevor **1 > U5:** 92; schon einmal **U3:** 66
behave [bɪ'heɪv] sich benehmen **U5:** 103
behind [bɪ'haɪnd] hinter **2 > Legend:** 110
bell [bel] Glocke **U1:** 10
belong to [bɪ'lɒŋ tə] gehören (zu) **2 > U2:** 29
below [bɪ'ləʊ] unter, unterhalb (von); unten **2 > U6:** 104; **below 0 °C** [bɪ'ləʊ 'zɪərəʊ dɪ'gri:z 'selsiəs] unter null Grad Celsius **2 > U6:** 104
best [best] bester/beste/bestes **1 > U4:** 74; *the best of friends* die besten Freunde *U5: 91*
better ['betə] besser **1 > U3:** 58
between [bɪ'twi:n] zwischen **U5:** 90
big [bɪg] groß **1 > U1:** 24; **bigger** größer **1 > U4:** 69; **bigger than** größer als **1 > U5:** 90
bike [baɪk] Fahrrad **1 > Intro:** 10; **ride a bike** Rad fahren **1 > U3:** 58; **mountain bike** Mountainbike **1 > U2:** 48; **mountain bike** Mountainbike fahren **U2:** 32
bird [bɜ:d] Vogel **2 > U2:** 33
biro ['baɪrəʊ] Kugelschreiber **1 > U1:** 32
birthday ['bɜ:θdeɪ] Geburtstag **1 > U3:** 62
biscuit ['bɪskɪt] Keks **1 > U4:** 74
black [blæk] schwarz **1 > Intro:** 14
blog [blɒg] Internet-Tagebuch **U4:** 74
blow up [bləʊ 'ʌp] in die Luft jagen **2 > U4:** 62
blue [blu:] blau **1 > Intro:** 10
board [bɔ:d] Tafel **1 > Intro:** 11; Brett (*hier:* Skateboard) **1 > U6:** 110; **boarder** Skateboardfahrer/Skateboardfahrerin **U1:** 29
boat [bəʊt] Boot, Schiff **2 > Legend:** 110
book [bʊk] Buch **1 > U1:** 26; buchen, reservieren **2 > U4:** 64; **phone book** Telefonbuch **1 > U2:** 44; **guide book** Reiseführer **U1:** 12
booking ['bʊkɪŋ] Buchung, Reservierung **U2:** 38

[ʊ] put [ə] again [eɪ] name [aɪ] time [ɔɪ] boy [əʊ] no [aʊ] house [ɪə] here [eə] chair [ʊə] sure

bored: you're bored [jɔː 'bɔːd] du langweilst dich, dir ist langweilig **U2:** 32; **I'm bored.** Ich langweile mich. **1 > U6:** 106

boring ['bɔːrɪŋ] langweilig **2 > Intro:** 7

born: I was born in ... [aɪ wəz 'bɔːn ɪn] Ich bin ... geboren. **2 > U2:** 40; **When were you born?** Wann bist du geboren? **2 > U2:** 40

both [bəʊθ] beide *U3: 53*

bottle: a bottle of ... [ə 'bɒtl əv] eine Flasche ... **1 > U3:** 55

bought → buy [bɔːt] *simple past* von **buy** **2 > U3:** 51

box [bɒks] Kasten, Kiste; *hier:* Glotze *U2: 37*; **lunch box** Butterbrotdose **1 > U3:** 56

boy [bɔɪ] Junge **1 > Intro:** 10

brand [brænd] Marke, Sorte **2 > U4:** 68; **brand name** Markenzeichen, -name **1 > U6:** 108

brave [breɪv] tapfer, mutig **U4:** 73

bread [bred] Brot **1 > U3:** 54

break [breɪk] Pause **U5:** 104; (zer)brechen, kaputtmachen **1 > U4:** 78

breakfast: have breakfast ['brekfəst] frühstücken **1 > U4:** 80; **Bed & Breakfast (B&B)** Frühstückspension, Zimmer mit Frühstück **U2:** 38

bridge [brɪdʒ] Brücke **U1:** 11

bring [brɪŋ] bringen, mitbringen **1 > U6:** 102

Britain ['brɪtn] Großbritannien **1 > U4:** 74

British ['brɪtɪʃ] britisch; Brite/Britin **2 > U1:** 13

broccoli ['brɒkəli] Brokkoli **1 > U3:** 53

brochure ['brəʊʃə] Broschüre, Prospekt **U1:** 16

broken ['brəʊkən] kaputt, defekt **1 > U2:** 42; gebrochen, zerbrochen **U4:** 85

brother ['brʌðə] Bruder **1 > U2:** 39

brought → bring [brɔːt] *simple past* von **bring** **2 > U5:** 87

brown [braʊn] braun **1 > Intro:** 14

brush [brʌʃ] bürsten; putzen **2 > U2:** 32

bubble ['bʌbl] Blase **U2:** 32

building ['bɪldɪŋ] Gebäude **2 > U3:** 50

burger ['bɜːgə] Hamburger **1 > U3:** 54

bus [bʌs] Bus **1 > U1:** 21; **open top bus** Bus mit offenem Dach U3: 48; **bus driver** Busfahrer/in **2 > U3:** 54; **bus stop** Bushaltestelle **1 > U5:** 88; **bus tour** Bus(rund)reise **1 > U6:** 102; **on the bus/train/...** im Zug/Bus/... **U3:** 56

business: for business [fə 'bɪznəs] geschäftlich **U1:** 8

busy ['bɪzi] beschäftigt **1 > U2:** 40; *get busy* sich mit etwas beschäftigen *U1: 15*; **busy shop** gut besuchter Laden **1 > U2:** 40

but [bʌt] aber **1 > U1:** 27

buy [baɪ] kaufen **1 > U4:** 68

by: fly by [flaɪ 'baɪ] vorbei-/vorüberfliegen *U1: 15*

Bye(-bye). [baɪ, bə 'baɪ] Tschüs. **1 > U1:** 28

C

C = Celsius: below 0 °C [bɪ'ləʊ 'zɪərəʊ dɪ'griːz 'selsiəs] unter null Grad Celsius **2 > U6:** 104

café ['kæfeɪ] Café **2 > U3:** 51

cage [keɪdʒ] Käfig **2 > U2:** 34

cake [keɪk] Kuchen **1 > U3:** 59

calculator ['kælkjuleɪtə] Taschenrechner **2 > U5:** 88

calendar ['kælɪndə] Kalender **2 > U4:** 72

call: phone call ['fəʊn kɔːl] (Telefon-)Anruf, (An-)Ruf **U2:** 46; anrufen **U3:** 46; nennen **U4:** 69; **call centre** Callcenter **U2:** 31

came [keɪm] kam/kamen **1 > U3:** 59

camera ['kæmərə] Kamera; Fotoapparat **2 > U3:** 51

campaign [kæm'peɪn] Aktion; Kampagne **2 > U1:** 18

camping holiday ['kæmpɪŋ hɒlədeɪ] Camping-Urlaub **2 > U5:** 87

campsite ['kæmpsaɪt] Campingplatz **2 > Intro:** 8

can [kæn] Dose, Büchse **2 > U4:** 63; können **1 > Intro:** 10; **Can I have a ...?** Kann ich eine(n)/ein ... haben? **1 > U1:** 32; **Can you spell ...?** Kannst du ... buchstabieren? **1 > U1:** 32; **What can you?** Was kannst du ...? **1 > Intro:** 10;

can't nicht können **1 > U5:** 91; *cannot* kann/kannst/können/könnte nicht *U1: 15*

canoe [kə'nuː] Kanu fahren **U2:** 32

capital ['kæpɪtl] Hauptstadt **U3:** 49

car [kɑː] Auto **1 > Intro:** 10; **car park** Parkhaus, Parkplatz **1 > U6:** 107; **car-boot sale** (eine Art) Trödelmarkt **1 > U4:** 68

caravan park ['kærəvæn pɑːk] Caravan/Wohnwagen-Campingplatz **2 > Intro:** 9

card [kɑːd] (Spiel-, Gruß-)Karte **3 > U2:** 32

careful ['keəfl] vorsichtig, sorgfältig **1 > U6:** 107

carnival ['kɑːnɪvəl] Karneval **U1:** 23

carrot ['kærət] Karotte, Möhre **1 > U3:** 53

carry ['kæri] tragen **U4:** 70

carton: a carton of ... [ə 'kɑːtn əv] ein Karton ... **1 > U3:** 55

case: pencil case ['penslkeɪs] Federmäppchen **1 > U1:** 32

cash [kæʃ] Bargeld *U3: 55*; *cash machine* Geldautomat *U3: 55*

castle ['kɑːsl] Burg, Schloss **2 > U5:** 80

cat [kæt] Katze, Kater **1 > U1:** 21

catch [kætʃ] fangen, erwischen **2 > Legend:** 108

caught → catch [kɔːt] *simple past* von **catch** U1: 21

cause [kɔːz] verursachen **U5:** 87

CD [siː'diː] CD **1 > U1:** 20; **CD player** CD-Player **1 > U3:** 62

celebrate ['selɪbreɪt] feiern **U3:** 49

cellphone *(AE)* ['selfəʊn] Handy **U4:** 85

cent [sent] Cent **2 > U5:** 88

central ['sentrəl] zentral, Zentral- **U1:** 12

centre ['sentə] Zentrum, Mittelpunkt **2 > U3:** 48

century ['sentʃʊri] Jahrhundert *U3: 53*

chair [tʃeə] Stuhl **1 > Intro:** 10

chance [tʃɑːns] Chance, Gelegenheit **U4:** 85

change [tʃeɪndʒ] verändern, wechseln **U5:** 91

charts (pl.) [tʃɑːts] Hitliste *U2: 37*

cheap [tʃiːp] billig **1 > U4:** 69; **the cheapest** am billigsten **1 > U6:** 107

[b] **b**ike [p] **p**en [d] **d**ay [t] **t**en [k] boo**k** [g] **g**o [ŋ] morni**ng** [l] **l**ike [r] **r**uler [v] se**v**en [w] **w**e

check [tʃek] (über)prüfen, kontrollieren **1 > U6:** 110
Cheers! [tʃɪəz] (hier) Tschüs! **1 > U6:** 115
cheese [tʃi:z] Käse **1 > U3:** 54; **cheeseburger** Cheeseburger **1 > U3:** 54
chewing gum ['tʃu:ɪŋ gʌm] Kaugummi **2 > U3:** 51
chicken ['tʃɪkɪn] Huhn **1 > U5:** 90
children ['tʃɪldrən] Kinder **1 > U3:** 60
Chill out! ['tʃɪl aʊt] Bleib(t) cool! **1 > U5:** 90
chip(s): chip shop ['tʃɪp ʃɒp] Pommes-frites-/Imbiss-Bude **1 > U3:** 59; **fish and chips** Fisch und Pommes frites **1 > U3:** 52
chocolate ['tʃɒklət] Schokolade **1 > U3:** 56; **hot chocolate** heiße Schokolade **2 > U5:** 82
choose [tʃu:z] (aus)wählen **U4:** 70
Christmas ['krɪsməs] Weihnachten **1 > ET:** 130; **Christmas Day** der 1. Weihnachtstag **1 > U5:** 98
church [tʃɜ:tʃ] Kirche **U1:** 27
cinema ['sɪnəmə] Kino **1 > U6:** 104
city ['sɪti] Stadt, Großstadt **2 > U1:** 22
class [klɑ:s] (Schul-)Klasse **1 > U1:** 24
classroom ['klɑ:sru:m] Klassenzimmer **1 > Intro:** 11
clean [kli:n] putzen **1 > U4:** 80; sauber **2 > U5:** 78; **cleaning** (das) Saubermachen **2 > U2:** 35
clear [klɪə] aufräumen, ausräumen **U4:** 704
clever ['klevə] schlau, klug **1 > U6:** 109
click [klɪk] (an-, hin-)klicken **2 > U5:** 77
cliff [klɪf] Klippe **U2:** 34
climb [klaɪm] klettern **U2:** 32
clock [klɒk] Uhr **1 > U6:** 102
close [kləʊz] schließen, zumachen **2 > U2:** 34; **closed** geschlossen, zu **2 > U2:** 31
clothes [kləʊðz] Kleidung, Kleider **1 > U4:** 69
cloud [klaʊd] Wolke *U2: 35*
cloudy ['klaʊdi] bewölkt, wolkig **2 > U6:** 104
club [klʌb] Klub; Verein **1 > U1:** 119; **youth club** Jugendclub, -zentrum **2 > U1:** 17
coal [kəʊl] Kohle **U2:** 31
coast [kəʊst] Küste **U2:** 32
code: dialling code ['daɪəlɪŋ kəʊd] Vorwahl **U3:** 56
coffee ['kəʊlə] Kaffee **U3:** *60*
cola ['kəʊlə] Cola **1 > U4:** 70
cold [kəʊld] kalt **2 > U4:** 62
collect [kə'lekt] (ein)sammeln **1 > U4:** 74
colour ['kʌlə] Farbe **1 > Intro:** 14
column ['kɒləm] Säule U1: 10
come [kʌm] kommen **1 > U3:** 58; **Come to ...** Komm(t) nach ... **1 > Intro:** 16; **come with us** komm(t) mit uns **1 > U5:** 89
comic ['kɒmɪk] Comic(heft) **1 > U3:** 55
company ['kʌmpəni] Firma, Unternehmen **2 > U6:** 94
competition [kɒmpə'tɪʃn] Wettbewerb **U1:** 29,
computer [kəm'pju:tə] Computer **1 > Intro:** 10
conceal [kən'si:l] verbergen, verheimlichen *U1: 15*
Congratulations! [kɒngrætʃʊ'leɪʃnz] Herzlichen Glückwunsch! **U3:** 56
console: games console ['geɪmz 'kɒnsəʊl] Spielkonsole **2 > U2:** 29
contact ['kɒntækt] sich in Verbindung setzen mit **2 > U6:** 94
cook ['kʊk] kochen **1 > U3:** 58; **cooking** (das) Kochen **2 > U5:** 82
cool [ku:l] cool, scharf, stark **2 > U1:** 18
coordinator [kəʊ'ɔ:dɪneɪtə] Koordinator/Koordinatorin, Organisator/Organisatorin *U5: 93*
copy ['kɒpi] kopieren, abschreiben **U1:** 21
cornflakes ['kɔ:nfleɪks] Cornflakes **1 > U3:** 61
cost [kɒst] kosten **1 > U4:** 73
cost → cost [kɒst] *simple past* von **cost** **U5:** 91
couch [kaʊtʃ] Couch, Sofa **U2:** 37; *couch potato* Dauerglotzer/in, (*wörtlich:* Sofakartoffel) *U2: 37*
could → can [kʊd] *simple past* von **can** **2 > U5:** 81; **couldn't** konnte/n nicht **2 > U5:** 81
count [kaʊnt] zählen **1 > U4:** 80
country ['kʌntri] Land **2 > U1:** 13; **in the country** auf dem Land **1 > U5:** 86
course: of course [əf 'kɔ:s] natürlich, selbstverständlich **2 > U4:** 62
cousin ['kʌzn] Cousin, Cousine/Kusine **1 > U5:** 89
cow [kaʊ] Kuh **1 > U3:** 58
crazy about sport ['kreɪzi əbaʊt 'spɔ:t] verrückt nach Sport **U2:** 31
cream: ice cream [aɪs 'kri:m] (Speise-)Eis **1 > U3:** 55
crime [kraɪm] Verbrechen, Kriminalität **U1:** 9
crisps *(pl.)* [krɪsps] Kartoffelchips **1 > U3:** 56
cross [krɒs] überqueren, kreuzen **2 > U3:** 46; **fingers crossed** Ich drücke die Daumen. **1 > U6:** 129
'cross (= across) [krɒs, ə'krɒs] (quer) über, durch; hinüber, herüber *U2: 35*
crying: I'm forever crying [aɪm fərevə 'kraɪɪŋ] ich werde ewig weinen *U2: 35*
cupboard ['kʌbəd] Schrank **1 > Intro:** 11
curtain ['kɜ:tn] Vorhang, Gardine **1 > U6:** 106
cushion ['kʊʃn] Kissen **1 > U6:** 106
customer ['kʌstəmə] Kunde/Kundin **1 > U2:** 41
cut ... in pieces [kʌt , ɪn 'pi:sɪz] in Stücke schneiden **1 > U6:** 110

D

dad [dæd] Papa, Vati **1 > U2:** 40
dance [dɑŋs] Tanz, Tanzveranstaltung *U4: 75*; tanzen **U1:** 28; **dancer** Tänzer/Tänzerin **U1:** 11
dancing ['dɑ:nsɪŋ] (das) Tanzen **2 > U4:** 61
dangerous ['deɪndʒərəs] gefährlich **2 > U1:** 18
dark [dɑ:k] dunkel **2 > U3:** 51
date [deɪt] Datum **2 > U4:** 72
daughter ['dɔ:tə] Tochter **1 > U3:** 60
day [deɪ] Tag **1 > U2:** 42; **every day** jeden Tag **1 > U3:** 53; **special day** besonderer Tag **1 > U4:** 74; *one day* eines Tages *U4: 75*; **day out** (Tages-)Ausflug **U2:** 30; **have a day out** einen Tagesausflug machen **1 > U5:** 86

[s] six [z] his [ʃ] she [tʃ] teacher [dʒ] jeans [j] yes [θ] thing [ð] the [i:] he [ɑ:] car [ɔ:] or

Dear ..., [dɪə] Liebe(r, s) ..., **2 > U1:** 16
December [dɪ'sembə] Dezember **1 > U5:** 98
deep [di:p] tief **U3:** 64
defy [dɪ'faɪ] trotzen, sich widersetzen *U1: 15*
degrees *(pl.)* [dɪ'gri:z] Grad **2 > U6:** 104
detail ['di:teɪl] Detail, Einzelheit **U1:** 16
dial [daɪəl] wählen *U3: 55*
dialling code ['daɪəlɪŋ kəʊd] Vorwahl **U3:** 56
dialogue ['daɪəlɒg] Dialog **2 > U1:** 21
diary ['daɪəri] Tagebuch **2 > U1:** 18
dictionary ['dɪkʃənri] Wörterbuch **1 > U2:** 37
did → do [dɪd] *simple past* von **do** **2 > U2:** 32; **No, I didn't (= did not).** Nein (habe ich nicht). **2 > U2:** 32
die [daɪ] sterben **2 > Legend:** 109
died → die [daɪd] *simple past* von *die* *U3: 53*
difference: (time) difference ['taɪm dɪfrəns] (Zeit-)Unterschied **2 > U6:** 97
different ['dɪfrənt] anderer/andere/anderes **1 > U1:** 24; verschieden **2 > Intro:** 9
difficult ['dɪfɪkəlt] schwierig, schwer **1 > U5:** 92
dinosaur ['daɪnəsɔ:] Dinosaurier **U1:** 10
discuss [dɪ'skʌs] diskutieren, besprechen *U5: 95*
dishwasher ['dɪʃwɒʃə] Geschirrspülmaschine **2 > U6:** 94
distribution [dɪstrɪ'bju:ʃn] Vertrieb *U4: 75*
district ['dɪstrɪkt] Distrikt, Bezirk *U5: 93*
do [du:] tun, machen **1 > U4:** 76
dock [dɒk] Hafen, Dock **2 > U3:** 46
doctor ['dɒktə] Arzt/Ärztin **1 > U3:** 53
Does: Does your cousin live ...? [dʌz jʊə kʌzn 'lɪv] Wohnt dein Cousin/deine Kusine ...? **1 > U5:** 89; **Yes, she does.** Ja (tut sie). **1 > U5:** 89; **No, she doesn't.** Nein (tut sie nicht). **1 > U5:** 89

dog [dɒg] Hund **1 > U1:** 21; **take the dog for a walk** mit dem Hund rausgehen/spazierengehen **2 > U1:** 19
doll [dɒl] Puppe **1 > U4:** 71
dollar ($) ['dɒlə] Dollar (US-Währung) **2 > U6:** 96
done: Well done! [wel 'dʌn] Gut gemacht! **1 > U5:** 93
door [dɔ:] Tür **1 > Intro:** 11
double ['dʌbl] doppelt, Doppel- **U3:** 56
down [daʊn] herunter, hinunter **U2:** 46
download ['daʊnləʊd] (Daten) herunterladen, downloaden **U4:** 76
downtown *(AE)* ['daʊntaʊn] Innenstadt, Stadtzentrum **U4:** 69
drank → drink [dræŋk] *simple past* von **drink** **U3:** 67
dream [dri:m] Traum **U4:** 84
drink [drɪŋk] Getränk **1 > U3:** 52; trinken **1 > U4:** 70; **The drinks are on me.** Die Getränke gehen auf mich., Ich bezahle die Getränke. U3: 51
drive [draɪv] fahren (ein Auto, Bus usw.) **2 > U6:** 102
driver: bus driver ['bʌs draɪvə] Busfahrer/in **2 > U3:** 54
driving ['draɪvɪŋ] (das) Autofahren **2 > U6:** 98
drummer ['drʌmə] Schlagzeuger/Schlagzeugerin **U4:** 70
drums *(pl.)* [drʌmz] Schlagzeug **U4:** 70
dry [draɪ] trocken **2 > U6:** 104
dustman ['dʌstmən] Müllmann **2 > U6:** 98
DVD [di: vi: 'di:] DVD (Digital Versatile Disk) **1 > U4:** 70; **DVD player** DVD-Spieler **2 > U2:** 29

E

each [i:tʃ] jede(r, s) **U5:** 92
early ['ɜ:li] früh, frühzeitig **1 > U6:** 107
earn [ɜ:n] verdienen **U5:** 91
Easter ['i:stə] Ostern U3: 53
easy ['i:zi] leicht, einfach **2 > U4:** 66
eat [i:t] essen **1 > U3:** 53; **eat fire** Feuer schlucken/speien **1 > U6:** 105
economy flyer [ɪ'kɒnəmi flaɪə] *hier:* Überflieger *U1: 15*

egg [eg] Ei **U5:** 103
eight [eɪt] acht **1 > Intro:** 15
eighteen [eɪ'ti:n] achtzehn **1 > U2:** 48
eighteenth [eʊ'ti:nθ] achzehnte(r, s) **2 > U4:** 72
eighth [eʊtθ] achte(r, s) **2 > U4:** 72
eighty ['eɪti] achtzig **1 > U2:** 48
electronic gadget [ɪlek'trɒnɪk 'gædʒɪt] Elektrogerät, -apparat **2 > U2:** 29
eleven [ɪ'levn] elf **1 > Intro:** 15
eleventh [ɪ'levnθ] elfte(r, s) **2 > U4:** 72
else: Anything else? [eniθɪŋ 'els] Sonst noch etwas? **1 > U4:** 75
email ['i:meɪl] E-Mail **2 > U1:** 16; als E-Mail verschicken, mailen **2 > U6:** 94
empty ['empti] leer **1 > U3:** 57
end [end] Ende **2 > Legend:** 110
engineer [endʒɪ'nɪə] Ingenieur/Ingenieurin, Techniker/Technikerin U5: 91
England ['ɪŋglənd] England **1 > Intro:** 16
English ['ɪŋglɪʃ] englisch **1 > U1:** 30; **in English** auf Englisch **1 > U1:** 32
enjoy [ɪn'dʒɔɪ] genießen **2 > U3:** 49
enormous [ɪ'nɔ:məs] ungeheuer groß **1 > U6:** 108
enough [ɪ'nʌf] genug **U4:** 70
err... [ɜ:] äh... U5: 104
euro ['jʊərəʊ] Euro **2 > U3:** 56
Europe ['jʊərəp] Europa **1 > Intro:** 16
European [jʊərə'pi:ən] Europäer/Europäerin **U5:** 90
evening: in the evening [ɪn ði 'i:vnɪŋ] abends **1 > U2:** 40; **Good evening.** Guten Abend. **1 > U1:** 28
event [ɪ'vent] Ereignis, Veranstaltung *U5: 93*
every: every day [evri 'deɪ] jeden Tag **1 > U3:** 53; *every now and then* ab und zu, hin und wieder *U1: 15*
everybody ['evribɒdi] jede(r, s), alle **2 > U5:** 83
everything ['evriθɪŋ] alles **1 > U2:** 42
everywhere ['evriweə] überall **2 > U6:** 99
example [ɪg'zɑ:mpl] Beispiel *U3: 55*; **for example** zum Beispiel **2 > U3:** 51

[u:] too [ɜ:] girl [i] sorry [u] July [ɪ] big [e] yes [æ] cat [ʌ] bus [ɒ] dog [ʊ] put [ə] again

except [ɪ'ksept] außer U5: 103
excited [ɪk'saɪtɪd] aufgeregt 2 > U5: 81
exciting [ɪk'saɪtɪŋ] aufregend, spannend 2 > U2: 35
Excuse me. [ɪk'skju:z mi] Entschuldigung./Entschuldigen Sie. 2 > U1: 24
exercise ['eksəsaɪz] Übung 1 > U1: 26
expect [ɪk'spekt] erwarten, annehmen, vermuten U3: 51
expensive: too expensive [tu: ɪk'spensɪv] zu teuer 1 > U4: 75
experience [ɪk'spɪərɪəns] Erfahrung, Erlebnis *U2: 30*
experiment [ɪk'sperɪmənt] Experiment, Versuch U1: 10
expert ['ekspɜ:t] Experte/Expertin, Fachmann/Fachfrau *U2: 37*
explain [ɪk'spleɪn] erklären U3: 67
extra ['ekstrə] Zusatz, Zugabe, Extra *U3: 55*

F

face [feɪs] Gesicht U3: 66
fact [fækt] Fakt, Tatsache U4: 74
factory ['fæktəri] Fabrik 2 > U3: 48
fair [feə] fair, gerecht 2 > U1: 18
fall [fɔ:l] fallen, stürzen U2: 47
family ['fæməli] Familie 1 > U2: 39
famous ['feɪməs] berühmt 1 > U6: 102
fan [fæn] Fan 1 > U1: 22
fantastic [fæn'tæstɪk] fantastisch, toll 2 > Intro: 7
far [fɑ:] weit U5: 94; *far away* weit weg *U2: 35*
farm [fɑ:m] Bauernhof, Farm 1 > U4: 69
fashion ['fæʃən] Mode *U2: 37*
fast [fɑ:st] schnell U5: 87
father ['fɑ:ðə] Vater 1 > U3: 60
favourite ['feɪvərɪt] Lieblings- 1 > Intro: 14
February ['februəri] Februar 1 > U5: 98
fed up: Asif was fed up. ['æsi:f wəz fed 'ʌp] Asif hatte die Nase voll. 1 > U6: 108
feed [fi:d] füttern, zu fressen geben 2 > U2: 32
feel [fi:l] (sich) fühlen, sich anfühlen U2: 47; **feel sorry for somebody (sb.)** jemanden (jdn.) bedauern, Mitleid mit jemandem (jdm.) haben U3: 67
fell → fall [fell] *simple past* von **fall** U3: 47
felt → feel [felt] *simple past* von **feel** U2: 47
felt-tip ['felttɪp] Filzstift 1 > U1: 32
ferry ['feri] Fähre 2 > U3: 46
few [fju:] wenige U5: 89; **a few** ein paar, einige 2 > U4: 63
field [fi:ld] Feld, Wiese 1 > U4: 69; **football field** Fußballplatz 1 > U5: 90
fifteen [fɪf'ti:n] fünfzehn 1 > U2: 48
fifteenth [fɪf'ti:nθ] fünfzehnte(r, s) 2 > U4: 72
fifth [fɪfθ] fünfte(r, s) 2 > U4: 72
fifty ['fɪfti] fünfzig 1 > U2: 48
film [fɪlm] Film 1 > U2: 43; **film guide** Filmführer, Filmprogrammheft 2 > U4: 73
find [faɪnd] finden 1 > U1: 21; **find out** herausfinden; entdecken 2 > U3: 48
fine [faɪn] gut 2 > Legend: 111
finger: fish fingers [fɪʃ 'fɪŋgəz] Fischstäbchen 2 > U5: 82; **fingers crossed** Ich drücke die Daumen. 1 > U6: 129
finish ['fɪnɪʃ] beenden, zu Ende machen 2 > U1: 14
fire: eat fire [i:t 'faɪə] Feuer schlucken/speien 1 > U6: 105
firework ['faɪəwɜ:k] Feuerwerkskörper 2 > U4: 62
first [fɜ:st] erste(r, s) 2 > U1: 14; zuerst, zum ersten Mal U1: 23; **at first** zuerst U3: 50; **May the first (= 1st May)** der erste Mai (1. Mai) 2 > U4: 72
fish: fish and chips [fɪʃ ənd 'tʃɪps] Fisch und Pommes frites 1 > U3: 52; **fish fingers** Fischstäbchen 2 > U5: 82
fishing ['fɪʃɪŋ] (das) Angeln 2 > U6: 99
fitness ['fɪtnəs] Fitness 1 > U4: 124
five [faɪv] fünf 1 > Intro: 15
fix the hook-ups [fɪks ðə 'hʊkʌps] das Verbindungskabel anschließen U5: 105
flag [flæg] Flagge, Fahne 1 > U5: 92
flat [flæt] Wohnung 1 > Intro: 18; *Platten, Reifenpanne U4: 75*; flach, eben U4: 69
floor: ground floor ['graʊnd flɔ:] Erdgeschoss 2 > U3: 51
flower ['flaʊə] Blume, Blüte 2 > U2: 35; **flower-bed** Blumenbeet 2 > U2: 35
flute [flu:t] (Quer-)Flöte U4: 70
fly [flaɪ] fliegen *U2: 35*; *fly by* vorbei-/vorüberfliegen *U1: 15*
flyer: economy flyer [ɪ'kɒnəmi flaɪə] *hier:* Überflieger *U1: 15*
foggy ['fɒgi] neblig 2 > U6: 104
follow ['fɒləʊ] folgen 1 > U5: 92
food [fu:d] Essen, Lebensmittel 1 > U3: 52
foot [fʊt] Fuß 1 > U6: 110; *on foot* zu Fuß *U1: 17*
football ['fʊtbɔ:l] Fußball 1 > U1: 22; **football field** Fußballplatz 1 > U5: 90
for [fɔ:] für 1 > U1: 26; **for example** zum Beispiel 2 > U3: 51; *for work/food/...* um Arbeit/Essen/... zu suchen *U3: 53*
foreign language [fɒrən 'læŋgwɪdʒ] Fremdsprache 2 > U6: 96
forest ['fɒrəst] Wald U5: 102
forever: I'm forever crying [aɪm fərevə 'kraɪɪŋ] ich werde ewig weinen *U2: 35*
forgot → forget [fə'gɒt] U2: 46 *simple past* von **forget**
forget: Don't forget! Vergesst/Vergiss nicht! 1 > U6: 102
form [fɔ:m] Form 2 > U3: 55; Formular U4: 70
forty ['fɔ:ti] vierzig 1 > U2: 48
forward: look forward to sth. [lʊk 'fɔ:wəd tə sʌmθɪŋ] sich auf etwas freuen U5: 103
found → find [faʊnd] *simple past* von **find** 2 > U5: 87
four [fɔ:] vier 1 > Intro: 15
fourteen [fɔ:'ti:n] vierzehn 1 > U2: 48
fourteenth [fɔ:'ti:nθ] vierzehnte(r, s) 2 > U4: 72
fourth (= 4th) [fɔ:θ] vierte(r, s) 2 > U4: 72
France [frɑ:ns] Frankreich 2 > Intro: 8
freak [fri:k] Freak, Fanatiker(in) U2: 37
free [fri:] frei, kostenlos 1 > U2: 40; **free time** Freizeit 1 > U4: 76
French [frentʃ] Französisch, französisch 2 > U1: 14

fresh [freʃ] frisch **U5:** 103
Friday ['fraɪdeɪ] Freitag **1 > U4:** 80
fridge [frɪdʒ] Kühlschrank **1 > U6:** 114
friend [frend] Freund/Freundin **1 > Intro:** 17; *the best of friends* die besten Freunde *U5: 91*
friendly ['frendli] freundlich, nett **1 > U2:** 38; **as friendly as** (genau)so freundlich wie **U4:** 76
frightened: They were frightened. [ðeɪ wə 'fraɪtnd] Sie hatten Angst. **2 > U5:** 82
from [frɒm] von, aus **1 > Intro:** 17; **from ... to** von ... bis **2 > U1:** 14; **from ... till** von ... bis **1 > U2:** 40; **Where are you from?** Wo kommst du her? **1 > U1:** 22
front: in front of [ɪn 'frʌnt əv] vor **1 > U2:** 39
fruit [fru:t] Obst **1 > U3:** 53; **fruit juice** (Frucht-) Saft **1 > U3:** 53
full of ['fʊl əv] voll (mit, von) **1 > U6:** 107
fun [fʌn] Spaß **1 > U4:** 70; **be fun** Spaß machen **1 > U2:** 40; *just for fun* nur so zum Spaß *U2: 37*
funny ['fʌni] lustig, witzig **1 > U6:** 110; komisch, merkwürdig **2 > U1:** 16
future ['fju:tʃə] Zukunft **2 > U6:** 101

G

gadget: electronic gadget [ɪlek'trɒnɪk 'gædʒɪt] Elektrogerät, -apparat **2 > U2:** 29
game [geɪm] Spiel **1 > U4:** 69; **video game** Videospiel **1 > U4:** 71; **games console** Spielkonsole **2 > U2:** 29
gameboy ['geɪmbɔɪ] Gameboy **1 > U4:** 73
garage ['gærɑ:ʒ] Garage **2 > U1:** 18
garden ['gɑ:dn] Garten **1 > U1:** 21; *gardener* Gärtner/Gärtnerin *U3: 53*
gate [geɪt] Tor, Pforte **2 > U2:** 30
gave → give [geɪv] *simple past* von **give** **U1:** 29
Gee! *(AE)* [dʒi:] Mensch!, Mann! U5: 104
geography [dʒi'ɒgrəfi] Geographie, Erdkunde **2 > U3:** 46
German ['dʒɜ:mən] deutsch **1 > U2:** 38; **in German** auf Deutsch **1 > U1:** 32
Germany ['dʒɜ:məni] Deutschland **1 > Intro:** 16
get [get] bekommen **1 > U5:** 85; erreichen **2 > Legend:** 110; holen **U4:** 70; gelangen, hinkommen **U5:** 94; **get back** zurückkommen/-finden **1 > U5:** 91; *get busy* sich mit etwas beschäftigen *U1: 15*; *get higher and higher* immer höher aufsteigen *U1: 15*; **get on** aufsteigen, einsteigen **2 > Legend:** 110; einsteigen, zusteigen *U1: 17*; **get on, get off service** Bus-Service zum Zu- und Aussteigen U3: 48; *get started* anfangen, beginnen *U5: 93*; **get up** aufstehen **1 > U4:** 80
gig [gɪg] Gig, Auftritt *U4: 75*
girl [gɜ:l] Mädchen **1 > Intro:** 10
girlfriend ['gɜ:lfrend] (feste) Freundin **1 > U1:** 27
give [gɪv] geben **U1:** 29; **Give my greetings to ...** Grüße mir ... **1 > U6:** 114
glad [glæd] froh **U3:** 49
glass [glɑ:s] Glas **2 > U3:** 51
go [gəʊ] gehen, fahren **1 > U3:** 41; **go along** entlanggehen **2 > U3:** 52; **go away** verreisen **1 > U5:** 87; **go by ...** mit dem/der ... fahren **2 > Intro:** 8; **go on holiday** in Urlaub gehen/fahren **2 > Intro:** 8; **go out for a meal** essen gehen **1 > U5:** 86; **go out in the car** eine Spazierfahrt machen **1 > U5:** 86; **Go straight on.** geradeaus (weiter)gehen **2 > U3:** 52; **go to the shops** einen Einkaufsbummel machen; einkaufen gehen **1 > U4:** 76; **go to town** in die (Innen-)Stadt fahren **1 > U6:** 106
goal [gəʊl] Tor **U3:** 56
golf [gɒlf] Golf **2 > U5:** 81
good: good (at) ['gʊd ət] gut (in) **1 > U1:** 26; **Good afternoon.** Guten Tag. (nachmittags) **1 > U1:** 28; *as good as* (genau)so gut wie *U4: 75*; **Good evening.** Guten Abend. **1 > U1:** 28; **good luck** (viel) Glück **U3:** 56; **Good morning.** Guten Morgen. **1 > U1:** 25; **good value** preisgünstig **2 > U4:** 68; **good-looking** gut aussehend, attraktiv **U4:** 76; **Your team is no good.** Dein Team /Deine Mannschaft taugt nichts. U3: 67
Goodbye. ['gʊdbaɪ] Auf Wiedersehen. **1 > U1:** 28
got → get [gɒt] *simple past* von **get** **2 > Legend:** 110; **got on → get on** *simple past* von **get on** **2 > Legend:** 110
grace [greɪs] Gnade; Tischgebet U3: 52
gram [græm] Gramm **2 > U4:** 68
grandfather ['grænfɑ:ðə] Großvater **1 > U3:** 60
grandma ['grænmɑ:] Oma **1 > U2:** 39
grandmother ['grænmʌðə] Großmutter **1 > U3:** 60
grass [grɑ:s] Gras **1 > U5:** 90
grave [greɪv] Grab *U3: 53*
gravity ['grævɪti] Schwerkraft *U1: 15*
great [greɪt] toll **1 > U3:** 53; groß, großartig **U5:** 91; **great at** super/großartig in **U1:** 27
green [gri:n] grün **1 > Intro:** 14
greetings: Give my greetings to ... [gɪv maɪ 'gri:tɪŋz tə] Grüße mir ... **1 > U6:** 114
ground floor ['graʊnd flɔ:] Erdgeschoss **2 > U3:** 51
group [gru:p] Gruppe **2 > U1:** 17
Grow up! ['grəʊ ʌp] Sei(d) mal vernünftig! **1 > U5:** 90
grumpy ['grʌmpi] mürrisch, brummig **1 > U5:** 90
guide book ['gaɪd bʊk] Reiseführer **U1:** 12
gum: chewing gum ['tʃu:ɪŋ gʌm] Kaugummi **2 > U3:** 51
gun [gʌn] Kanone *U3: 53*
gym [dʒɪm] Turnhalle, Sporthalle **U4:** 72
gypsy ['dʒɪpsi] Zigeuner/Zigeunerin *U5: 91*

H

had [hæd] hatte/hatten **1 > U3:** 58
haggis ['hægɪs] schottisches Gericht aus Schafsinnereien U3: 52

half (*pl.:* **halves**) [hɑːf, hɑːvz] Hälfte **U2:** 34; **half past** halb *(Uhrzeit)* **2 > U3:** 51; **half-brother** Halbbruder **1 > U2:** 39
Halloween [hæləʊ'iːn] Halloween **1 > U5:** 98
hamburger ['hæmbɜːgə] Hamburger **U1:** 25
hamster ['hæmstə] Hamster **2 > U2:** 34
handbook ['hændbʊk] Gebrauchsanweisung *U3: 54*
happen ['hæpən] passieren, geschehen **2 > U6:** 95; **What's happening?** Was ist los?/Was geht hier vor? **2 > U4:** 64
happy ['hæpi] glücklich, froh **1 > U1:** 26
hard(er) [hɑːd] hart (härter); schwierig(er) **2 > U1:** 18
hardware ['hɑːdweə] Hardware **1 > U4:** 69
hate [heɪt] hassen, gar nicht mögen **2 > U1:** 17
have [hæv] haben **1 > U3:** 54; essen, trinken **U3:** 60; **I don't have** Ich habe keinen/keine/kein **1 > U3:** 55; **he doesn't have** er hat keinen/keine/kein **1 > U3:** 57; **Can I have a ...?** Kann ich eine(n)/ein ... haben? **1 > U1:** 32; **have a day out** einen Tagesausflug machen **1 > U5:** 86; **have a good time** sich gut amüsieren **2 > U4:** 65; **have a race** um die Wette laufen **1 > U5:** 92; **have a wash** sich waschen **1 > U4:** 80; **have breakfast** frühstücken **1 > U4:** 80; **have to** müssen **2 > U6:** 96
he's (= he is) [hiːz] er ist **1 > U1:** 25
headphones ['hedfəʊnz] Kopfhörer **2 > U2:** 29
healthy ['helθi] gesund **1 > U3:** 53
hear [hɪə] hören **2 > U1:** 15
heard → hear [hɜːd] *simple past* von **hear** **2 > Legend:** 109
heavenly ['hevənli] himmlisch, göttlich *U1: 15*
helicopter ['helɪkɒptə] Hubschrauber **U2:** 47
helmet ['helmɪt] Helm **1 > U6:** 110
help [help] helfen **1 > U4:** 74
helpful ['helpfəl] hilfreich, behilflich **U4:** 76
her [hɜː] ihr/ihre **1 > U2:** 39
here [hɪə] hier **1 > U1:** 22; **here are** hier sind **1 > U2:** 38; **Here you are.** (hier) Bitte. **1 > U1:** 32; **here's (= here is)** hier ist **1 > Intro:** 18
Hey! [heɪ] Hey! **1 > U4:** 75
Hi. [haɪ] Hallo. **1 > U1:** 26
high [haɪ] hoch **2 > U5:** 80; **high school** (US) Gesamtschule für 13- bis 18-Jährige **U5:** 99; *High Street* Hauptstraße, Einkaufsstraße *U3: 55*; *get higher and higher* immer höher aufsteigen *U1: 15*
hike [haɪk] wandern **U2:** 32; **hiker** Wanderer **U5:** 94
hill [hɪl] Hügel, Berg **2 > U3:** 45
him [hɪm] ihn; ihm **2 > Intro:** 8
his [hɪz] sein/seine **1 > U1:** 27
history ['hɪstri] Geschichte, Vergangenheit **2 > U3:** 45
hit ['hɪt] Hit, Schlager **1 > U4:** 81; treffen, schlagen, stoßen **U3:** 66; **hit → hit** *simple past* von **hit** **U3:** 66
hobby ['hɒbi] Hobby **1 > U3:** 58; **What's your hobby?** Welches Hobby hast du? **1 > U4:** 76
hold [həʊld] (fest)halten **2 > U4:** 65
hole [həʊl] Loch *U3: 55*
holiday ['hɒlədeɪ] Urlaub, Urlaubs-; Ferien **1 > U5:** 87; **public holiday** gesetzlicher Feiertag **1 > U5:** 86; **on holiday** im Urlaub **1 > U6:** 115; **go on holiday** in Urlaub gehen/fahren **2 > Intro:** 8
home [həʊm] Zuhause, Heim, Heimat **U1:** 10; nach Hause **1 > U3:** 59; **at home** zu Hause **1 > U2:** 36
home page, homepage ['həʊmpeɪdʒ] Homepage, Startseite **2 > U1:** 25
homesick: be/get homesick [bɪ, get 'həʊmsɪk] Heimweh haben/bekommen **2 > U5:** 84
homework ['həʊmwɜːk] Hausaufgabe(n) **1 > U5:** 94
hook-up: fix the hook-ups [fɪks ðə 'hʊkʌps] das Verbindungskabel anschließen U5: 105
hope [həʊp] hoffen **1 > U6:** 109
horse [hɔːs] Pferd **1 > U5:** 96
hospital ['hɒspɪtl] Krankenhaus **2 > U3:** 53
hostel: youth hostel ['juːθ hɒstl] Jugendherberge **U2:** 38
hot [hɒt] heiß **2 > U4:** 62; **hot chocolate** heiße Schokolade **2 > U5:** 82; **hot dog** Hotdog **1 > U3:** 59
hotel [həʊ'tel] Hotel **1 > U6:** 114
hour ['aʊə] Stunde **2 > U1:** 18
house [haʊs] Haus **1 > Intro:** 10; **at ... house** bei ... zu Hause **1 > U2:** 42; **leave the house** das Haus verlassen **1 > U4:** 80
how [haʊ] wie **1 > U6:** 110; **How are things?** Wie geht's?, Wie läuft's? *(ugs.)* **U3:** 56; **How are you?** Wie geht es dir/euch/Ihnen? **1 > U6:** 114; **how many?** wie viele? **2 > U4:** 62; **How much is it?** Was kostet das? **1 > U4:** 75; **how much?** wie viel? **2 > U4:** 62; **How old are you?** Wie alt bist du? **1 > U1:** 22
human ['hjuːmən] menschlich, Menschen- **2 > U3:** 50
hundred ['hʌndrəd] hundert **1 > U2:** 48; **hundreds** Hunderte U1: 23
hungry: I'm hungry. [aɪm 'hʌŋgri] Ich habe Hunger. **1 > U3:** 52
hurry: Hurry! ['hʌri] Beeilt euch!/Beeil dich! **1 > U6:** 109
hurt [hɜːt] verletzt **2 > U2:** 31

I

I [aɪ] ich **1 > Intro:** 10; **I'm (= I am)** ich bin **1 > Intro:** 17
ice cream [aɪs 'kriːm] (Speise-)Eis **1 > U3:** 55
iced tea [aɪst 'tiː] Eistee **1 > U3:** 55
idea [aɪ'dɪə] Idee, Gedanke **1 > U3:** 54; Vorstellung, Ahnung, Meinung **U3:** 51; **have no idea** keine Ahnung haben **1 > U6:** 108
ideal [aɪ'dɪəl] ideal **U2:** 32
idol ['aɪdl] Idol, Star **U4:** 68
ill [ɪl] krank **1 > U3:** 58
important [ɪm'pɔːtnt] wichtig **2 > U4:** 72
in [ɪn] in, auf **1 > Intro:** 10; **in English** auf Englisch **1 > U1:** 32; **in German** auf Deutsch **1 > U1:** 32; **in the country** auf dem Land **1 > U5:** 86; **in the morning** morgens **1 > U2:** 40

[ʃ] **sh**e [tʃ] tea**ch**er [dʒ] **j**eans [j] **y**es [θ] **th**ing [ð] **th**e [iː] h**e** [ɑː] c**ar** [ɔː] **or** [uː] t**oo** [ɜː] g**ir**l

Indian ['ɪndiən] indisch; Inder/in 2 > U2: 33
Industrial Revolution [ɪndʌstriəl revə'lu:ʃn] industrielle Revolution 2 > U3: 48
industry ['ɪndəstri] Industrie 2 > U3: 48
information technology (IT) [ɪnfəmeɪʃn tek'nɒlədʒi] Informationstechnologie 2 > U1: 14
inline skating ['ɪnlaɪn skeɪtɪŋ] Inlineskating 2 > U6: 102
insist [ɪn'sɪst] bestehen auf, beharren auf *U5: 91*
instrument: play an instrument [pleɪ ən 'ɪnstrəmənt] ein Instrument spielen 1 > U6: 105
interest ['ɪntrəst] Interesse; Hobby 2 > U2: 28
interested in ['ɪntrəstɪd ɪn] interessiert an 1 > U4: 75
interesting ['ɪntrəstɪŋ] interessant 1 > U5: 86; **more interesting than** interessanter als 2 > U3: 50
international [ɪntə'næʃənl] international 1 > U3: 65
Internet ['ɪntənet] Internet 2 > U1: 25; **surf the Internet** im Internet surfen U1: 27
interview ['ɪntəvju:] Interview U1: 9; befragen, interviewen 2 > U3: 46
into ['ɪntə] in ... (hinein) 2 > U5: 82
intonation [ɪntə'neɪʃn] Intonation, Tonfall U3: 57
invitation [ɪnvɪ'teɪʃn] Einladung 2 > U4: 64
Ireland: Northern Ireland [nɔ:ðən 'aɪələnd] Nordirland 2 > U1: 12
Irn-Bru [ɜ:n 'bru:] schottisches Limonadengetränk U3: 51
is [ɪz] ist 1 > Intro: 14; **Is it ...?** Ist es ...? 1 > Intro: 14; **Is that ...?** Ist das ...? 1 > U1: 30; **isn't (= is not)** ist nicht 1 > U2: 40
island ['aɪlənd] Insel U3: 48
issue ['ɪʃju:, 'ɪsju:] (Streit-)Frage, Thema, Angelegenheit *U5: 93*
it's (= it is) [ɪts] es ist (er/sie ist, nicht Personen) 1 > U1: 25
its [ɪts] sein/seine, ihr/ihre 1 > U3: 62

J

jam: traffic jam ['træfɪk dʒæm] Stau *U5: 93*
January ['dʒænjuəri] Januar 1 > U5: 98
jeans *(pl.)* [dʒi:nz] Jeans 1 > U6: 107
job [dʒɒb] Aufgabe 1 > U3: 58; Arbeit, Arbeitsplatz, Stelle U1: 8
join [dʒɔɪn] sich anschließen; mitmachen *U5: 93*
joke [dʒəʊk] Witz, Scherz 2 > U1: 25
journey ['dʒɜ:ni] (lange) Reise, Fahrt 2 > U5: 78
juggle ['dʒʌgl] jonglieren 1 > U6: 105; **juggler** Jongleur, Gaukler/Gauklerin U1: 11
juice: fruit juice ['fru:t dʒu:s] (Frucht-) Saft 1 > U3: 53
July [dʒu'laɪ] Juli 1 > U5: 98
jump off [dʒʌmp 'ɒf] herunter-, hinunterspringen von, herunter-, hinunterhüpfen von U2: 46
junction ['dʒʌŋktʃn] Ausfahrt *U2: 30*
June [dʒu:n] Juni 1 > U5: 98
junior railcard [dʒu:njə 'reɪlkɑ:d] „Bahncard" für Jugendliche U3: 54
junk [dʒʌŋk] Gerümpel, altes Zeug, Müll U4: 70
jury ['dʒʊəri] Jury U4: 72
just: Just a minute. [dʒʌst ə 'mɪnɪt] Einen Augenblick. 1 > U2: 43; *just for fun* nur so zum Spaß *U2: 37*; **Just phone me.** Ruf(t) mich einfach an. 1 > U6: 110

K

keen [ki:n] eifrig, kühn, verwegen *U1: 15*
ketchup ['ketʃəp] Ketschup 1 > U3: 54
key [ki:] Schlüssel 2 > U6: 97
kid [kɪd] Kind, Jugendliche(r) 2 > U1: 18
kilometer [kɪləmi:tə] Kilometer U3: 64
kill [kɪl] töten, umbringen 2 > U4: 62
kilt [kɪlt] Schottenrock U3: 51
kind [kaɪnd] Art, Sorte *U3: 53*; *what kind of* was für *U2: 37*
king ['kɪŋ] König 2 > U4: 62
kingdom: United Kingdom (UK) [junaɪtɪd 'kɪŋdəm] Vereinigtes Königreich 2 > U1: 12
kitchen ['kɪtʃɪn] Küche 1 > U2: 37
kite [kaɪt] Drachen 1 > U4: 71
knew → know [kju:] *simple past* von **know** U1: 21
know [nəʊ] kennen 1 > U5: 92; **know the way** den Weg kennen 1 > U5: 92

L

lake [leɪk] (Binnen-)See 2 > U6: 94
land [lænd] landen 2 > U6: 97
landline ['lændlaɪn] Festnetz *U3: 55*
language ['læŋgwɪdʒ] Sprache U1: 9; **foreign language** Fremdsprache 2 > U6: 96
last [lɑ:st] letzte(r, s) 2 > U1: 19; **at last** endlich U2: 46
late [leɪt] spät 1 > U2: 40; **till late** bis spät 1 > U2: 40; **he is late** er kommt zu spät, er verspätet sich U3: 56; **run late** sich verspäten, Verspätung haben U3: 56; **late parking** das Überziehen der Parkzeit 1 > U6: 109; **Better late than never.** Lieber spät als gar nicht. 1 > U5: 93; **See you later.** Bis später. 1 > U1: 28; **later** ['leɪtə] später U2: 46; **latest** neueste(r, s) U3: 61
laugh [lɑ:f] lachen 2 > U3: 50
lay [laɪ] *simple past* von **lie** 2 > U5: 82
lead singer [li:d 'sɪŋə] Leadsänger/Leadsängerin U4: 85
leaf (*pl.*: **leaves**) [li:f] Blatt, Blätter 2 > U4: 62
leaflet ['li:flet] Flugblatt, Werbeprospekt, Handzettel U1: 29
learn [lɜ:n] lernen U1: 8; **learn about** etwas erfahren über 1 > U6: 102
leave [li:v] (stehen) lassen 1 > U4: 71; lassen, verlassen 2 > U3: 49; **leave the house** das Haus verlassen 1 > U4: 80; *on the left* links, auf der linken Seite *U1: 17*
left: to the left [tə ðə 'left] links 1 > U5: 92

[i] sorry [u] July [ɪ] big [e] yes [æ] cat [ʌ] bus [ɒ] dog [ʊ] put [ə] again [eɪ] name [aɪ] time

left → leave [left] *simple past* von **leave** **2 > U3:** 49

legend ['ledʒənd] Legende, Sage **2 > Legend:** 108

lemonade [lemə'neɪd] Limonade **1 > U3:** 55

less [les] weniger **U5:** 87

lesson ['lesn] (Unterrichts-)Stunde **1 > U1:** 32

Let's ... [lets] Lass(t) uns ... **1 > U2:** 41

letter ['letə] Brief **1 > U6:** 106

lettuce ['letɪs] (Kopf-)Salat **1 > U3:** 53

level ['levl] Ebene, Höhe **U3:** 50

library ['laɪbrəri] Bibliothek, Bücherei **1 > U6:** 104

lie (on) [laɪ] liegen (auf) **2 > U5:** 81

life [laɪf] Leben **2 > U3:** 48; **Run for your life!** Renn/t um dein/euer Leben! **U2:** 47

lift [lɪft] Fahrstuhl, Aufzug **2 > U3:** 51

light [laɪt] Licht, Lampe **2 > U5:** 82; hell **2 > U6:** 97

like [laɪk] mögen **1 > U5:** 85; **be like** (sein/aussehen) wie **2 > U3:** 51; **I'd like ... (= I would like)** Ich hätte gern .../Ich möchte ... **1 > U4:** 75; **What would you like ...?** Was würdest du gern ...? **2 > U4:** 61; **I don't like ...** Ich mag ... nicht. **1 > U5:** 94; **What is/was/were ... like?** Wie ist/war/waren ...? **2 > U2:** 36

line [laɪn] Linie, Strecke **U5:** 90; **assembly line** Fließband U5: 91

link [lɪŋk] Link; Verbindung **2 > U1:** 25

list [lɪst] auflisten *U2: 37*; **make a list** eine Liste schreiben **2 > U4:** 64

listen (to) ['lɪsn tə] hören, sich anhören **1 > U4:** 70

little: a little [ə 'lɪtl] ein bisschen, ein wenig **2 > U4:** 63

live [lɪv] wohnen **1 > U5:** 89; *live off* leben von *U4: 75*; **Does your cousin live ...?** Wohnt dein Cousin/deine Kusine ...? **1 > U5:** 89

living room ['lɪvɪŋ ru:m] Wohnzimmer **1 > U2:** 37

local ['ləʊkl] örtlich, am/vom Ort **1 > U6:** 102

Londoner ['lʌndənə] Londoner/Londonerin **U1:** 9

long [lɒŋ] lang **1 > U5:** 86; **as long as** solange **U5:** 91

look [lʊk] gucken, schauen **1 > U2:** 41; (nach)schauen **1 > U3:** 54; **look after** sich kümmern um; betreuen **1 > U6:** 107; **look at** anschauen **1 > U1:** 26; *look for* suchen *U1: 17*; **look forward to sth.** sich auf etwas freuen **U5:** 103; **looked at → look at** *simple past* von **look at** **2 > U2:** 35

lose [lu:z] verlieren **U3:** 67

lost → lose [lɒst] *simple past* von **lose** **U3:** 67; **Lost in the maze.** Verloren im Irrgarten. **1 > U5:** 90

lot: a lot of [ə 'lɒt əv] eine Menge, viel, viele **2 > U2:** 34; **lots of** viel, viele; eine Menge **1 > U3:** 54

loud [laʊd] laut **U2:** 47

loudspeaker ['laʊdspi:kə] Lautsprecher **U5:** 92

love [lʌv] Liebe **U5:** 91; lieben, sehr mögen **2 > U2:** 29

luck: good luck [gʊd 'lʌk] (viel) Glück **U3:** 56

lucky ['lʌki] glücklich, Glücks- **1 > U2:** 42; **we were lucky** wir hatten Glück **U2:** 47; **You're lucky!** Du hast Glück! **1 > U2:** 40

lunch [lʌntʃ] Mittag(essen) **2 > U1:** 15; **lunch box** Butterbrotdose **1 > U3:** 56

M

machine [mə'ʃi:n] Maschine, Gerät **2 > U3:** 50

mad about ['mæd əbaʊt] verrückt nach **2 > U2:** 29

made → make [meɪd] *simple past* von **make** **2 > U3:** 49

magazine [mægə'zi:n] Zeitschrift **1 > U4:** 69

magic show ['mædʒɪk ʃəʊ] Zaubershow **2 > U4:** 61

maize [meɪz] Mais **1 > U5:** 90

make [meɪk] machen **1 > U2:** 37; **we're making** wir machen (gerade) **2 > U1:** 20

mall [mɔ:l] Einkaufszentrum **2 > U6:** 94

man (*pl.:* **men**) [mæn, men] Mann **1 > U6:** 113

many ['meni] viele **2 > U3:** 48; **how many?** wie viele? **2 > U4:** 62

map [mæp] Landkarte, Stadtplan **2 > U3:** 52

March [mɑ:tʃ] März **1 > U5:** 98

marching band ['mɑ:tʃɪŋ bænd] (Blas-)Kapelle U4: 69

market ['mɑ:kɪt] Markt **1 > U6:** 102; **market hall** Markthalle **1 > U6:** 107

mask [mɑ:sk] Maske **2 > U4:** 63

match [mætʃ] Spiel, Wettkampf **1 > U5:** 86

mate [meɪt] Freund, Kumpel (*ugs.*) **U1:** 27

maths [mæθs] Mathe(matik) **1 > U1:** 26

matter: it doesn't matter [ɪt dʌznt 'mætə] Das macht doch nichts. **2 > U5:** 84; **What's the matter?** Was ist denn (los)? **U4:** 73

May [meɪ] Mai **1 > U5:** 98

may [meɪ] vielleicht werden; können, dürfen *U5: 91*

maze: Lost in the maze. [lɒst ɪn ðə 'meɪz] Verloren im Irrgarten. **1 > U5:** 90

me [mi:] mich, mir **1 > U3:** 58; **it's me** ich bin's **U3:** 56

meal [mi:l] Mahlzeit, (zubereitetes) Essen **1 > U3:** 53; **go out for a meal** essen gehen **1 > U5:** 86; **pot-luck meal** Essen, zu dem alle Gäste etwas mitbringen **2 > U6:** 97

mean [mi:n] bedeuten, meinen **2 > U1:** 16; geizig, kleinlich **U3:** 51

meet [mi:t] sich treffen (mit) **1 > U4:** 70; treffen **2 > U6:** 98; **I'll meet you at the station.** Ich hole dich vom Bahnhof ab. **U3:** 56,U3:57

memory ['meməri] Speicher; Gedächtnis, Erinnerung U3: 61

mess [mes] Durcheinander **1 > U6:** 106

message ['mesɪdʒ] Nachricht **1 > U6:** 114; **text message** SMS-Nachricht **1 > U6:** 105

met → meet [met] *simple past* von **meet** **2 > U6:** 98

metre ['mi:tə] Meter **2 > Legend:** 109

middle ['mɪdl] Mitte **1 > U5:** 91; **middle school** Schule für 11- bis 14-Jährige **U4:** 69

mile [maɪl] Meile **U4:** 69; **a mile up** eine Meile hoch U4: 69
milk [mɪlk] Milch **1 > U3:** 55; **milkman** Milchmann **2 > U6:** 98; **milkshake** Shake **1 > U3:** 55
million ['mɪljən] Million **1 > U4:** 74
mind: never mind [nevə 'maɪnd] macht nichts **1 > U2:** 42
mineral water ['mɪnərəl wɔːtə] Mineralwasser **1 > U3:** 55
minigolf ['mɪnigɒlf] Minigolf **2 > Intro:** 11
minus ['maɪnəs] minus **2 > U6:** 104
minute ['mɪnɪt] Minute **1 > U2:** 43; **Just a minute.** Einen Augenblick. **1 > U2:** 43
miss [mɪs] verpassen; vermissen **2 > U1:** 15; **one word is missing** ein Wort fehlt **U2:** 40
mix everything ['mɪks evriθɪŋ] alles miteinander vermischen **1 > U6:** 110
mixer ['mɪksə] Mixer **1 > U6:** 110
mobile ['məʊbaɪl] Handy, Mobiltelefon **U1:** 27
model train [mɒdl 'treɪn] Modelleisenbahn **1 > U4:** 76
modern ['mɒdn] modern **2 > U3:** 48
mom *(AE)* [mɒm] Mutti, Mama **U4:** 72
Monday ['mʌndeɪ] Montag **1 > U4:** 80
money ['mʌni] Geld **1 > U4:** 71; **no money** kein Geld **1 > U4:** 71; **pocket money** Taschengeld **1 > U5:** 85
monster ['mɒnstə] Monster, Ungeheuer **U2:** 40
month [mʌnθ] Monat **1 > U5:** 98
more interesting than [mɔːr 'ɪntrəstɪŋ] interessanter als **2 > U3:** 50
morning: in the morning [ɪn ðə 'mɔːnɪŋ] morgens **1 > U2:** 40; **Good morning.** Guten Morgen. **1 > U1:** 25
mosque [mɒsk] Moschee U3: 53
most [məʊst] die meisten **2 > U3:** 48; **most popular** beliebteste(r, s) **2 > U3:** 51
mother ['mʌðə] Mutter **1 > U1:** 24; **Mother's Day** Muttertag U3: 53
motor ['məʊtə] Motor **U5:** 87; **motorhome** Wohnmobil U5: 87
mountain ['maʊntən] Berg **2 > Intro:** 9; **mountain bike** Mountainbike **1 > U2:** 48
mouse (*pl.*: **mice**) [maʊs, maɪs] Maus (*pl.* Mäuse) **2 > U2:** 35
move [muːv] (um)ziehen *(Wohnort)* **U3:** 50; *move* (sich) bewegen *U1: 15*; **their family has moved** ihre Familie ist umgezogen **U3:** 50
MP3 player [empiː'θriː 'pleɪə] MP3-Player, MP3-Spieler **Intro:** 6
Mr ['mɪstə] Herr (Anrede) **1 > U1:** 28
Mrs ['mɪsɪz] Frau (Anrede) **1 > U1:** 24
much [mʌtʃ] viel **1 > U5:** 91; **How much is it?** Was kostet das? **1 > U4:** 75; **how much?** wie viel? **2 > U4:** 62
mum [mʌm] Mutti, Mama **1 > U1:** 28
museum [mju'ziːəm] Museum **1 > U5:** 99
music ['mjuːzɪk] Musik **1 > U4:** 70
must [mʌst] müssen **2 > U1:** 17; **you mustn't** du darfst/Sie dürfen nicht **2 > U2:** 34
my [maɪ] mein/meine **1 > Intro:** 14

N

name: What's your name? [wɒts jɔː 'neɪm] Wie heißt du? **1 > U1:** 22
national ['næʃənl] national, National-, Landes- **U2:** 31
Native Americans ['neɪtɪv ə'merɪkənz] amerikanische Ureinwohner **U5:** 90
near [nɪə] in der Nähe von, nahe **1 > U5:** 89; *to be near you* um dir nahe zu sein, um in deiner Nähe zu sein *U2: 35*; **Where's the nearest ...?** Wo ist der/die/das nächst(e) ...? **2 > U3:** 52
need [niːd] brauchen **1 > U6:** 110; *need to* müssen *U2: 37*
neighbour ['neɪbə] Nachbar/Nachbarin **1 > U2:** 39
nervous ['nɜːvəs] nervös, aufgeregt **U4:** 72,
never ['nevə] nie, niemals **1 > U5:** 86; *I've never been* ich war (noch) nie, ich bin (noch) nie gewesen *U5: 91*; **never mind** macht nichts **1 > U2:** 42; **Better late than never.** Lieber spät als gar nicht. **1 > U5:** 93
new [njuː] neu **1 > Intro:** 18
newspaper ['njuːzpeɪpə] Zeitung **2 > U4:** 63
next [nekst] nächster/nächste/nächstes **1 > U4:** 74; als Nächstes **1 > U6:** 110; **next to** neben **1 > U2:** 37
nice [naɪs] nett **1 > U1:** 24; **will be very nice** wird sehr schön sein **1 > U6:** 106
night [naɪt] Nacht, (später) Abend **2 > U4:** 62
nine [naɪn] neun **1 > Intro:** 15
nineteen [naɪn'tiːn] neunzehn **1 > U2:** 48
nineteenth [naɪn'tiːnθ] neunzehnte(r, s) **2 > U4:** 72
ninety ['naɪnti] neunzig **1 > U2:** 48
ninth [naɪnθ] neunte(r, s) **2 > U4:** 72
no [nəʊ] nein **1 > U1:** 22; kein/e **1 > U4:** 74; **No, I didn't (= did not).** Nein (habe ich nicht). **2 > U2:** 32; **No, she doesn't.** Nein (tut sie nicht). **1 > U5:** 89; **Your team is no good.** Dein Team /Deine Mannschaft taugt nichts. U3: 67
nobody ['nəʊbədi] niemand, keiner **U4:** 76
noise [nɔɪz] Lärm, Geräusch **2 > Legend:** 109
noisy ['nɔɪzi] laut, lärmend **2 > U3:** 51
north [nɔːθ] Norden; nördlich **2 > U3:** 45
Northern Ireland [nɔːðən 'aɪələnd] Nordirland **2 > U1:** 12
not [nɒt] nicht **1 > U1:** 22
note [nəʊt] Notiz, (kurzer) Brief **1 > U6:** 115
nothing ['nʌθɪŋ] nichts **U1:** 27
notice ['nəʊtɪs] bemerken **U3:** 66
November [nəʊ'vembə] November **1 > U5:** 98
now [naʊ] jetzt **1 > U1:** 26; *every now and then* ab und zu, hin und wieder *U1: 15*
number ['nʌmbə] Zahl, Nummer **1 > Intro:** 15

[g] **g**o	[ŋ] morni**ng**	[l] **l**ike	[r] **r**uler	[v] se**v**en	[w] **w**e	[s] **s**ix	[z] hi**s**	[ʃ] **sh**e	[tʃ] tea**ch**er	[dʒ] **j**eans

O

o'clock: two o'clock [tu: ə'klɒk] zwei Uhr 1 > **U3:** 64; **at ... o'clock** um ... Uhr 1 > **U3:** 64
October [ɒk'təʊbə] Oktober 1 > **U5:** 98
of course [əf 'kɔ:s] natürlich, selbstverständlich 2 > **U4:** 62
offer: special offer [speʃl 'ɒfə] Sonderangebot 2 > **U4:** 68
office ['ɒfɪs] Büro, Amt **U2:** 31; **post office** Postamt 2 > **U3:** 52; **tourist office** Fremdenverkehrsamt; Auskunft 2 > **U3:** 52
officer ['ɒfɪsə] (Polizei-)Beamter/ Beamtin 2 > **U3:** 52
often ['ɒfn] oft 1 > **U4:** 70
oil [ɔɪl] Öl **U3:** 49
OK ['əʊkeɪ] O.K., in Ordnung 1 > **U1:** 26
old [əʊld] alt 1 > **U2:** 38; **How old are you?** Wie alt bist du? 1 > **U1:** 22; **oldest** älteste 2 > **U3:** 48
on [ɒn] auf; an 1 > **U1:** 23; *on foot* zu Fuß *U1: 17*; **The drinks are on me.** Die Getränke gehen auf mich., Ich bezahle die Getränke. U3: 51; **on Sundays** sonntags, am Sonntag 1 > **U4:** 70; **on the train/bus/...** im Zug/Bus/... **U3:** 56
once [wʌns] einmal **U4:** 70
one [wʌn] ein(e/r), eins 1 > **Intro:** 15; *one-way street* Einbahnstraße *U1: 17*; **the small one/s** der/die/das kleine, die kleineren 2 > **U4:** 68
online [ɒn'laɪn] online, im Internet *U1: 17*
only ['əʊnli] nur, bloß 1 > **U2:** 43; erst **U5:** 87
open ['əʊpən] öffnen, aufmachen 1 > **U1:** 26; geöffnet 1 > **U2:** 40; **open top bus** Bus mit offenem Dach U3: 48
opinion [ə'pɪniən] Meinung **U4:** 72
opposite ['ɒpəzɪt] Gegenteil 2 > **U2:** 35
option ['ɒpʃn] Möglichkeit, Alternative *U3: 55*
or [ɔ:] oder 1 > **Intro:** 19
orange ['ɒrɪndʒ] Apfelsine, Orange 1 > **U3:** 53
order: alphabetical order [ælfə'betɪkl 'ɔ:də] alphabetische Reihenfolge 2 > **U1:** 23; bestellen 2 > **U4:** 64
organisation [ɔ:gənaɪ'zeɪʃn] Organisation 1 > **U4:** 74
organise ['ɔ:gənaɪz] organisieren, veranstalten 2 > **U1:** 17
other ['ʌðə] andere, weitere 1 > **U2:** 37; **some others** manche andere 2 > **U1:** 18 18
our ['aʊə] unser/unsere 1 > **U1:** 20
outdoor ['aʊtdɔ:] im Freien, draußen **U2:** 31
outside [aut'saɪd] draußen; nach draußen 2 > **U3:** 51
over ['əʊvə] über, mehr als 2 > **U1:** 14; **over there** dort/da drüben 1 > **U5:** 93
own [əʊn] eigen **U3:** 49
owner ['əʊnə] Besitzer/in 2 > **U2:** 32

P

p.m. [pi: 'em] nachmittags, abends 2 > **U6:** 92
packet ['pækɪt] Schachtel; Paket, Päckchen 2 > **U1:** 18
pad [pæd] Schützer 1 > **U6:** 110
page [peɪdʒ] Seite 1 > **U1:** 26; **home page** Homepage, Startseite 2 > **U5:** 77
paint [peɪnt] malen 1 > **U4:** 76
pair [peə] Paar **U5:** 97
Pakistan [pækɪ'stɑ:n] Pakistan 1 > **U2:** 39
Pardon? ['pɑ:dən] Wie bitte? **U5:** 94
parents *(pl.)* ['peərənts] Eltern 1 > **U2:** 39
park [pɑ:k] Park 1 > **U5:** 87
parking: late parking [leɪt 'pɑ:kɪŋ] das Überziehen der Parkzeit 1 > **U6:** 109
parliament ['pɑ:ləmənt] Parlament 2 > **U4:** 62
part [pɑ:t] Teil **U3:** 49
partner ['pɑ:tnə] Partner- 2 > **U1:** 15; **ask a partner about** eine(n) Partner/in fragen über/ nach 2 > **U2:** 31
party ['pɑ:ti] Party, Feier 1 > **U2:** 49
pass [pɑ:s] vorbeigehen, -fahren, -ziehen *U2: 35*
past [pɑ:st] Vergangenheit 2 > **U3:** 48
past: half past [hɑ:f 'pɑ:st] halb 2 > **U3:** 51; **quarter to/past** Viertel vor/nach ... 2 > **U5:** 82
path [pɑ:θ] Weg, Pfad **U2:** 46
pay (for) ['peɪ fə] bezahlen, zahlen (für) 2 > **U6:** 96
pen [pen] Füller 1 > **U1:** 32
pence *(pl.)* [pens] Pence 2 > **U5:** 88
pencil ['pensl] Bleistift 1 > **U1:** 32; **pencil case** Federmäppchen 1 > **U1:** 32
people ['pi:pl] Leute, Menschen 1 > **U4:** 70
pepper ['pepə] Paprika(schote) 1 > **U3:** 53
per [pə] pro *U3: 55*; **per cent (%)** Prozent **U5:** 89
perhaps [pə'hæps] vielleicht 1 > **U1:** 24
personality [pɜ:sə'nælɪti] Persönlichkeit *U2: 37*
pet shop ['pet ʃɒp] Tierhandlung 1 > **U6:** 104
phone [fəʊn] anrufen 1 > **U5:** 93; **Just phone me.** Ruf(t) mich einfach an. 1 > **U6:** 110; **phone book** Telefonbuch 1 > **U2:** 44; **(phone) call** (Telefon-)Anruf, (An-)Ruf **U2:** 46
photo ['fəʊtəʊ] Foto 1 > **Intro:** 11; **take photos (of)** Fotos von ... machen 1 > **U4:** 76
phrase [freɪz] (Rede-)Wendung, Ausdruck 2 > **U1:** 21
picnic ['pɪknɪk] Picknick 1 > **U5:** 84
picture ['pɪktʃə] Bild 1 > **Intro:** 10
piece [pi:s] Stück **U4:** 71; **cut ... in pieces** in Stücke schneiden 1 > **U6:** 110
pig [pɪg] Schwein 1 > **U5:** 90
pink [pɪŋk] rosa 1 > **Intro:** 14
pirate ['paɪrət] Pirat/in 2 > **Legend:** 109
pity: That's a pity. [ðæts ə 'pɪti] Das ist schade. **U1:** 29
pizza ['pi:tsə] Pizza 2 > **U5:** 86
place [pleɪs] Ort, Stelle 1 > **U4:** 78
plan [plæn] Plan, Vorhaben 1 > **U6:** 109; planen 1 > **U6:** 112
plane [pleɪn] Flugzeug 2 > **Intro:** 9
plasma TV ['plæzmə tɪ: vi:] Plasma-TV, -Fernseher 2 > **U6:** 94

[j] yes [θ] thing [ð] the [i:] he [ɑ:] car [ɔ:] or [u:] too [ɜ:] girl [i] sorry [u] July [ɪ] big [e] yes

plate [pleɪt] Teller **2 > U4:** 63
play [pleɪ] spielen **1 > U4:** 70; **play an instrument** ein Instrument spielen **1 > U6:** 105; **play sport** Sport treiben **1 > U4:** 70; **Did you play with ...?** Hast du mit ... gespielt? **2 > U2:** 32
played → play [pleɪ] *simple past* von **play** **2 > Intro:** 9
player: CD player [si: di: 'pleɪə] CD-Player **1 > U3:** 62; **DVD player** DVD-Spieler **2 > U2:** 29; **MP3 player** MP3-Player, MP3-Spieler **Intro:** 6
please [pli:z] bitte **1 > U1:** 26
pocket ['pɒkɪt] Tasche **U1:** 29; **pocket money** Taschengeld **1 > U5:** 85
podcast ['pɒdkɑ:st] digitale Internet-Radioshow zum Downloaden *U4: 75*
poem ['pəʊɪm] Gedicht **2 > U5:** 89
poet ['pəʊɪt] Dichter/Dichterin **U3:** 52
point [pɔɪnt] Punkt **U4:** 72
police [pə'li:s] Polizei **2 > U3:** 51; **police station** Polizeiwache, Polizeirevier **2 > U3:** 52
policeman [pɒ'li:smən] Polizist *U3: 53*
pollution [pə'lu:ʃn] (Umwelt-)Verschmutzung **U5:** 87
poor [pʊə] arm **2 > Legend:** 108; schwach, dürftig **U3:** 61
pop: pop group ['pɒp gru:p] Popgruppe **1 > U5:** 94; **pop music** Popmusik **1 > U4:** 74
popular ['pɒpjələ] beliebt **1 > U3:** 53; **most popular** beliebteste(r, s) **2 > U3:** 51, **popular with** beliebt bei **U2:** 34
portion ['pɔ:ʃn] Portion **1 > U3:** 53
post office ['pəʊst ɒfɪs] Postamt **2 > U3:** 52
postcard ['pəʊstkɑ:d] Postkarte **1 > U5:** 93
postcode ['pəʊstkəʊd] Postleitzahl **2 > U5:** 85
poster ['pəʊstə] Poster **1 > U3:** 61
pot-luck meal [pɒt lʌk 'mɪ:l] Essen, zu dem alle Gäste etwas mitbringen **2 > U6:** 97
potato (*pl.:* **-oes**) [pə'teɪtəʊ] Kartoffel **1 > U3:** 53; **baked potato** [beɪkt pə'teɪtəʊ] gebackene Kartoffel **2 > U4:** 62; *couch potato* Dauerglotzer/in, (*wörtlich:* Sofakartoffel) *U2: 37*
pound [paʊnd] Pfund (britisches Geld) **1 > U2:** 43
practise ['præktɪs] üben **U4:** 70
preposition [prepə'zɪʃn] Präposition **2 > U1:** 23
present ['preznt] Gegenwart **2 > U3:** 48; Geschenk **2 > U4:** 66
price [praɪs] (Kauf-)Preis **1 > U4:** 75
principal *(AE)* ['prɪnsɪpl] Schulleiter/Schulleiterin, Direktor/Direktorin **U4:** 72
print [prɪnt] drucken **2 > U6:** 95
prize [praɪz] Preis, Gewinn **U1:** 29
problem ['prɒbləm] Problem **1 > U4:** 70
programme ['prəʊgræm] (Fernseh-)Sendung **1 > U2:** 42; Programm **U4:** 72
project ['prɒdʒekt] Projekt **U5:** 88
proud [praʊd] stolz **U1:** 9
PS ['pi: ɛs] PS/Postskript(um) **2 > U6:** 98
pub [pʌb] Kneipe, Lokal **2 > U1:** 19
public holiday [pʌblɪk 'hɒlədeɪ] gesetzlicher Feiertag **1 > U5:** 86
pull up [pʊl 'ʌp] hochziehen **U2:** 47
puncture ['pʌŋktʃə] Loch, Reifenschaden, Platten *U2: 37*
pupil ['pju:pl] Schüler/Schülerin **1 > U5:** 96
puppy ['pʌpi] Welpe, Hundejunges **U5:** 103
push [pʊʃ] schieben **1 > U6:** 110
put: put (on) [pʊt ɒn] (hin)stellen (auf) **1 > U3:** 58; **put in** hineintun, -stecken **1 > U4:** 71; **put together** zusammensetzen **U1:** 23; *put up* aufstellen, errichten *U3: 53*

Q

quarter to/past ['kwɔ:tə tə/pɑ:st] Viertel vor/nach ... **2 > U5:** 82
queen [kwi:n] Königin **U1:** 10
question ['kwestʃən] Frage **2 > U1:** 16
quick [kwɪk] schnell, flott *U1: 15*
quiet ['kwaɪət] ruhig, leise, still **2 > U5:** 78
quite [kwaɪt] recht, ziemlich *U1: 15*
quiz [kwɪz] Quiz **1 > U2:** 44

R

race [reɪs] Wettlauf, Rennen **1 > U5:** 92; **have a race** um die Wette laufen **1 > U5:** 92; **race against** um die Wette laufen **1 > U5:** 92
radio ['reɪdiəʊ] Radio, Rundfunk **1 > U2:** 48
railcard: junior railcard [dʒu:njə 'reɪlkɑ:d] „Bahncard" für Jugendliche U3: 54
rain [reɪn] regnen **2 > U5:** 81
rainy ['reɪni] regnerisch **2 > U5:** 84
raise [reɪz] steigern, erhöhen *U5: 93*
ran [ræn] lief/liefen **1 > U6:** 109
rap [ræp] „rappen" **U4:** 70; *rap rhymes* Reime „rappen" *U1: 15*; **rapper** Rapper/Rapperin **U4:** 73
rat [ræt] Ratte **2 > U2:** 35
read [ri:d] lesen **1 > U4:** 70
reading ['ri:dɪŋ] (das) Lesen **2 > U2:** 28
ready ['redi] fertig **1 > U5:** 92
really ['rɪəli] sehr, echt **2 > U2:** 35; wirklich **U4:** 72,; **not really** eigentlich nicht **U1:** 27
record ['rekɔ:d] (Schall-)Platte *U4: 75*; aufnehmen, aufzeichnen **2 > U4:** 73
video recorder [vɪdiəʊ rɪ'kɔ:də] Videorekorder **1 > U2:** 42
red [red] rot **1 > Intro:** 10
relative ['relətɪv] Verwandte/Verwandter **U3:** 53
remember [rɪ'membə] sich erinnern; daran denken **2 > U4:** 62
remind sb. [rɪ'maɪnd sʌmbədi] jdn. erinnern *U5: 93*
rent [rent] mieten, leihen **2 > U6:** 96
repair [rɪ'peə] reparieren **1 > U6:** 105

[æ] cat [ʌ] bus [ɒ] dog [ʊ] put [ə] again [eɪ] name [aɪ] time [ɔɪ] boy [əʊ] no [aʊ] house [ɪə] here

report [rɪ'pɔ:t] Bericht; Umfrage 2 > **U1:** 18; berichten *U5: 95*
rest [rest] Rest **U4:** 84
restaurant ['restrɒnt] Restaurant 2 > **U2:** 33
result [rɪ'zʌlt] Ergebnis **U4:** 72
retire [rɪ'taɪə] sich zurückziehen, zurücktreten *U1: 15*
return [rɪ'tɜ:n] zurückkehren *U3: 53*
revolution: Industrial Revolution [ɪndʌstriəl revə'lu:ʃn] industrielle Revolution 2 > **U3:** 48
rhyme: rap rhymes [ræp 'raɪmz] Reime „rappen" *U1: 15*
rich [rɪtʃ] reich 2 > **Legend:** 108
ride [raɪd] reiten **U2:** 32; **ride a bike** Rad fahren 1 > **U3:** 58
right [raɪt] Recht *U4: 75*
right [raɪt] richtig, korrekt 1 > **U2:** 43; **Right or wrong?** richtig oder falsch 2 > **U1:** 25; rechts, nach rechts *U1: 17*; **to the right** rechts 1 > **U5:** 92; **You're right.** Du hast Recht./Stimmt. 1 > **U1:** 27
ringtone ['rɪŋtəʊn] Klingelton *U3: 55*
river ['rɪvə] Fluss 2 > **U5:** 80
road [rəʊd] Straße 1 > **Intro:** 18
rock [rɒk] Fels, Stein **U2:** 46; **rock band** Rockband **U4:** 70
roll [rəʊl] Brötchen 1 > **U3:** 54
room [ru:m] Zimmer, Raum 1 > **U1:** 32; **living room** Wohnzimmer 1 > **U2:** 37
round [raʊnd] um ... herum 2 > **U3:** 46
rubber ['rʌbə] Radiergummi 1 > **U1:** 32
rubbish ['rʌbɪʃ] Abfall, Müll 2 > **U4:** 62
rugby ['rʌgbi] Rugby **U2:** 31
rule [ru:l] Regel, Vorschrift **U2:** 46
ruler ['ru:lə] Lineal 1 > **U1:** 32
run [rʌn] rennen, laufen 1 > **U4:** 78; **Run for your life!** Renn/t um dein/euer Leben! **U2:** 47; **run late** sich verspäten, Verspätung haben **U3:** 56

S

safe [seɪf] sicher **U2:** 47
said [sed] sagte/sagten 1 > **U3:** 58
sail [seɪl] segeln **U2:** 32
sale: car-boot sale [kɑ: 'bu:t seɪl] (eine Art) Trödelmarkt 1 > **U4:** 68
same: the same as [ðə 'seɪm əz] genauso wie; dasselbe wie 1 > **U4:** 75
sand [sænd] Sand **U2:** 46
sandwich ['sænwɪtʃ] Sandwich (belegtes Brot) 1 > **U3:** 56
sandy ['sændi] sandig, Sand- **U2:** 46
sat → sit [sæt] *simple past* von **sit** **U2:** 46
Saturday ['sætədeɪ] Samstag/Sonnabend 1 > **U4:** 80; **on Saturday** am Samstag/Sonnabend 1 > **U4:** 81
sauce [sɔ:s] Soße 1 > **U3:** 59
sauna ['sɔ:nə] Sauna 2 > **U6:** 94
sausage ['sɒsɪdʒ] Würstchen, Wurst 2 > **U4:** 62
save [seɪv] sparen *U1: 17*
saw [sɔ:] sah/sahen 1 > **U5:** 91
say [seɪ] sagen 1 > **U3:** 53; **they say** man sagt U3: 51
scene [si:n] Szene; Ort **U5:** 92
school [sku:l] Schule 1 > **Intro:** 10; **at school** in der Schule 1 > **Intro:** 10; **middle school** Schule für 11- bis 14-Jährige **U4:** 69; **high school** (US) Gesamtschule für 13- bis 18-Jährige **U5:** 99
science ['saɪəns] (Natur-)Wissenschaft 2 > **U1:** 17
Scotland ['skɒtlənd] Schottland 2 > **U1:** 12
Scottish ['skɒtɪʃ] schottisch **U3:** 48
sea [si:] Meer, die See 1 > **U5:** 87
search [sɜ:tʃ] (durch)suchen **U2:** 32
seaside: at the seaside [ət ðə 'si:saɪd] am Meer 1 > **U5:** 86
season ['si:zn] Jahreszeit 1 > **U5:** 99; Saison *U2: 37*; *season ticket* Jahreskarte, Dauerkarte *U2: 37*
second ['sekənd] Sekunde **U5:** 91; zweite(r, s) (= 2nd) 2 > **U4:** 72; **second-hand** gebraucht 1 > **U4:** 69
see [si:] sehen 1 > **Intro:** 10; **See you later.** Bis später. 1 > **U1:** 28
seem [si:m] scheinen **U4:** 71
sell [sel] verkaufen 1 > **U4:** 69
send [send] senden, schicken 1 > **U4:** 74
sent → send [sent] *simple past* von **send** 2 > **U3:** 47
sentence ['sentəns] Satz 2 > **U1:** 20
September [sep'tembə] September 1 > **U5:** 98
service ['sɜ:vɪs] Dienst, Service **U3:** 54
seven ['sevn] sieben 1 > **Intro:** 15
seventeen [sevn'ti:n] siebzehn 1 > **U2:** 48
seventeenth [sevn'ti:nθ] siebzehnte(r, s) 2 > **U4:** 72
seventh ['sevnθ] siebte(r, s) 2 > **U4:** 72
seventy ['sevnti] siebzig 1 > **U2:** 48
she [ʃi:] sie 1 > **U1:** 25; **she's (= she is)** sie ist 1 > **U1:** 25
sheep (*pl.:* **sheep**) [ʃi:p] Schaf, Schafe 1 > **U5:** 90
Sheriff ['ʃerɪf] Sheriff 1 > **U2:** 49
shine: the sun is shining [ðə sʌn ɪz 'ʃaɪnɪŋ] die Sonne scheint 1 > **U2:** 42
ship [ʃɪp] Schiff 2 > **Legend:** 111
shirt [ʃɜ:t] Hemd (*hier:* Fußballtrikot) 1 > **U6:** 107
shone → shine [ʃɒn] *simple past* von **shine** U1: 21
shop [ʃɒp] Laden, Geschäft 1 > **Intro:** 18; **busy shop** gut besuchter Laden 1 > **U2:** 40; **chip shop** Pommes-frites-/Imbiss-Bude 1 > **U3:** 59; **shopping centre** Einkaufszentrum 1 > **U6:** 109; **go to the shops** einen Einkaufsbummel machen; einkaufen gehen 1 > **U4:** 76
short [ʃɔ:t] kurz **U3:** 52; **too short** zu kurz 2 > **Intro:** 7
should [ʃʊd] sollte/solltest/sollten/solltet **U1:** 9
shout [ʃaʊt] rufen, schreien **U1:** 284
show [ʃəʊ] (Fernseh-, Radio-)Sendung 1 > **U5:** 94; zeigen 2 > **U6:** 94; **Show me, please.** Zeig(t) es mir bitte. 1 > **U6:** 110
sick [sɪk] deprimiert, betroffen; krank, übel **U4:** 85
side [saɪd] Seite 2 > **U6:** 98
sight [saɪt] Sehenswürdigkeit **U1:** 9
sightseeing ['saɪtsi:ɪŋ] Besichtigung, Besichtigung von Sehenswürdigkeiten **U1:** 12
sign [saɪn] Schild 1 > **U5:** 91
silly ['sɪli] blöd, albern **U2:** 46

[eə] chair [ʊə] sure [b] bike [p] pen [d] day [t] ten [k] book [g] go [ŋ] morning [l] like [r] ruler

sing [sɪŋ] singen **1 > U6:** 105
singer ['sɪŋə] Sänger/Sängerin **U3:** 52
sink [sɪŋk] Spül-/Waschbecken U5: 103
sister ['sɪstə] Schwester **1 > U2:** 39
sit [sɪt] sich setzen; sitzen **1 > U1:** 25; **sit down** sich hinsetzen **1 > U1:** 25; **Sit here.** Setz dich hierhin. **1 > U1:** 25
situation [sɪtʃu'eɪʃn] Situation **2 > Legend:** 109
six [sɪks] sechs **1 > Intro:** 15
sixteen [sɪk'sti:n] sechzehn **1 > U2:** 48
sixteenth [sɪks'ti:nθ] sechzehnte(r, s) **2 > U4:**72
sixth [sɪksθ] sechste(r, s) **2 > U4:** 72
sixty ['sɪksti] sechzig **1 > U2:** 48
skate [skeɪt] „skaten", Skateboard fahren **U1:** 28
skateboard ['skeɪtbɔ:d] Skateboard **2 > Intro:** 11; **skateboarder** Skateboardfahrer/Skateboardfahrerin **U1:** 20; **go skateboarding** zum Skateboarden gehen **U1:** 14, 40
skates [skeɪts] Inlineskates, Rollschuhe **2 > Intro:** 8
skating ['skeɪtɪŋ] Roll-, Schlittschuhlaufen **2 > U1:** 18
skiing ['ski:ɪŋ] (das) Skilaufen, Skisport **U4:** 69
skill [skɪl] Fähigkeit **U3:** 59
skunk [skʌŋk] Stinktier **U5:** 105
sky [skaɪ] Himmel *U1: 15*
sleep [sli:p] schlafen **2 > U5:** 82
sleeping ['sli:pɪŋ] (das) Schlafen **2 > U5:** 82
slept → sleep [slept] *simple past* von **sleep** **2 > U5:** 87
slogan ['sləʊgən] Slogan, Werbespruch **1 > U6:** 112
small [smɔ:l] klein **1 > U2:** 37
smell [smel] riechen **U5:** 104
smile [smaɪl] Lächeln **U3:** 66; lächeln **1 > U6:** 109; **smile at somebody (sb.)** jemanden (jdn.) anlächeln, jemandem (jdm.) zulächeln **U3:** 67
smoke [sməʊk] rauchen **2 > U1:** 18
snack [snæk] Snack **2 > U1:** 15
snow [snəʊ] Schnee **U3:** 51; schneien **2 > U6:** 104
snowboarding ['snəʊbɔ:dɪŋ] Snowboard fahren, snowboarden **U4:** 69
snowy ['snəʊi] verschneit **2 > U6:** 99
so [səʊ] so **1 > U5:** 90; daher, deshalb **U4:** 70; **not so popular as ...** nicht so beliebt wie ... **U5:** 90
soap ['səʊp] *hier:* TV-Seifenoper **2 > U1:** 19
soccer ['sɒkə] Fußball U4: 69
sock [sɒk] Socke, Strumpf **2 > U4:** 63
software ['sɒftweə] Software **1 > U4:** 69
sold → sell [səʊld] *simple past* von **sell** **2 > U5:** 87
solo ['səʊləʊ] Solo **U4:**
some [sʌm] einige, ein paar **1 > Intro:** 11; **some others** manche andere **2 > U1:** 18
somebody ['sʌmbədi] jemand **2 > U5:** 82
something ['sʌmθɪŋ] etwas **2 > U1:** 16
sometimes ['sʌmtaɪmz] manchmal **1 > U5:** 86
son [sʌn] Sohn **1 > U3:** 60
song [sɒŋ] Lied **2 > U1:** 25
soon [su:n] bald **2 > U2:** 35
sorry: I'm sorry. [aɪm 'sɒri] Es tut mir leid. **1 > U1:** 27; **feel sorry for somebody (sb.)** jemanden (jdn.) bedauern, Mitleid mit jemandem (jdm.) haben **U3:** 67
sound [saʊnd] Klang, Geräusch **U3:** 59
soup [su:p] Suppe **2 > U4:** 62
souvenir [su:və'nɪə] Souvenir, Andenken **1 > U6:** 102
space [speɪs] Platz, Raum **2 > U6:** 96
spaghetti [spə'geti] Spagetti **1 > U3:** 59
Spain [speɪn] Spanien **2 > Intro:** 11
speak [spi:k] sprechen **2 > U1:** 18
special: special day ['speʃl deɪ] besonderer Tag **1 > U4:** 74; **special offer** Sonderangebot **2 > U4:** 68
speech [spi:tʃ] Rede, Ansprache **U3:** 52
speed [spi:d] rasen, schnell fahren *U1: 15*
spell: Can you spell ...? [kən ju spel] Kannst du ... buchstabieren? **1 > U1:** 32
spelling ['spelɪŋ] (Recht-)Schreibung, Schreibweise **U2:** 40
spend (time/money) [spend] verbringen (Zeit), ausgeben (Geld) **U3:** 50,U3:51
spent → spend [sepnt] *simple past* von **spend** **U3:** 50
spoke → speak [spəʊk] *simple past* von **speak** **U4:** 84
sport [spɔ:t] Sport **1 > U4:** 70; **play sport** Sport treiben **1 > U4:** 70; **sports centre** Sportzentrum **1 > U6:** 104
sporty ['spɔ:ti] sportlich *U2: 37*
spring [sprɪŋ] Frühling **1 > U5:** 86
stall [stɔ:l] (Verkaufs-)Stand **1 > U4:** 69
stallholder ['stɔ:lhəʊldə] Standbesitzer/in **1 > U4:** 69
stamp [stæmp] Briefmarke **2 > U5:** 85
stand [stænd] stehen **1 > U2:** 39; **stand up** aufstehen, aufrecht stehen **1 > U4:** 78; **they're standing** sie stehen **1 > U2:** 39
star [stɑ:] Star **1 > U4:** 74; **You're a star!** Du bist ein Schatz! *(ugs.)* U4: 76
stare [stæə] (an)starren *U1: 15*
start [stɑ:t] Start **1 > U5:** 92; beginnen, starten **1 > U3:** 53; **(they) started eating** (sie) fingen an zu essen **2 > U3:** 50
state [steɪt] (Bundes-)Staat, (Bundes-)Land **U4:** 70,
station ['steɪʃn] Bahnhof **2 > U3:** 48; **police station** Polizeiwache, Polizeirevier **2 > U3:** 52; **TV station** Fernsehsender **U4:** 84; **I'll meet you at the station.** Ich hole dich vom Bahnhof ab. **U3:** 56,U3:57
statue ['stætʃu:] Statue U3: 50
stay [steɪ] bleiben **1 > U5:** 87; **we stayed (with) → stay** *simple past* von **stay** **2 > Intro:** 8
steal [sti:l] stehlen **U1:** 27
stepfather ['stepfɑ:ðə] Stiefvater **1 > U3:** 60
stepmother ['stepmʌðə] Stiefmutter **1 > U3:** 60
sticker ['stɪkə] Sticker, Aufkleber **2 > U2:** 29
still [stɪl] bewegungslos, still **1 > U6:** 105; noch **2 > U2:** 35
stole → steal [stəʊl] *simple past* von **steal** **U1:** 27

[v] seven [w] we [s] six [z] his [ʃ] she [tʃ] teacher [dʒ] jeans [j] yes [θ] thing [ð] the [i:] he

stood → stand [stʊd] *simple past* von **stand** **U1:** 28
stop [stɒp] anhalten **U1:** 12, 443; **bus stop** Bushaltestelle **1 > U5:** 88; **Stop it!** Hör(t) auf! **1 > U5:** 90
stormy ['stɔːmi] stürmisch *U2: 35*
story ['stɔːri] Geschichte, Erzählung **2 > Legend:** 108; **... the story is about ...** ... die Geschichte handelt von ... **U1:** 16
straight: Go straight on. [gəʊ streɪt 'ɒn] geradeaus (weiter)gehen **2 > U3:** 52
strange [streɪndʒ] seltsam, sonderbar **U3:** 50
street [striːt] Straße **2 > Intro:** 9; *one-way street* Einbahnstraße *U1: 17*; *High Street* Hauptstraße, Einkaufsstraße *U3: 55*
string [strɪŋ] Schnur, Bindfaden **2 > U3:** 53
strong [strɒŋ] stark **U3:** 47
structure ['strʌktʃə] Struktur **U3:** 60
student ['stjuːdnt] Schüler/in; Student/in **2 > U1:** 14
study ['stʌdi] lernen, studieren **U1:** 8
stuff [stʌf] Zeug *U4: 75*
stupid ['stjuːpɪd] blöd, dämlich **1 > U1:** 23
style [staɪl] Stil **1 > U6:** 108
subject ['sʌbdʒɪkt] (Schul-)Fach **2 > U1:** 20
suburb ['sʌbɜːb] Vorort **2 > U6:** 94
successful [sə'ksesfl] erfolgreich **U5:** 90
suddenly ['sʌdnli] plötzlich, auf einmal **2 > U2:** 30
summer ['sʌmə] Sommer **1 > U5:** 86
sun [sʌn] Sonne **1 > U2:** 42; **the sun is shining** die Sonne scheint **1 > U2:** 42
Sunday ['sʌndeɪ] Sonntag **1 > U4:** 69; **on Sundays** sonntags, am Sonntag **1 > U4:** 70
sunny ['sʌni] sonnig **2 > U6:** 104
super ['suːpə] super, toll **1 > U3:** 58
supermarket ['suːpəmɑːkɪt] Supermarkt **1 > U5:** 87
sure: be sure [bi 'ʃʊə] sicher sein **1 > U5:** 92
surf the Internet [sɜːf ði 'ɪntənet] im Internet surfen **U1:** 27
surprise [sə'praɪz] Überraschung; Überraschungs- **1 > U3:** 58; **surprised** überrascht **2 > U6:** 98
SUV (= sports utility vehicle) [esjuː'viː] Geländewagen U5: 87
sweatshirt ['swetʃɜːt] Sweatshirt **1 > U3:** 62
sweet [swiːt] Süßigkeit, Bonbon **1 > U4:** 79; süß, niedlich **2 > U2:** 35
swim [swɪm] schwimmen **1 > U5:** 85
swimming ['swɪmɪŋ] (das) Schwimmen **2 > U1:** 17; **swimming pool** Schwimmbad, Freibad; Schwimmbecken **2 > Intro:** 11
swimsuit ['swɪmsuːt] Badeanzug, Badehose **U2:** 36

T

T-shirt ['tiːʃɜːt] T-Shirt **1 > U2:** 50
table ['teɪbl] Tisch **1 > Intro:** 10; **table tennis** Tischtennis **1 > U6:** 105
take [teɪk] nehmen **2 > U3:** 47; hinfahren, bringen **U4:** 84; *hier:* dauern, brauchen **U5:** 89; **take photos (of)** Fotos von ... machen **1 > U4:** 76; **take the dog for a walk** mit dem Hund rausgehen/spazierengehen **2 > U1:** 19; *he will take to the air* er wird an der Luft Gefallen finden, er wird sich an die Luft gewöhnen *U1: 15*; **take-away ...** ... zum Mitnehmen **1 > U3:** 53
talk: talk about ['tɔːk əbaʊt] sprechen über **2 > U4:** 60; **she talked (to)** redete/sprach (mit); hat mit ... gesprochen/geredet **2 > U1:** 18
task [tɑːsk] Aufgabe **U1:** 16
tax [tæks] Steuer *U4: 75*
taxi ['tæksi] Taxi **2 > U6:** 97
tea [tiː] Tee **2 > U5:** 82; **iced tea** Eistee **1 > U3:** 55
teach [tiːtʃ] lehren, beibringen *U5: 93*
teacher ['tiːtʃə] Lehrer/Lehrerin **1 > Intro:** 10
team [tiːm] Team, Mannschaft **1 > U1:** 23
technology: information technology (IT) [ɪnfəmeɪʃn tek'nɒlədʒi] Informationstechnologie **2 > U1:** 14
teddy bear ['tedi beə] Teddybär **1 > U4:** 73
teenage ['tiːneɪdʒ] Teenager-, für/von Teenager **U2:** 36; **teenager** Teenager **Intro:** 6
teeth [tiːθ] Zähne **1 > U4:** 80
telephone ['telɪfəʊn] Telefon **1 > U6:** 115
tell [təʊld] erzählen, berichten **2 > U3:** 47; **tell (about)** erzählen, berichten (über) **2 > U1:** 16
telly addict [teli'ædɪkt] fernsehkrank *U2: 37*
temperature ['temprətʃə] Temperatur **2 > U6:** 104
ten [ten] zehn **1 > Intro:** 15
tennis ['tenɪs] Tennis **1 > U4:** 76
tent [tent] Zelt **2 > U5:** 82
tenth [tenθ] zehnte/zehnter/zehntes **2 > U4:** 64
terrible ['terəbl] schrecklich, furchtbar **1 > U1:** 23
terrific [tə'rɪfɪk] fantastisch, toll **1 > U4:** 69; wunderbar, hervorragend **U1:** 15
test [test] Test, Prüfung, Klassenarbeit **1 > U6:** 129; testen, prüfen **2 > U5:** 82
text [tekst] Text **U4:** 74; **text message** SMS-Nachricht **1 > U6:** 105
than: bigger than ['bɪgə ðən] größer als **1 > U5:** 90; **more interesting than** interessanter als **2 > U3:** 50
thank [θæŋk] danken **2 > U6:** 95; **Thank you.** Danke (schön). **1 > U1:** 26; **Thanks.** Danke. **1 > U3:** 58
that's (= that is) [ðæts] das ist **1 > U4:** 75
the [ðə] der/die/das **1 > Intro:** 10
theatre ['θɪətə] Theater **2 > U5:** 78
their [ðeə] ihr/ihre **1 > U3:** 56
them [ðem] sie, ihnen **1 > U4:** 71
theme park ['θiːm pɑːk] Freizeitpark **1 > U5:** 86
then [ðen] dann **1 > U3:** 59; *every now and then* ab und zu, hin und wieder *U1: 15*
there [ðeə] da, dort **1 > U2:** 39; **over there** dort/da drüben **1 > U5:** 93; **there is/are** es gibt **1 > U4:** 74

[ɑː] car [ɔː] or [uː] too [ɜː] girl [i] sorry [u] July [ɪ] big [e] yes [æ] cat [ʌ] bus [ɒ] dog [ʊ] put

these [ðiːz] diese **2 > U6: 93**
they [ðeɪ] sie **1 > U1: 24**; **they're (= they are)** sie sind **1 > U1: 24**
thing [θɪŋ] Ding, Sache **1 > U1: 20**; **How are things?** Wie geht's?, Wie läuft's? *(ugs.)* **U3: 56**
think [θɪŋk] denken, glauben **2 > U1: 15**; **What do you think ...?** Was meinst/glaubst du ...? **1 > U6: 108**
third (= 3rd) [θɜːd] dritte(r, s) **2 > U4: 72**
thirsty: I'm thirsty. [aɪm ˈθɜːsti] Ich habe Durst. **1 > U3: 55**
thirteen [θɜːˈtiːn] dreizehn **1 > U2: 48**
thirteenth [tɜːˈtiːnθ] dreizehnte(r, s) **1 > U2: 48**
thirtieth [ˈθɜːtiəθ] dreißigste(r, s) **2 > U4: 72**
thirty [ˈθɜːti] dreißig **2 > U4: 72**
this [ðɪs] dies **1 > U3: 58**
those [ðəʊz] die (da), jene (dort) **U3: 67**
though [ðəʊ] jedoch, aber; obwohl **U5: 90**
thought → think [θɔːt] *simple past* von **think** **2 > U5: 87**
thousand [ˈθaʊznd] tausend **1 > U5: 90**; **thousands** Tausende U1: 23
three [θriː] drei **1 > Intro: 15**
through [θruː] durch, hindurch **2 > U4: 66**
Thursday [ˈθɜːzdeɪ] Donnerstag **1 > U4: 80**
tick [tɪk] ab-/anhaken *U5: 95*
ticket [ˈtɪkɪt] Eintrittskarte; Fahrkarte **2 > U2: 29**
tidy [ˈtaɪdi] aufräumen **2 > U6: 96**
till: from ... till [frəm , tɪl] von ... bis **1 > U2: 40** 40; **till late** bis spät **1 > U2: 40**
time [taɪm] Zeit, Uhrzeit **1 > U3: 64**; Mal U1: 9; **have time** Zeit haben **2 > U2: 30**; **free time** Freizeit **1 > U4: 76**; **have a good time** sich gut amüsieren **2 > U4: 65**; **What time is it?** Wie spät ist es? **1 > U3: 64**; **times** mal **2 > U1: 14**
timetable [ˈtaɪmteɪbl] Stundenplan, Tagesablauf **1 > U6: 102**
tin [tɪn] Dose, Büchse **2 > U4: 68**
tip [tɪp] Hinweis, Tipp **1 > U5: 92**
tired [ˈtaɪəd] müde **1 > U4: 75**
title [ˈtaɪtl] Titel, Überschrift **U2: 36**
to [tu] zu, nach **1 > U3: 57**; **quarter to/past** Viertel vor/nach ... **2 > U5: 82**
toast [təʊst] Toast **U3: 60**
today [təˈdeɪ] heute **1 > U2: 42**
together [təˈgeðə] zusammen, gemeinsam **U4: 85**
toilet [ˈtɔɪlət] Toilette **1 > U2: 37**
told → tell [təʊld] *simple past* von **tell** **2 > U3: 47**
tomato *(pl.: -oes)* [təˈmɑːtəʊ] Tomate **1 > U3: 53**
tomorrow [təˈmɒrəʊ] morgen **1 > U6: 106**
tonight [təˈnaɪt] heute Nacht, heute Abend **2 > U5: 82**
too [tuː] auch **1 > Intro: 16**; **too expensive** zu teuer **1 > U4: 75**
took → take [tʊk] *simple past* von **take** **2 > U3: 47**
tool [tuːl] Werkzeug **1 > U4: 69**
top: at the top [æt ðə ˈtɒp] oben, am oberen Ende, an der Spitze **U2: 47**; *at the top (of)* oben, am oberen Ende, an der Spitze (von) *U2: 37*; **open top bus** Bus mit offenem Dach U3: 48; *top up* aufstocken *U3: 55*
torch [tɔːtʃ] Taschenlampe **2 > U5: 82**
tour [tʊə] Führung, Besichtigung **2 > U3: 51**
tourism [ˈtʊərɪzəm] Tourismus **1 > U6: 103**
tourist [ˈtʊərɪst] Tourist/Touristin **U1: 16**; **tourist office** Fremdenverkehrsamt; Auskunft **2 > U3: 52**
towards [təˈwɔːdz] entgegen, in Richtung auf, auf ... zu **U3: 67**
town [taʊn] Stadt **1 > Intro: 16**
toy [tɔɪ] Spielzeug **1 > U4: 68**
tradition [trəˈdɪʃn] Tradition **U3: 49**
traffic [ˈtræfɪk] Verkehr **U1: 9**; *traffic jam* Stau *U5: 93*
train [treɪn] Zug **1 > U1: 32**; **model train** Modelleisenbahn **1 > U4: 76**; **on the train/bus/...** im Zug/Bus/... **U3: 56**
tram [træm] Tram, Straßenbahn **2 > U3: 48**
transport *(no pl.)* [ˈtrænspɔːt] Transport, Verkehr, Beförderung **U5: 90**
travel [ˈtrævl] reisen **2 > U6: 97**; *hier:* fahren, gelangen, hinkommen **U5: 48, 88**
travelcard [ˈtrævlkɑːd] Tageskarte *U1: 17*
tree [triː] Baum **U3: 53**
trick [trɪk] Trick, Kunststück **U1: 28**
tried → try [traɪ] *simple past* von **try** **2 > U6: 102**
trip: (school) trip [trɪp] (Schul-)Ausflug **2 > U1: 17**
trouble [ˈtrʌbl] Ärger, Schwierigkeiten **U2: 47**
true [truː] wahr **U5: 51**
try [traɪ] versuchen, (aus)probieren **2 > U3: 50**
tube [tjuːb] U-Bahn *(besonders in London) U1: 17*
Tuesday [ˈtjuːzdeɪ] Dienstag **1 > U4: 80**
Turkey [ˈtɜːki] Türkei **2 > Intro: 11**
turn [tɜːn] (sich) umdrehen, wenden **U2: 47**; **turn left/right** nach links/rechts abbiegen **2 > U3: 52**
TV [tiːˈviː] Fernseher, Fernsehapparat **1 > U2: 42**; **watch TV** fernsehen **1 > U4: 70** 70; **TV station** Fernsehsender **U4: 84**
twelve [twelv] zwölf **1 > Intro: 15**
twelfth [twelθ] zwölfte(r, s) **2 > U4: 72**
twentieth [ˈtwentiəθ] zwanzigste(r, s) **2 > U4: 72**
twenty [ˈtwenti] zwanzig **1 > U2: 48**
twice [twaɪs] zweimal **U4: 85**
two [tuː] zwei **1 > Intro: 15**
typical [ˈtɪpɪkl] typisch **1 > U4: 74**

U

ultra [ˈʌltrə] ultra *U2: 37*
uncle [ˈʌŋkl] Onkel **1 > U3: 60**
under [ˈʌndə] unter **2 > U2: 30**
underground [ˈʌndəgraʊnd] U-Bahn **U1: 12**
understand [ʌndəˈstænd] verstehen **1 > U6: 107**
unfriendly [ʌnˈfrendli] unfreundlich **1 > U1: 23**
unhappy [ʌnˈhæpi] unglücklich **2 > U2: 31**
uniform [ˈjuːnɪfɔːm] Uniform **2 > U1: 16**

[ə] again [eɪ] name [aɪ] time [ɔɪ] boy [əʊ] no [aʊ] house [ɪə] here [eə] chair [ʊə] sure [b] bike

United Kingdom (UK) [junaɪtɪd 'kɪŋdəm] Vereinigtes Königreich **2 > U1:** 12
unlucky [ʌn'lʌki] glücklos, unglücklich **2 > U6:** 101
up [ʌp] (hin/her)auf, nach oben **2 > U3:** 51
update ['ʌpdeɪt] Aktualisierung **1 > U3:** 63
us [ʌs] uns **1 > U5:** 89
USA [ju: es 'eɪ] USA, die Vereinigten Staaten **1 > U5:** 98
use [ju:z] verwenden, benutzen **2 > U2:** 35
usually ['ju:ʒuəli] normalerweise **1 > U6:** 114

V

vacation *(AE)* [və'keɪʃn] Ferien, Urlaub **U5:** 87
vacuum cleaner ['vækjuəm kli:nə] Staubsauger **2 > U3:** 50
valley ['væli] Tal **U2:** 31
value: good value [gʊd 'vælju:] preisgünstig **2 > U4:** 68
van [væn] Kleinbus *U4: 75*
vegetables ['vedʒtəblz] Gemüse **1 > U3:** 53
verb [vɜ:b] Verb **2 > U3:** 51
very ['veri] sehr **1 > U1:** 23
victim ['vɪktɪm] Opfer *U2: 37*
video ['vɪdiəʊ] Video **1 > U2:** 40; **video game** Videospiel **1 > U4:** 71; **video recorder** Videorekorder **1 > U2:** 42
village ['vɪlɪdʒ] Dorf **1 > U2:** 38
visit ['vɪzɪt] Besuch *U1: 17*; besuchen **1 > U5:** 85
visitor ['vɪzɪtə] Besucher/Besucherin **U3:** 65
voice [vɔɪs] Stimme **2 > U3:** 51
volleyball ['vɒlibɔ:l] Volleyball **2 > Intro:** 11
voucher ['vaʊtʃə] Gutschein *U2: 37*

W

waggon ['wægən] (Pferde-)Wagen U5: 90
wait [weɪt] warten **1 > U5:** 92; *can't wait* nicht abwarten können, es nicht erwarten können *U5: 91*
wake [weɪk] wecken **2 > U1:** 15
walk [wɔ:k] Spaziergang **2 > U1:** 19; (spazieren) gehen **1 > U5:** 86; **take the dog for a walk** mit dem Hund rausgehen/spazierengehen **2 > U1:** 19; *walkable* (zu Fuß) begehbar, zurücklegbar *U5: 93*; **we have walked** wir sind gegangen, wir gingen **U3:** 50
Walkman ['wɔ:kmən] Walkman **1 > U4:** 69
wall [wɔ:l] Mauer **1 > U5:** 91
wallpaper ['wɔ:lpeɪpə] Tapete **1 > U6:** 106
want [wɒnt] wollen **1 > U4:** 73; **want a word** sich unterhalten wollen, ein Wort wechseln wollen **U1:** 28
warden ['wɔ:dən] Aufsicht, Aufseher/Aufseherin **U2:** 46
warm [wɔ:m] warm **2 > U5:** 81
was [wɒz] war **1 > U3:** 58
wash: have a wash [hæv ə 'wɒʃ] sich waschen **1 > U4:** 80; **wash up** abwaschen, spülen **1 > U3:** 58
wasn't (= was not) [wɒznt] war nicht **2 > U2:** 31
watch [wɒtʃ] zuschauen, sich ansehen **2 > U4:** 65; **watch TV** fernsehen **1 > U4:** 70
water ['wɔ:tə] Wasser **1 > U4:** 73; **mineral water** Mineralwasser **1 > U3:** 55; **water sports** Wassersport **U2:** 34
waxworks ['wækswɜ:ks] Wachsfiguren(kabinett) U1: 10
way [weɪ] Art, Weise, Möglichkeit **U1:** 16; **on the way** auf dem Weg, unterwegs **1 > U6:** 109; **know the way** den Weg kennen **1 > U5:** 92; *our way* in unsere Richtung, zu uns her *U5: 91*; **Do it this way.** Mach(t) es so. **1 > U6:** 110
we [wi:] wir **1 > Intro:** 11; **we're (= we are)** wir sind **1 > U1:** 23
wear [weə] tragen, anhaben (Kleidung) **2 > U1:** 16
weather ['weðə] Wetter **1 > U6:** 114
Web (= World Wide Web) [web] Netz (= Internet) **2 > U1:** 24
webcam ['webkæm] Webcam, Webcamera **U1:** 27
website ['web saɪt] Website **2 > U1:** 16
Wednesday ['wenzdeɪ] Mittwoch **1 > U4:** 80
week [wi:k] Woche **1 > U4:** 72
weekday ['wi:kdeɪ] Wochentag **1 > U4:** 80
weekend [wi:k'end] Wochenende **1 > U4:** 80
Welcome! ['welkəm] Willkommen! **1 > U5:** 93
well [wel] nun, also **1 > U2:** 40; **Well done!** Gut gemacht! **1 > U5:** 93
Welsh [welʃ] walisisch; (die) Waliser **2 > U1:** 16
went → go [went] *simple past* von **go** **2 > Intro:** 8
were [wɜ:] waren **1 > U4:** 75; **weren't (= were not)** warst/wart/waren nicht **2 > U2:** 31
west [west] Westen **U5:** 90
wet [wet] nass, feucht **2 > U2:** 30
what [wɒt] welche/welcher/welches **1 > U2:** 43; **What a ...** Was für ein/eine ... **1 > U6:** 109; **What about ...?** Wie wäre es mit ...? **1 > U3:** 54; **What can you?** Was kannst du ...? **1 > Intro:** 10; **What do you think ...?** Was meinst/glaubst du ...? **1 > U6:** 108; **What time is it?** Wie spät ist es? **1 > U3:** 64; **What's your name?** Wie heißt du? **1 > U1:** 22; **What's?** Was ist ...? **1 > Intro:** 11
wheel [wi:l] Rad **2 > U4:** 69
when [wen] wann **1 > U3:** 64; als, wenn **2 > U5:** 82; **When were you born?** Wann bist du geboren? **2 > U2:** 40
where [weə] wo **1 > U2:** 40; **Where are you from?** Wo kommst du her? **1 > U1:** 22
which ...? [wɪtʃ] welche(r, s) ...? **2 > U5:** 76
whisky ['wɪski] Whisky **U3:** 51
white [waɪt] weiß **1 > Intro:** 10
who [hu:] wer **1 > U3:** 60; **who's (= who is)** wer ist **1 > U5:** 93; **Who is it?** Wer ist es? **1 > U3:** 60
why [waɪ] warum **2 > U1:** 19; **that's why** deshalb, daher **U4:** 70; **Why not?** Warum nicht? **1 > U3:** 60
wild [waɪld] wild **U5:** 102
will [wɪl] werden **2 > U6:** 96; **will be very nice** wird sehr schön sein **1 > U6:** 106

[p] **p**en [d] **d**ay [t] **t**en [k] boo**k** [g] **g**o [ŋ] morni**ng** [l] **l**ike [r] **r**uler [v] se**v**en [w] **w**e [s] **s**ix

win [wɪn] gewinnen, siegen **1 > U6:** 129
wind [wɪnd] Wind **U3:** 47
window ['wɪndəʊ] Fenster **1 > Intro:** 11
windy ['wɪndi] windig **2 > U6:** 104
winner ['wɪnə] Sieger/Siegerin **1 > U5:** 93
winning ['wɪnɪŋ] (das) Gewinnen **2 > U1:** 20
winter ['wɪntə] Winter **1 > U5:** 99
wish: Best wishes [best 'wɪʃɪz] Viele Grüße **1 > U6:** 129; **Wish you were here.** Ich wünschte, du wärst hier. **2 > U5:** 85
with [wɪð] mit; bei **1 > U1:** 25
without [wɪ'ðaʊt] ohne **2 > U1:** 18
woman ['wʊmən] Frau **2 > U3:** 52
won → win [wɒn] *simple past* von **win** **U3:** 56
won't (= will not) [wəʊnt] werden/wird nicht **2 > U1:** 18; **won't (= will not) have time.** Wir werden keine Zeit haben. **1 > U6:** 107
wood [wʊd] Holz; (kleinerer) Wald **2 > U4:** 62
word [wɜːd] Wort **1 > U1:** 29; **want a word** sich unterhalten wollen, ein Wort wechseln wollen **U1:** 28; **one word is missing** ein Wort fehlt **U2:** 40; **he ate his words** er änderte seine Meinung U4: 85
wore → wear [wɔː] *simple past* von **wear** U1: 21
work [wɜːk] Arbeit **U5:** 87; arbeiten **1 > U2:** 40; **worker** Arbeiter/Arbeiterin **U5:** 91
world [wɜːld] Welt **2 > U3:** 48; *world wide* weltweit *U5: 93*
worry: Don't worry. ['dəʊnt wʌri] Mach dir keine Sorgen. **1 > U6:** 109
worse [wɜːs] schlimmer, schlechter **U4:** 72
worst: the worst [ðə 'wɜːst] der/die/das schlimmste, der/die/das schlechteste **U4:** 72
would [wʊd]**: I'd like ... (= I would like)** Ich hätte gern .../ich möchte ... **1 > U4:** 75; **wrong** [rɒŋː] falsch **2 > U1:** 25 **What would you like ...?** Was würdest du gern ...? **2 > U4:** 61
Wow! [waʊ] Krass!/Wahnsinn! **2 > U6:** 94
write [raɪt] schreiben **1 > U1:** 26
writing ['raɪtɪŋ] Schreiben **1 > U2:** 121
I wouldn't like to ... [aɪ wʊdnt laɪk tə] Ich würde nicht gern ... **U2:** 33
wrong [rɒŋː] falsch **2 > U1:** 25
wrote → write [rəʊt] *simple past* von **write** **2 > U3:** 47

Y

year [jɪə] Jahr, Jahrgang **1 > U1:** 25
yellow ['jeləʊ] gelb **1 > Intro:** 14
yes [jes] ja **1 > U1:** 22; **Yes, she does.** Ja (tut sie). **1 > U5:** 89
yesterday ['jestədeɪ] gestern **2 > U2:** 30
yogurt ['jɒgət] Jogurt **1 > U3:** 56
you [juː] du/ihr/Sie **1 > U1:** 23; **you and your ...** du mit deinem/deiner ... **1 > U4:** 73; **you're (= you are)** du bist/ihr seid/Sie sind **1 > U1:** 23
young [jʌŋ] jung **1 > U6:** 105
your [jɔː] dein/euer/Ihr **1 > Intro:** 11
yourself [jɔː'self] du/dir/dich (selbst) *U5: 95*
youth: youth club ['juːθ klʌb] Jugendclub, -zentrum **2 > U1:** 17; **youth hostel** Jugendherberge **U2:** 38

Z

zero / 0 ['zɪərəʊ] null **2 > U6:** 104
zoo [zuː] Zoo **1 > U5:** 86

[z] **his** [ʃ] **she** [tʃ] **teacher** [dʒ] **jeans** [j] **yes** [θ] **thing** [ð] **the** [iː] **he** [ɑː] **car** [ɔː] **or** [uː] **too**

ALPHABET

a	[eɪ]
b	[biː]
c	[siː]
d	[diː]
e	[iː]
f	[ef]
g	[dʒiː]
h	[eɪtʃ]
i	[aɪ]
j	[dʒeɪ]
k	[keɪ]
l	[el]
m	[em]
n	[en]
o	[əʊ]
p	[piː]
q	[kjuː]
r	[ɑː]
s	[es]
t	[tiː]
u	[juː]
v	[viː]
w	['dʌbljuː]
x	[eks]
y	[waɪ]
z	[zed]

SOUNDS

[iː]	meet, team, he
[ɑː]	answer, class, car
[ɔː]	or, ball, door
[uː]	ruler, blue, too
[ɜː]	girl, word, her
[i]	radio, video, sorry
[u]	July, February
[ɪ]	in, milk, big
[e]	empty, yes, bed
[æ]	cat, black
[ʌ]	bus, come
[ɒ]	on, dog, what
[ʊ]	put, good, woman
[ə]	again, today, sister

[eɪ]	eight, name, play
[aɪ]	I, time, my
[ɔɪ]	boy, toilet
[əʊ]	old, no, road
[aʊ]	house, now
[ɪə]	near, here, we're
[eə]	there, chair
[ʊə]	you're, sure

[b]	bike, hobby, job
[p]	pen, pupil, shop
[d]	day, window, good
[t]	ten, football, at
[k]	car, lucky, book
[g]	go, again, bag
[ŋ]	wrong, morning
[l]	like, old, small
[r]	ruler, friend, biro
[v]	very, seven, have
[w]	we, swim
[s]	six, poster, yes
[z]	zoo, visit, his
[ʃ]	she, action, English
[tʃ]	child, teacher, match
[dʒ]	jeans, German, badge
[j]	yes, you, young
[θ]	thing, maths, month
[ð]	the, father, with

ORDINAL NUMBERS

1st	**first**	[fɜːst]
2nd	**second**	['sekənd]
3rd	**third**	[θɜːd]
4th	**fourth**	[fɔːθ]
5th	**fifth**	[fɪfθ]
6th	**sixth**	[sɪksθ]
7th	**seventh**	['sevnθ]
8th	**eighth**	[eɪtθ]
9th	**ninth**	[naɪnθ]
10th	**tenth**	[tenθ]
11th	**eleventh**	[ɪ'levnθ]
12th	**twelfth**	[twelfθ]
13th	**thirteenth**	[θɜː'tiːnθ]
14th	**fourteenth**	[fɔː'tiːnθ]
15th	**fifteenth**	[fɪf'tiːnθ]
16th	**sixteenth**	[sɪks'tiːnθ]
17th	**seventeenth**	[sevn'tiːnθ]
18th	**eighteenth**	[eɪ'tiːnθ]
19th	**nineteenth**	[naɪn'tiːnθ]
20th	**twentieth**	['twentiəθ]
21st	**twenty-first**	[twenti'fɜːst]
22nd	**twenty-second**	[twenti'sekənd]
23rd	**twenty-third**	[twenti'θɜːd]
24th	**twenty-fourth**	[twenti'fɔːθ]
25th	**twenty-fifth**	[twenti'fɪfθ]
26th	**twenty-sixth**	[twenti'sɪksθ]
27th	**twenty-seventh**	[twenti'sevnθ]
28th	**twenty-eighth**	[twenti'eɪtθ]
29th	**twenty-ninth**	[twenti'naɪnθ]
30th	**thirtieth**	['θɜːtiəθ]

Alphabetische Liste der Wörter aus Band 1, Band 2 und Band 3 (Deutsch-Englisch)

A

ab: ab und zu every now and then [everi naʊ ənd 'ðen]
abbiegen: nach links/rechts abbiegen turn left/right [tɜ:n 'left / 'raɪt]
Abend: (später) Abend night [naɪt]; **heute Abend** tonight [tə'naɪt]; **Guten Abend.** Good evening. [gʊd 'i:vnɪŋ]
abends in the evening [ɪn ði 'i:vnɪŋ]; p.m. [pi: 'em]
aber but [bʌt]; though [ðəʊ]
Abfall rubbish ['rʌbɪʃ]
abgesehen: abgesehen von apart from [ə'pɑ:t frəm]
abhaken tick [tɪk]
Abhängige/r addict ['ædɪkt]
abholen: ich hole dich vom Bahnhof ab. I'll meet you at the station. [aɪl 'mi:t ju: ət ðə 'steɪʃn]
abschreiben copy ['kɒpi]
abseilen abseil ['æbseɪl]
abwarten: nicht abwarten können can't wait [kɑ:nt 'weɪt]
abwaschen wash up [wɒʃ 'ʌp]
Abzeichen badge [bædʒ]
acht eight [eɪt]; **achte(r, s)** eighth [eʊtθ]
achtzehn eighteen [eɪ'ti:n]; **achzehnte(r, s)** eighteenth [eʊ'ti:nθ]
achtzig eighty ['eɪti]
Action action ['ækʃn]
Admiral admiral ['ædmɪrəl]
Adresse address [ə'dres]
äh... err... [ɜ:]
Ahnung idea [aɪ'dɪə]; **keine Ahnung haben** have no idea [hæv nəʊ aɪ'dɪə]
Aktion campaign [kæm'peɪn]; action ['ækʃn]
aktiv active ['æktɪv]
Aktivität action ['ækʃn]; activity [æk'tɪvəti]
Aktualisierung update ['ʌpdeɪt]
Akzent accent ['æksent]
albern silly ['sɪli]
Album album ['ælbəm]
alle all [ɔ:l]; everybody ['evribɒdi]
allein alone [ə'ləʊn]
alles everything ['evriθɪŋ]
alphabetisch: alphabetische Reihenfolge alphabetical order [ælfə'betɪkl 'ɔ:də]
als as [æz]; **größer als** bigger than ['bɪgə ðən]; **interessanter als** more interesting than [mɔ:r 'ɪntrəstɪŋ]
also well [wel]
alt old [əʊld]; **Wie alt bist du?** How old are you? [haʊ 'əʊld ə ju:]
Alternative option ['ɒpʃn]
älteste oldest ['əʊldɪst]
Amerika America [ə'merɪkə]
Amerikaner/in American [ə'merɪkən]
amerikanisch American [ə'merɪkən]; **amerikanische Ureinwohner** native Americans ['neɪtɪv ə'merɪkənz]
Amt office ['ɒfɪs]
amüsieren: sich gut amüsieren have a good time [həv ə gʊd 'taɪm]
an at [æt]; on [ɒn]
Andenken souvenir [su:və'nɪə]
andere other ['ʌðə]; **manch andere** some others [sʌm 'ʌðəz]; **andere(r, s)** different ['dɪfrənt]; **ein/e andere(r, s)** another [ə'nʌðə]
ändern: er änderte seine Meinung he ate his words [hi 'eɪt hɪz wɜ:dz]
anfangen get started [get 'stɑ:tɪd]; **(sie) fingen an zu essen** (they) started eating [i:tɪŋ]
anfühlen: sich anfühlen feel [fi:l]
Angelegenheit issue ['ɪʃju:, 'ɪsju:]
Angeln: (das) Angeln fishing ['fɪʃɪŋ]
Angst: Angst haben be frightened [bi 'fraɪtənd]; **Sie hatten Angst.** They were frightened. [ðeɪ wə 'fraɪtnd]
anhaben wear *(Kleidung)* [weə]
anhaken tick [tɪk]
anhalten stop [stɒp]
anhören: sich anhören listen (to) ['lɪsn tə]
ankommen arrive [ə'raɪv]
Ankunft arrival [ə'raɪvl]
anlächeln: jemanden (jdn.) anlächeln smile at somebody (sb.) ['smaɪl ət sʌmbədi]
annehmen expect [ɪk'spekt]
Anruf: (Telefon-)Anruf (phone)call ['fəʊn kɔ:l]
anrufen phone [fəʊn]; call [kɔ:l]; **Ruf(t) mich einfach an.** Just phone me. [jəst 'fəʊn mi]
anschauen look at ['lʊk ət]
anschließen: sich anschließen join [dʒɔɪn]; **das Verbindungskabel anschließen** fix the hook-ups [fɪks ðə 'hʊkʌps]
Anschrift address [ə'dres]
ansehen: sich ansehen watch [wɒtʃ]
Ansprache speech [spi:tʃ]
Antwort answer ['ɑ:nsə]
antworten answer ['ɑ:nsə]
Anzeige advert ['ædvɜ:t]
Apfel apple ['æpl]
Apfelsine orange ['ɒrɪndʒ]
April April ['eɪprəl]
Arbeit job [dʒɒb]; work [wɜ:k]; **um Arbeit/Essen/... zu suchen** for work/food/... [fə 'wɜ:k 'fu:d]
arbeiten work [wɜ:k]
Arbeiter/Arbeiterin worker ['wɜ:kə]
Arbeitsplatz job [dʒɒb]
Ärger trouble ['trʌbl]
arm poor [pʊə]
arrogant arrogant ['ærəgənt]
Art way [weɪ]; kind [kaɪnd]; kind [kaɪnd]
Arzt/Ärztin doctor ['dɒktə]
attraktiv good-looking [gʊd'lʊkɪŋ]
auch too [tu:]; also ['ɔ:lsəʊ]
auf in [ɪn]; on [ɒn]; **(hin/her)auf** up [ʌp]; **auf ... zu** towards [tə'wɔ:dz]; **Auf Wiedersehen.** Goodbye. ['gʊdbaɪ]
Aufführung act [ækt]
Aufgabe job [dʒɒb]; task [tɑ:sk]
aufgeregt excited [ɪk'saɪtɪd]; nervous ['nɜ:vəs]
aufhören: Hör(t) auf! Stop it! ['stɒp ɪt]
Aufkleber sticker ['stɪkə]
auflisten list [lɪst]
aufmachen open ['əʊpən]
Aufmerksamkeit awareness [ə'weənəs]
aufnehmen record [rɪ'kɔ:d]
aufräumen tidy ['taɪdi]; clear [klɪə]

[i:] he	[ɑ:] car	[ɔ:] or	[u:] too	[ɜ:] girl	[i] sorry	[u] July	[ɪ] big	[e] yes	[æ] cat	[ʌ] bus	[ɒ] dog

aufrecht: aufrecht stehen stand up [stænd 'ʌp]
aufregend exciting [ɪk'saɪtɪŋ]
Aufseher/Aufseherin warden ['wɔ:dən]
Aufsicht warden ['wɔ:dən]
aufstehen stand up [stænd 'ʌp]; get up [get 'ʌp]
aufsteigen get on [gɒt 'ɒn]; **immer höher aufsteigen** get higher and higher [get haɪər ənd 'haɪə]
aufstellen put up [pʊt 'ʌp]
aufstocken top up [tɒp 'ʌp]
Auftritt act [ækt]; gig [gɪg]
aufzeichnen record [rɪ'kɔ:d]
Aufzug lift [lɪft]
Augenblick: Einen Augenblick. Just a minute. [dʒʌst ə 'mɪnɪt]
August August ['ɔ:gəst]
aus from [frɒm]
Ausdruck phrase [freɪz]
Ausfahrt junction ['dʒʌŋktʃn]
Ausflug: (Schul-)Ausflug (school)trip [trɪp]; **(Tages-) Ausflug** day out [deɪ 'aʊt]
ausgeben spend (time/money) [spend]
Auskunft tourist office [ˌtʊərɪst ɒfɪs]
ausprobieren try [traɪ]
ausräumen clear [klɪə]
aussehen: gut aussehend good-looking [gʊd'lʊkɪŋ]
außer apart from [ə'pɑ:t frəm]; except [ɪ'ksept]
Außerirdischer alien ['eɪliən]
Auto car [kɑ:]; **(das) Autofahren** driving ['draɪvɪŋ]

B

Badeanzug swimsuit ['swɪmsu:t]
Badehose swimsuit ['swɪmsu:t]
Badezimmer bathroom ['bɑ:θru:m]
„Bahncard" für Jugendliche junior railcard [dʒu:njə 'reɪlkɑ:d]
Bahnhof station ['steɪʃn]; **Ich hole dich vom Bahnhof ab.** I'll meet you at the station. [aɪl 'mi:t ju: ət ðə 'steɪʃn]
bald soon [su:n]
Ball ball [bɔ:l]
Banane banana [bə'nɑ:nə]
Band band [bænd]
Bank bank [bæŋk]
Bargeld cash [kæʃ]
Baseball baseball ['beɪsbɔ:l]
Basiswissen: Lesen basic reading [beɪsɪk 'ri:dɪŋ]
Batterie battery (*pl.* -ies) ['bætərɪ]
Basketball basketball ['bɑ:skɪtbɔ:l]
Bauernhof farm [fɑ:m]
Baum tree [tri:]
Bayer/Bayerin Bavarian [bə'veəriən]
bayerisch Bavarian [bə'veəriən]
Bayern Bavaria [bə'veəriə]
Beamter/Beamtin: (Polizei-)Beamter/Beamtin officer ['ɒfɪsə]
beantworten answer ['ɑ:nsə]
bedauern: jemanden (jdn.) bedauern feel sorry for somebody (sb.) [fi:l 'sɒri fə sʌmbədi]
bedeuten mean [mi:n]
beeilen: Beeilt euch!/Beeil dich! Hurry! ['hʌri]
beenden finish ['fɪnɪʃ]
Beförderung transport ['trænspɔ:t] *(no pl)*
befragen interview ['ɪntəvju:]
begehbar: (zu Fuß) begehbar walkable ['wɔ:kəbl]
beginnen start [stɑ:t]; get started [get 'stɑ:tɪd]
beharren: beharren auf insist [ɪn'sɪst]
behilflich helpful ['helpfəl]
bei at [æt]; with [wɪð]; **bei ... zu Hause** at ... house [ət haʊs]
beibringen teach [ti:tʃ]
beide both [bəʊθ]
beinahe almost ['ɔ:lməʊst]
Beispiel example [ɪg'zɑ:mpl]; **zum Beispiel** for example [fər ɪg'zɑ:mpl]
bekommen get [get]
beliebt popular ['pɒpjʊlə]; **nicht so beliebt wie ...** not so popular as ... [nɒt səʊ 'pɒpjʊlə æz]; **beliebteste(r, s)** most popular [məʊst 'pɒpjʊlə]
bemerken notice ['nəʊtɪs]
benehmen: sich benehmen behave [bɪ'heɪv]
benutzen use [ju:z]
bereits already [ɔ:l'redi]
Berg mountain ['maʊntən]; hill [hɪl]
Bericht report [rɪ'pɔ:t]
berichten tell [təʊld]; report [rɪ'pɔ:t]; tell (about) ['tel əbaʊt]
berühmt famous ['feɪməs]
beschäftigen: sich mit etwas beschäftigen get busy [get 'bɪzi]
beschäftigt busy ['bɪzi]
Besichtigung tour [tʊə]; **Besichtigung von Sehenswürdigkeiten** sightseeing ['saɪtsi:ɪŋ]
Besitzer/in owner ['əʊnə]
besonders: besonderer Tag special day ['speʃl deɪ]
besprechen discuss [dɪ'skʌs]
besser better ['betə]
beste(r, s) best [best]
bestehen: bestehen auf insist [ɪn'sɪst]
bestellen order ['ɔ:də]
Besuch visit ['vɪzɪt]
besuchen visit ['vɪzɪt]
Besucher/Besucherin visitor ['vɪzɪtə]
betreuen look after [lʊk 'ɑ:ftə]
betroffen sick [sɪk]
Bett bed [bed]
Beutel bag [bæg]
bevor before [bɪ'fɔ:]
bewegen: (sich) bewegen move [mu:v]
bewegungslos still [stɪl]
bewölkt cloudy ['klaʊdi]
bewundern admire [əd'maɪə]
Bewusstsein awareness [ə'weənəs]
bezahlen pay (for) ['peɪ fə]; **ich bezahle die Getränke.** The drinks are on me. [ðə drɪnks ɑ:r ɒn 'mi:]
Bezirk district ['dɪstrɪkt]
Bibliothek library ['laɪbrəri]
Bier beer [bɪə]
Bild picture ['pɪktʃə]
billig cheap [tʃi:p]; **am billigsten** the cheapest [ðə 'tʃi:pɪst]
bin: ich bin I'm (= I am) [aɪm, aɪ 'æm]
Bindfaden string [strɪŋ]
bis: von ... bis from ... till [frəm tɪ]; **von ... bis** from ... to [frəm, tə]; **bis spät** till late [tɪl leɪt]; **Bis später.** See you later. [si: ju 'leɪtə]
bisschen: ein bisschen a little [ə 'lɪtl]
bitte please [pli:z]; **Bitte (sehr).** Here you are. [hɪə ju 'ɑ:]; **(hier) Bitte.** Here you are. ['hɪə ju ɑ:]; **Wie bitte?** Pardon? ['pɑ:dən]
Blase bubble ['bʌbl]
Blatt leaf (*pl.* leaves) [li:f]
blau blue [blu:]
bleiben stay [steɪ]; **Bleib(t) cool!** Chill out! ['tʃɪl aʊt]
Bleistift pencil ['pensl]

[ʊ] put [ə] again [eɪ] name [aɪ] time [ɔɪ] boy [əʊ] no [aʊ] house [ɪə] here [eə] chair [ʊə] sure

blöd stupid ['stju:pɪd]; silly ['sɪli]
bloß only ['əʊnli]
Blume flower ['flaʊə]
Blumenbeet flower-bed ['flaʊəbed]
Blüte flower ['flaʊə]
Bohne bean [bi:n]; **gebackene Bohnen (in Tomatensoße)** baked beans [beɪkt 'bi:nz]
Bonbon sweet [swi:t]
Boot boat [bəʊt]
böse angry ['æŋgri]
brauchen need [ni:d]; take [teɪk]
braun brown [braʊn]
brechen: (zer)brechen break [breɪk]
Brett board [bɔ:d]
Brief letter ['letə]; **(kurzer) Brief** note [nəʊt]
Briefmarke stamp [stæmp]
bringen bring [brɪŋ]; take [teɪk]
Brite/Britin British ['brɪtɪʃ]
britisch British ['brɪtɪʃ]
Brokkoli broccoli ['brɒkəli]
Broschüre brochure ['brəʊʃə]
Brot bread [bred]
Brötchen roll [rəʊl]
Brücke bridge [brɪdʒ]
Bruder brother ['brʌðə]
brummig grumpy ['grʌmpi]
Buch book [bʊk]
buchen book [bʊk]
Bücherei library ['laɪbrəri]
Büchse can [kæn]; tin [tɪn]
buchstabieren: Kannst du ... buchstabieren? Can you spell ...? [kən ju spel]
Buchung booking ['bʊkɪŋ]
Bundesland state [steɪt]
Bundesstaat state [steɪt]
Burg castle ['kɑ:sl]
Büro office ['ɒfɪs]
bürsten brush [brʌʃ]
Bus bus [bʌs]; **Bus mit offenem Dach** open top bus [əʊpən tɒp 'bʌs]; **Bus(rund)reise** bus tour ['bʌs tʊə]; **Bus-Service zum Zu- und Aussteigen** get on, get off service [get 'ɒn get 'ɒf sɜ:vɪs]; **im Bus/Zug/...** on the train/bus/... [ɒn ðə 'treɪn 'bʌs]
Busfahrer/in bus driver ['bʌs draɪvə]
Bushaltestelle bus stop ['bʌs stɒp]
Butterbrotdose lunch box ['lʌntʃ bɒks]
Button badge [bædʒ]]

C

Café café ['kæfeɪ]
Callcenter call centre ['kɔ:l sentə]
Camping-Urlaub camping holiday ['kæmpɪŋ hɒlədeɪ]
Campingplatz campsite ['kæmpsaɪt]
Caravan-Campingplatz caravan park ['kærəvæn pɑ:k]
CD CD [si:'di:]; **CD-Player** CD player [si: di: 'pleɪə]
Celsius: unter null Grad Celsius below 0 °C [bɪ'ləʊ 'zɪərəʊ dɪ'gri:z 'selsiəs]
Cent cent [sent]
Chance chance [tʃɑ:ns]
Cheeseburger cheeseburger ['tʃi:zbɜ:gə]
Cola cola ['kəʊlə]
Comic(heft) comic ['kɒmɪk]
Computer computer [kəm'pju:tə]
Cornflakes cornflakes ['kɔ:nfleɪks]
Couch couch [kaʊtʃ]
Cousin/Cousine cousin ['kʌzn]

D

da there [ðeə]; **da drüben** over there [əʊvə 'ðeə]
Dach: Bus mit offenem Dach open top bus [əʊpən tɒp 'bʌs]
daher so [səʊ]; that's why ['ðæts waɪ]
dämlich stupid ['stju:pɪd]
Danke: Danke (schön). Thank you. ['θæŋk ju]; Thanks. [θæŋks]
danken thank [θæŋk]
dann then [ðen]
darstellen act [ækt]
das: das ist that's (= that is) [ðæts]
dasselbe: dasselbe wie the same as [ðə 'seɪm əz]
Datum date [deɪt]
Dauerglotzer/in couch potato ['kaʊtʃ pəteɪtəʊ]
Dauerkarte season ticket [si:zn 'tɪkɪt]
dauern take [teɪk]
Daumen: Ich drücke die Daumen. fingers crossed ['fɪŋəz krɒst]
defekt broken ['brəʊkən]
dein your [jɔ:]
denken think [θɪŋk]; **daran denken** remember [rɪ'membə]
deprimiert sick [sɪk]
der/die/das the [ðə]
deshalb so [səʊ]; that's why ['ðæts waɪ]
Detail detail ['di:teɪl]
deutsch German ['dʒɜ:mən]; **auf Deutsch** in German [ɪn 'dʒɜ:mən]
Deutschland Germany ['dʒɜ:məni]
Dezember December [dɪ'sembə]
Dialog dialogue ['daɪəlɒg]
Dichter/Dichterin poet ['pəʊɪt]
die (da) those [ðəʊz]
Dienst service ['sɜ:vɪs]
Dienstag Tuesday ['tju:zdeɪ]
dies this [ðɪs]
diese these [ði:z]
digital: digitale Internet-Radioshow zum Downloaden podcast ['pɒdkɑ:st]
Ding thing [θɪŋ]
Dinosaurier dinosaur ['daɪnəsɔ:]
Direktor/Direktorin principal ['prɪnsɪpl] *(AE)*
diskutieren discuss [dɪ'skʌs]
Distrikt district ['dɪstrɪkt]
Dock dock [dɒk]
Dollar dollar ($) ['dɒlə]
Donnerstag Thursday ['θɜ:zdeɪ]
doppelt, Doppel- double ['dʌbl]
Dorf village ['vɪlɪdʒ]
dort there [ðeə]; **dort drüben** over there [əʊvə 'ðeə]
Dose can [kæn]; tin [tɪn]
downloaden download ['daʊnləʊd]
Drachen kite [kaɪt]
draußen outside [aʊt'saɪd]; outdoor ['aʊtdɔ:]
drei three [θri:]
dreißig thirty ['θɜ:ti]; **dreißigste(r, s)** thirtieth ['θɜ:tiəθ]
dreizehn thirteen [θɜ:'ti:n]; **dreizehnte(r, s)** thirteenth [tɜ:'ti:nθ]
dritte(r, s) third (= 3rd) [θɜ:d]
drucken print [prɪnt]
drücken: Ich drücke die Daumen. fingers crossed ['fɪŋəz krɒst]
du you [ju:]; **du bist** you're (= you are) [jʊə]; **du mit deinem/deiner ...** you and your ... ['ju ənd jɔ:]; **du/dir/dich (selbst)** yourself [jɔ:'self]
Dudelsack bagpipes ['bægpaɪps]
dunkel dark [dɑ:k]
durch through [θru:]; 'cross (= across) [krɒs (ə'krɒs)]
Durcheinander mess [mes]

dürfen may [meɪ]; **du darfst nicht/Sie dürfen nicht** you mustn't ['mʌsnt]
dürftig poor [pɔ:]
Durst: Ich habe Durst. I'm thirsty. [aɪm 'θɜ:sti]
DVD DVD [di: vi: 'di:]; **DVD-Spieler** DVD player [di: vi: 'di: pleɪə]

E

E-Mail email ['i:meɪl]; **als E-Mail verschicken** email ['i:meɪl]
eben flat [flæt]
Ebene level ['levl]
echt really ['rɪəli]
Ei egg [eg]
eifrig keen [ki:n]
eigen own [əʊn]
eigentlich: eigentlich nicht not really [nɒt 'ri:əli]
ein(e, r) one [wʌn]
ein/eine a [ə]; an [æn]
Einbahnstraße one-way street [wʌnweɪ stri:t]
einfach easy ['i:zi]; **Ruf(t) mich einfach an.** Just phone me. [jəst 'fəʊn mi]
einige some [sʌm]; a few [ə 'fju:]
einkaufen: einkaufen gehen go to the shops [gəʊ tə ðə 'ʃɒps]
Einkaufsbummel: einen Einkaufsbummel machen go to the shops [gəʊ tə ðə 'ʃɒps]
Einkaufsstraße High Street ['haɪ stri:t]
Einkaufszentrum shopping centre ['ʃɒpɪŋ sentə]; mall [mɔ:l]
Einladung invitation [ɪnvɪ'teɪʃn]
einmal once [wʌns]; **auf einmal** suddenly ['sʌdnli]
eins one [wʌn]
einsteigen get on [get 'ɒn]
eintreffen arrive [ə'raɪv]
Eintrittskarte ticket ['tɪkɪt]
Einzelheit detail ['di:teɪl]
Eis: (Speise-)Eis ice cream [aɪs 'kri:m]
Eistee iced tea [aɪst 'ti:]
Elektrogerät, -apparat electronic gadget [ɪlek'trɒnɪk 'gædʒɪt]
elf eleven [ɪ'levn]
elfte(r, s) eleventh [ʊ'levnθ]
Eltern parents ['peərənts] *(pl.)*
Ende end [end]; **am oberen Ende** at the top [æt ðə 'tɒp]; **am oberen Ende** at the top (of) [ət ðə 'tɒp (əv)]; **zu Ende machen** finish ['fɪnɪʃ]
endlich at last [ət 'lɑ:st]
England England ['ɪŋglənd]
englisch English ['ɪŋglɪʃ]; **auf Englisch** in English [ɪn 'ɪŋglɪʃ]
entdecken find out [faɪnd 'aʊt]
entgegen towards [tə'wɔ:dz]
entlang along [ə'lɒŋ]; **entlanggehen** go along [gəʊ ə'lɒŋ]
entschuldigen: Entschuldigen Sie. Excuse me. [ɪk'skju:z mi]
Entschuldigung. Excuse me. [ɪk'skju:z mi]
er: er ist he's (= he is) [hi:z]
Erdgeschoss ground floor ['graʊnd flɔ:]
Erdkunde geography [dʒi'ɒgrəfi]
Ereignis event [ɪ'vent]
erfahren: etwas erfahren über learn about ['lɜ:n əbaʊt]
Erfahrung experience [ɪk'spɪərɪəns]
erfolgreich successful [sə'ksesfl]
Ergebnis result [rɪ'zʌlt]
erhöhen raise [reɪz]
erinnern: sich erinnern remember [rɪ'membə]; **jdn. erinnern** remind sb. [rɪ'maɪnd sʌmbədi]
Erinnerung memory ['meməri]
erklären explain [ɪk'spleɪn]
Erlebnis experience [ɪk'spɪərɪəns]
erreichen get [get]
errichten put up [pʊt 'ʌp]
erst only ['əʊnli]
erste(r, s) first [fɜ:st]; **zum ersten Mal** first [fɜ:st]; **der erste Mai (1. Mai)** May the first (= 1st May) [meɪ ðə 'fɜ:st]
Erwachsene/r adult ['ædʌlt]
erwarten expect [ɪk'spekt]; **es nicht erwarten können** can't wait [kɑ:nt 'weɪt]
erwischen catch [kætʃ]
erzählen tell (about) ['tel əbaʊt]
Erzählung story ['stɔ:ri]
es: es ist it's (= it is) [ɪts]
Essen food [fu:d]; **(zubereitetes) Essen** meal [mi:l]; **Essen, zu dem alle Gäste etwas mitbringen** pot-luck meal [pɒt lʌk 'mɪ:l]
essen eat [i:t]; have [hæv]; **(sie) fingen an zu essen** (they) started eating [i:tɪŋ]; **essen gehen** go out for a meal [gəʊ aʊt fər ə 'mi:l]
etwas something ['sʌmθɪŋ]
euer your [jɔ:]
Euro euro ['jʊərəʊ]
Europa Europe ['jʊərəp]
Europäer/Europäerin European [jʊərə'pi:ən]
ewig: ich werde ewig weinen I'm forever crying [aɪm fərevə 'kraɪɪŋ]
Experiment experiment [ɪk'sperɪmənt]
Experte/Expertin expert ['ekspɜ:t]
Extra extra ['ekstrə]

F

Fabrik factory ['fæktəri]
Fach: (Schul-)Fach subject ['sʌbdʒɪkt]
Fachmann/Fachfrau expert ['ekspɜ:t]
Fähigkeit skill [skɪl]
Fahne flag [flæg]
Fähre ferry ['feri]
fahren go [gəʊ]; travel ['trævl]; drive [draɪv]; **in Urlaub fahren** go on holiday [gəʊ ɒn 'hɒlədeɪ]; **in die (Innen-)stadt fahren** go to town [gəʊ tə 'taʊn]; **mit dem/der ... fahren** go by ... [gəʊ baɪ]; **schnell fahren** speed [spi:d]
Fahrkarte ticket ['tɪkɪt]
Fahrrad bike [baɪk]
Fahrstuhl lift [lɪft]
Fahrt journey ['dʒɜ:ni]
fair fair [feə]
Fakt fact [fækt]
fallen fall [fɔ:l]
falsch wrong [rɒŋ]
Familie family ['fæməli]
Fan fan [fæn]
Fanatiker(in) freak [fri:k]
fangen catch [kætʃ]
fantastisch terrific [tə'rɪfɪk]; fantastic [fæn'tæstɪk]
Farbe colour ['kʌlə]
Farm farm [fɑ:m]
fast almost ['ɔ:lməʊst]
Februar February ['februəri]
Federmäppchen pencil case ['penslkeɪs]

[s] **s**ix [z] hi**s** [ʃ] **sh**e [tʃ] tea**ch**er [dʒ] **j**eans [j] **y**es [θ] **th**ing [ð] **th**e [i:] h**e** [ɑ:] c**ar** [ɔ:] **or**

fehlen: ein Wort fehlt one word is missing [wʌn wɜːd ɪz 'mɪsɪŋ]
Feier party ['pɑːti]
feiern celebrate ['selɪbreɪt]
Feiertag: gesetzlicher Feiertag public holiday [pʌblɪk 'hɒlədeɪ]
Feld field [fiːld]
Fels rock [rɒk]
Fenster window ['wɪndəʊ]
Ferien holiday ['hɒlədeɪ]; vacation [və'keɪʃn] *(AE)*
fernsehen watch TV [wɒtʃ tiː'viː]
Fernseher, Fernsehapparat TV [tiː'viː]
Fernsehsender TV station [tiː'viː 'steɪʃn]
fertig ready ['redi]
Festnetz landline ['lændlaɪn]
feucht wet [wet]
Feuer: Feuer schlucken/speien eat fire [iːt 'faɪə]
Feuerwerkskörper firework ['faɪəwɜːk]
Film film [fɪlm]
Filmführer film guide ['fɪlm gaɪd]
Filmprogrammheft film guide ['fɪlm gaɪd]
Filzstift felt-tip ['felttɪp]
finden find [faɪnd]
Firma company ['kʌmpəni]
Fisch: Fisch und Pommes frites fish and chips [fɪʃ ənd 'tʃɪps]; **Fischstäbchen** fish fingers [fɪʃ 'fɪŋgəz]
Fitness fitness ['fɪtnəs]
flach flat [flæt]
Flagge flag [flæg]
Flasche: eine Flasche ... a bottle of ... [ə 'bɒtl əv]
fliegen fly [flaɪ]
Fließband assembly line [ə'sembli laɪn]
Flöte: (Quer-)Flöte flute [fluːt]
flott quick [kwɪk]
Flugblatt leaflet ['liːflet]
Flugzeug plane [pleɪn]
Fluss river ['rɪvə]
folgen follow ['fɒləʊ]
Form form [fɔːm]
Formular form [fɔːm]
Foto photo ['fəʊtəʊ]; **Fotos von ... machen** take photos (of) [teɪk 'fəʊtəʊz əv]
Fotoapparat camera ['kæmərə]
Frage question ['kwestʃən]; **(Streit-)Frage** issue ['ɪʃjuː, 'ɪsjuː]
fragen ask [ɑːsk]; **eine(n) Partner/in fragen über/nach** ask a partner about [ɑːsk ə 'pɑːtnə əbaʊt]; **sie fragt nach** she's asking about [ʃiːz 'ɑːskɪŋ ə'baʊt]
Frankreich France [frɑːns]
Französisch, französisch French [frentʃ]
Frau woman ['wʊmən]; Mrs *(Anrede)* ['mɪsɪz]
Freak freak [friːk]
frei free [friː]; **im Freien** outdoor ['aʊtdɔː]
Freibad swimming pool ['swɪmɪŋ puːl]
Freitag Friday ['fraɪdeɪ]
Freizeit free time ['friː taɪm]
Freizeitpark theme park ['θiːm pɑːk]
Fremdenverkehrsamt tourist office [ˌtʊərɪst ɒfɪs]
Fremdsprache foreign language [fɒrən 'læŋgwɪdʒ]
fressen: zu fressen geben feed [fiːd]
freuen: sich auf etwas freuen look forward to sth. [lʊk 'fɔːwəd tə sʌmθɪŋ]
Freund mate *(ugs.)* [meɪt]; **Freund/Freundin** friend [frend]; **Freundin** girlfriend ['gɜːlfrend]; **die besten Freunde** the best of friends [ðə 'best əv 'frendz]
freundlich friendly ['frendli]
frisch fresh [freʃ]
froh happy ['hæpi]; glad [glæd]
früh early ['ɜːli]
Frühling spring [sprɪŋ]
Frühstück: Zimmer mit Frühstück B&B (Bed & Breakfast) [bed ənd 'brekfəst]
frühstücken have breakfast ['brekfəst]
Frühstückspension B&B (Bed & Breakfast) [bed ənd 'brekfəst]
frühzeitig early ['ɜːli]
fühlen: (sich) fühlen feel [fiːl]
Führung tour [tʊə]
Füller pen [pen]
fünf five [faɪv]; **fünfte(r, s)** fifth [fɪfθ]
fünfzehn fifteen [fɪf'tiːn]; **fünfzehnte(r, s)** fifteenth [fɪf'tiːnθ]
fünfzig fifty ['fɪfti]
für for [fɔː]; **was für** what kind of [wɒt 'kaɪnd əv]
furchtbar terrible ['terəbl]
Fuß foot [fʊt]; **zu Fuß** on foot [ɒn 'fʊt]
Fußball football ['fʊtbɔːl]; soccer ['sɒkə]
Fußballplatz football field ['fʊtbɔːl fiːld]
Fußballtrikot shirt [ʃɜːt]
füttern feed [fiːd]

G

Gameboy gameboy ['geɪmbɔɪ]
ganz: der/die/das ganze all [ɔːl]
Garage garage ['gærɑːʒ]
Gardine curtain ['kɜːtn]
Garten garden ['gɑːdn]
Gärtner/Gärtnerin gardener ['gɑːdənə]
Gaukler/Gauklerin juggler ['dʒʌglə]
gebacken: gebackene Bohnen (in Tomatensoße) baked beans [beɪkt 'biːnz]; **gebackene Kartoffel** baked potato [beɪkt pə'teɪtəʊ]
Gebäude building ['bɪldɪŋ]
geben give [gɪv]; **es gibt** there is/are [ðeə iz/ɑː]
geboren: Ich bin ... geboren. I was born in ... [aɪ wəz 'bɔːn ɪn]; **Wann bist du geboren?** When were you born? ['wen wə ju bɔːn]
Gebrauchsanweisung handbook ['hændbʊk]
gebraucht second-hand [sekənd'hænd]
gebrochen broken ['brəʊkn]
Geburtstag birthday ['bɜːθdeɪ]
Gedächtnis memory ['meməri]
Gedanke idea [aɪ'dɪə]
Gedicht poem ['pəʊɪm]
gefährlich dangerous ['deɪndʒərəs]
Gefallen: er wird an der Luft Gefallen finden he will take to the air [hi wɪl teɪk tə ði 'eə]
gegen against [ə'geɪnst]; at about *(Uhrzeit)* [ə'baʊt]
Gegenteil opposite ['ɒpəzɪt]
Gegenwart present ['preznt]
gehen go [gəʊ]; **(spazieren) gehen** walk [wɔːk]; **in Urlaub gehen** go on holiday [gəʊ ɒn 'hɒlədeɪ]; **geradeaus (weiter)gehen** Go straight on. [gəʊ streɪt 'ɒn]; **Die Getränke gehen auf mich.** The drinks are on me. [ðə drɪnks ɑːr ɒn 'miː]; **ging so** not

[uː] too [ɜː] girl [i] sorry [u] July [ɪ] big [e] yes [æ] cat [ʌ] bus [ɒ] dog [ʊ] put [ə] again

bad [nɒt 'bæd]; **Wie geht es dir/euch/Ihnen?** How are you? [haʊ ə 'juː]; **Was geht hier vor?** What's happening? [wɒts 'hæpənɪŋ]; **es geht so** not bad [nɒt 'bæd]; **Wie geht's?** How are things? *(ugs.)* [həʊ ə 'θɪŋz]
gehören: gehören (zu) belong to [bɪ'lɒŋ tə]
geizig mean [miːn]
Geländewagen SUV (= sports utility vehicle) [esjuː'viː]
gelangen travel ['trævl]; get [get]
gelb yellow ['jeləʊ]
Geld money ['mʌni]; **kein Geld** no money [nəʊ 'mʌni]
Geldautomat cash machine ['kæʃ məʃiːn]
Gelegenheit chance [tʃɑːns]
gemacht: Gut gemacht! Well done! [wel 'dʌn]
gemeinsam together [tə'geðə]
Gemüse vegetables ['vedʒtəblz]
genauso: genauso freundlich wie as friendly as [əz 'frendli əz]; **genauso gut wie** as good as [æz 'gʊd əz]; **genauso wie** the same as [ðə 'seɪm əz]
genießen enjoy [ɪn'dʒɔɪ]
genug enough [ɪ'nʌf]
geöffnet open ['əʊpən]
Geographie geography [dʒi'ɒgrəfi]
geradeaus: geradeaus (weiter)gehen Go straight on. [gəʊ streɪt 'ɒn]
Gerät machine [mə'ʃiːn]
Geräusch noise [nɔɪz]; sound [saʊnd]
gerecht fair [feə]
Gericht: schottisches Gericht aus Schafsinnereien haggis ['hægɪs]
Gerümpel junk [dʒʌŋk] *(AE)*
Gesamtschule: (US) Gesamtschule für 13- bis 18-Jährige high school ['haɪ skuːl]
Geschäft shop [ʃɒp]
geschäftlich for business [fə 'bɪznəs]
geschehen happen ['hæpən]
Geschenk present ['preznt]
Geschichte history ['hɪstri]; story ['stɔːri]; **... die Geschichte handelt von ...** ... the story is about ... [ðə 'stɔːri ɪz ə'baʊt]
Geschirrspülmaschine dishwasher ['dɪʃwɒʃə]
geschlossen closed [kləʊzd]
gesetzlich: gesetzlicher Feiertag public holiday [pʌblɪk 'hɒlədeɪ]
Gesicht face [feɪs]
gestern yesterday ['jestədeɪ]
gesund healthy ['helθi]
Getränk drink [drɪŋk]; **Die Getränke gehen auf mich./Ich bezahle die Getränke.** The drinks are on me. [ðə drɪnks ɑːr ɒn 'miː]
Gewinn prize [praɪz]
gewinnen win [wɪn]
Gewinnen: (das) Gewinnen winnning ['wɪnɪŋ]
gewöhnen: er wird sich an die Luft gewöhnen he will take to the air [hi wɪl teɪk tə ði 'eə]
Gig gig [gɪg]
Glas glass [glɑːs]
glauben think [θɪŋk]; **Was glaubst du ...?** What do you think ...? [wɒt də ju 'θɪŋk]
Glocke bell [bel]
Glotze box [bɒks]
Glück: wir hatten Glück we were lucky [wiː wə 'lʌki]; **(viel) Glück** good luck [gʊd 'lʌk]; **Du hast Glück!** You're lucky! [jɔː 'lʌki]
glücklich happy ['hæpi]; **glücklich, Glücks-** lucky ['lʌki]
glücklos unlucky [ʌn'lʌki]
Glückwunsch: Herzlichen Glückwunsch! Congratulations! [kɒngrætʃʊ'leɪʃnz]
Gnade grace [greɪs]
Golf golf [gɒlf]
göttlich heavenly ['hevənli]
Grab grave [greɪv]
Grad degrees [dɪ'griːz] *(pl.)*; **unter null Grad Celsius** below 0 °C [bɪ'ləʊ 'zɪərəʊ dɪ'griːz 'selsiəs]
Gramm gram [græm]
Gras grass [grɑːs]
Grillparty barbecue ['bɑːbɪkjuː]
groß big [bɪg]; great [greɪt]; **ungeheuer groß** enormous [ɪ'nɔːməs]
großartig great [greɪt]; **großartig in** great at ['greɪt ət]
Großbritannien Britain ['brɪtn]
größer bigger ['bɪgə]; **größer als** bigger than ['bɪgə ðən]
Großmutter grandmother ['grænmʌðə]
Großstadt city ['sɪti]
Großvater grandfather ['grænfɑːðə]
grün green [griːn]
Gruppe group [gruːp]; **(Musik-)Gruppe** band [bænd]
Gruß: Viele Grüße Best wishes [best 'wɪʃɪz]
grüßen: Grüße mir ... Give my greetings to ... [gɪv maɪ 'griːtɪŋz tə]
gucken look [lʊk]
gut fine [faɪn]; **gut (in)** good (at) ['gʊd ət]; **gut aussehend** good-looking [gʊd'lʊkɪŋ]; **gut besuchter Laden** busy shop [bɪzi 'ʃɒp]; **Gut gemacht!** Well done! [wel 'dʌn]; **Guten Abend.** Good evening. [gʊd 'iːvnɪŋ]; **Guten Morgen.** Good morning. [gʊd 'mɔːnɪŋ]; **Guten Tag. (nachmittags)** Good afternoon. [gʊd ɑːftə'nuːn]
Gutschein voucher ['vaʊtʃə]

H

haben have [hæv]; **Kann ich eine(n)/ein ... haben?** Can I have a ...? [kən aɪ 'hæv ə]; **habe keinen/keine/kein** I don't have [aɪ 'dəʊnt hæv]; **er hat keinen/keine/kein** he doesn't have [hi 'dʌznt hæv]
Hafen dock [dɒk]
halb half past [hɑːf 'pɑːst]
Halbbruder half-brother ['hɑːfbrʌðə]
Hälfte half (*pl.*: halves) [hɑːf, hɑːvz]
Hallo Hi [haɪ]
Halloween Halloween [hæləʊ'iːn]
halten: (fest)halten hold [həʊld]
Hamburger hamburger ['hæmbɜːgə]; burger ['bɜːgə]
Hamster hamster ['hæmstə]
handeln: ... die Geschichte handelt von ... ... the story is about ... [ðə 'stɔːri ɪz ə'baʊt]
Handlung action ['ækʃn]
Handy mobile ['məʊbaɪl]; cellphone ['selfəʊn] *(AE)*
Handzettel leaflet ['liːflet]
Hardware hardware ['hɑːdweə]
hart: hart (härter) hard(er) [hɑːd]
hassen hate [heɪt]
hätte: Ich hätte gern .../Ich möchte ... I'd like ... (= I would like) [aɪd 'laɪk]
Hauptstadt capital ['kæpɪtl]

Hauptstraße High Street ['haɪ striːt]
Haus house [haʊs]; **das Haus verlassen** leave the house ['liːv ðə haʊs]; **zu Hause** at home [ət 'həʊm]; home [həʊm]
Hausaufgabe(n) homework ['həʊmwɜːk]
Heim home [həʊm]
Heimat home [həʊm]
Heimweh haben/bekommen be/get homesick [bɪ̥get 'həʊmsɪk]
heiß hot [hɒt]; **heiße Schokolade** hot chocolate [hɒt 'tʃɒklət]
heißen: Wie heißt du? What's your name? [wɒts jɔː 'neɪm]
helfen help [help]
hell light [laɪt]
Helm helmet ['helmɪt]
Hemd shirt [ʃɜːt]
her: zu uns her our way [aʊə 'weɪ]
herauf up [ʌp]
herausfinden find out [faɪnd 'aʊt]
Herbst autumn ['ɔːtəm]
Herkunft background ['bækgraʊnd]
Herr Mr *(Anrede)* ['mɪstə]
herüber 'cross (= across) [krɒs (ə'krɒs)]
herum around [ə'raʊnd]; **um ... herum** round [raʊnd]
herunter down [daʊn]; **herunterhüpfen von** jump off [dʒʌmp 'ɒf]; **(Daten) herunterladen** download ['daʊnləʊd]; **herunterspringen von** jump off [dʒʌmp 'ɒf]
hervorragend terrific [tə'rɪfɪk]
herzlich: Herzlichen Glückwunsch! Congratulations! [kɒngrætʃʊ'leɪʃnz]
heute today [tə'deɪ]; **heute Nacht, heute Abend** tonight [tə'naɪt]
hier here [hɪə]; **hier ist** here's (= here is) ['hɪəz]; **hier sind** here are [hɪə ɑː]
hilfreich helpful ['helpfəl]
Himmel sky [skaɪ]
himmlisch heavenly ['hevənli]
hin: hin und wieder every now and then [everi naʊ ənd 'ðen]
hinauf up [ʌp]
hindurch through [θruː]
hineintun, -stecken put in [pʊt ɪn]
hinfahren take [teɪk]
hinkommen get [get]; travel ['trævl]
hinsetzen: sich hinsetzen sit down [sɪt 'daʊn]
hinstellen: hinstellen (auf) put (on) [pʊt ɒn]
hinter behind [bɪ'haɪnd]
Hintergrund background ['bækgraʊnd]
hinüber 'cross (= across) [krɒs (ə'krɒs)]
hinunter down [daʊn]; **hinunterhüpfen von** jump off [dʒʌmp 'ɒf]; **hinunterspringen von** jump off [dʒʌmp 'ɒf]
Hinweis tip [tɪp]
Hit hit ['hɪt]
Hitliste charts [tʃɑːts] *(pl)*
Hobby hobby ['hɒbi]; interest ['ɪntrəst]; **Welches Hobby hast du?** What's your hobby? ['wɒts jə hɒbi]
hoch high [haɪ]; **eine Meile hoch** a mile up [ə maɪl 'ʌp]
hochziehen pull up [pʊl 'ʌp]
hoffen hope [həʊp]
Höhe level ['levl]
höher: immer höher aufsteigen get higher and higher [get haɪər ənd 'haɪə]
holen get [get]
Holz wood [wʊd]
Homepage homepage ['həʊmpeɪdʒ]
hören listen (to) ['lɪsn tə]; hear [hɪə]
Hotdog hot dog ['hɒt dɒg]
Hotel hotel [həʊ'tel]
Hubschrauber helicopter ['helɪkɒptə]
Hügel hill [hɪl]
Huhn chicken ['tʃɪkɪn]
Hund dog [dɒg]; **mit dem Hund rausgehen** take the dog for a walk ['teɪk ðə dɒg fə ə wɔːk]
Hundejunges puppy ['pʌpi]
hundert hundred ['hʌndrəd]
Hunderte hundreds ['hʌndrɪdz]
Hunger: Ich habe Hunger. I'm hungry. [aɪm 'hʌŋgri]

I

ich I [aɪ]; **ich bin's** it's me [ɪts 'miː]
ideal ideal [aɪ'dɪəl]
Idee idea [aɪ'dɪə]
Idol idol ['aɪdl]
ihm him [hɪm]
ihn him [hɪm]
ihnen them [ðem]
Ihr your [jɔː]
ihr/ihre her [hɜː]; its [ɪts]; their [ðeə]; **ihr** you [juː]
im: im Zug/Bus/... on the bus/train/... [ɒn ðə 'treɪn 'bʌs]
Imbiss-Bude chip shop ['tʃɪp ʃɒp]
immer always ['ɔːlweɪz]
in in [ɪn]; at [æt]; **in ... (hinein)** into ['ɪntə]
Inder/in Indian ['ɪndiən]
indisch Indian ['ɪndiən]
Industrie industry ['ɪndəstri]
industriell: industrielle Revolution Industrial Revolution [ɪndʌstriəl revə'luːʃn]
Informationstechnologie information technology (IT) [ɪnfəmeɪʃn tek'nɒlədʒi]
Ingenieur/Ingenieurin engineer [endʒɪ'nɪə]
Inlineskates skates [skeɪts]
Inlineskating inline skating ['ɪnlaɪn skeɪtɪŋ]
Innenstadt downtown ['daʊntaʊn] *(AE)*
Insel island ['aɪlənd]
Instrument: ein Instrument spielen play an instrument [pleɪ ən 'ɪnstrəmənt]
interessant interesting ['ɪntrəstɪŋ]; **interessanter als** more interesting than [mɔːr 'ɪntrəstɪŋ]
Interesse interest ['ɪntrəst]
interessiert: interessiert an interested in ['ɪntrəstɪd ɪn]
international international [ɪntə'næʃnəl]
Internet Internet ['ɪntənet]; **im Internet** online [ɒn'laɪn]; **im Internet surfen** surf the Internet [sɜːf ði 'ɪntənet]; **Internet-Tagebuch** blog [blæg]
Interview interview ['ɪntəvjuː]
interviewen interview ['ɪntəvjuː]
Intonation intonation [ɪntə'neɪʃn]
irgendein/e any ['eni]
irgendwelche any ['eni]
Irrgarten: Verloren im Irrgarten. Lost in the maze. [lɒst ɪn ðə 'meɪz]
ist is [ɪz]; **Ist das ...?** Is that ...? [ɪz ðæt]; **Ist es ...?** Is it ...? [ɪz ɪt]; **ist nicht** isn't (= is not) ['ɪznt]

[d] **d**ay	[t] **t**en	[k] boo**k**	[g] **g**o	[ŋ] morni**ng**	[l] **l**ike	[r] **r**uler	[v] se**v**en	[w] **w**e	[s] **s**ix	[z] hi**s**

J

ja yes [jes]; **Ja (tut sie).** Yes, she does. [jes ʃi 'dʌz]
jagen: in die Luft jagen blow up [bləʊ 'ʌp]
Jahr year [jɪə]
Jahreskarte season ticket [si:zn 'tɪkɪt]
Jahreszeit season ['si:zn]
Jahrgang year [jɪə]
Jahrhundert century ['sentʃʊri]
Januar January ['dʒænjuəri]
Jeans jeans [dʒi:nz] *(pl.)*
jede(r, s) everybody ['evribɒdi]; each [i:tʃ]; any ['eni]; **jeden Tag** every day [evri 'deɪ]
jedoch though [ðəʊ]
jemand somebody ['sʌmbədi]
jene: jene (dort) those [ðəʊz]
jetzt now [naʊ]
Jogurt yogurt ['jɒgət]
Jongleur juggler ['dʒʌglə]
jonglieren juggle ['dʒʌgl]
Jugendclub youth club ['ju:θ klʌb]
Jugendherberge youth hostel ['ju:θ hɒstl]
Jugendliche(r) kid [kɪd]
Jugendzentrum youth club ['ju:θ klʌb]
Juli July [dʒu'laɪ]
jung young [jʌŋ]
Junge boy [bɔɪ]
Juni June [dʒu:n]
Jury jury ['dʒʊəri]

K

Kaffee coffee ['kɒfi]
Käfig cage [keɪdʒ]
Kalender calendar ['kælɪndə]
kalt cold [kəʊld]
Kamera camera ['kæmərə]
Kampagne campaign [kæm'peɪn]
Kanone gun [gʌn]
Kanu fahren canoe [kə'nu:]
Kapelle: (Blas-)Kapelle marching band ['mɑ:tʃɪŋ bænd]
kaputt broken ['brəʊkən]
kaputtmachen break [breɪk]
Karneval carnival ['kɑ:nɪvəl]
Karotte carrot ['kærət]
Karte: (Spiel-, Gruß-)Karte card [kɑ:d]
Kartoffel potato (*pl.* -oes) [pə'teɪtəʊ]; **gebackene Kartoffel** baked potato [beɪkt pə'teɪtəʊ]
Kartoffelchips crisps [krɪsps] *(pl.)*
Karton: ein Karton ... a carton of ... [ə 'kɑ:tn əv]
Käse cheese [tʃi:z]
Kasten box [bɒks]
Kater cat [kæt]
Katze cat [kæt]
kaufen buy [baɪ]
Kaufpreis price [praɪs]
Kaugummi chewing gum ['tʃu:ɪŋ gʌm]
kein/e not any [nɒt 'eni]; **keine Ahnung haben** have no idea [hæv nəʊ aɪ'dɪə]
keiner nobody ['nəʊbədi]
Keks biscuit ['bɪskɪt]
Keller basement ['beɪsmənt] *(AE)*
kennen know [nəʊ]; **den Weg kennen** know the way [nəʊ ðə 'weɪ]
Ketschup ketchup ['ketʃəp]
Kilometer kilometer ['kɪləmi:tə]
Kind kid [kɪd]; **Kinder** children ['tʃɪldrən]
Kino cinema ['sɪnəmə]
Kirche church [tʃɜ:tʃ]
Kissen cushion ['kʊʃn]
Kiste box [bɒks]
Klang sound [saʊnd]
Klasse: (Schul-)Klasse class [klɑ:s]
Klassenarbeit test [test]
Klassenzimmer classroom ['klɑ:sru:m]
Kleider clothes [kləʊðz]
Kleidung clothes [kləʊðz]
klein small [smɔ:l]; **der/die/das kleine** the small one/s [ðə 'smɔ:l wʌn]; **die kleineren** the small one/s [ðə 'smɔ:l wʌnz]
Kleinbus van [væn]
kleinlich mean [mi:n]
klettern climb [klaɪm]
klicken: (an-, hin-)klicken click [klɪk]
Klimaanlage air-conditioning '['eə kəndɪʃnɪŋ]
Klimatisierung air-conditioning ['eə kəndɪʃnɪŋ]
Klingelton ringtone ['rɪŋtəʊn]
Klippe cliff [klɪf]
Klub club [klʌb]
klug clever ['klevə]
Kneipe pub [pʌb]
kochen cook ['kʊk]
Kochen: (das) Kochen cooking ['kʊkɪŋ]
Kohle coal [kəʊl]
komisch funny ['fʌni]
kommen come [kʌm]; get [get]; **Wo kommst du her?** Where are you from? [weə ə ju: 'frɒm]; **komm(t) mit uns** come with us [kʌm wɪð 'ʌs]; **Komm(t) nach ...** Come to ... [kʌm tə]
König king ['kɪŋ]
Königin queen [kwi:n]
Königreich: Vereinigtes Königreich United Kingdom (UK) [junaɪtɪd 'kɪŋdəm]
können can [kæn]; may [meɪ]; **nicht können** can't [kɑ:nt]; **Kann ich eine(n)/ein ... haben?** Can I have a ...? [kən aɪ 'hæv ə]; **kann/kannst/können/könnt nicht** cannot ['kænɒt]
Kontostand balance ['bæləns]
kontrollieren check [tʃek]
Koordinator/Koordinatorin coordinator [kəʊ'ɔ:dɪneɪtə]
Kopfhörer headphones ['hedfəʊnz]
kopieren copy ['kɒpi]
korrekt right [raɪt]
kosten cost [kɒst]; **was kostet das?** How much is it? [haʊ 'mʌtʃ ɪz ɪt]
kostenlos free [fri:]
krank ill [ɪl]; sick [sɪk]
Krankenhaus hospital ['hɒspɪtl]
krass: Krass! Wow! [waʊ]
kreuzen cross [krɒs]
Kriminalität crime [kraɪm]
Küche kitchen ['kɪtʃɪn]
Kuchen cake [keɪk]
Kugelschreiber biro ['baɪrəʊ]
Kuh cow [kaʊ]
Kühlschrank fridge [frɪdʒ]
kühn keen [ki:n]
kümmern: sich kümmern um look after [lʊk 'ɑ:ftə]
Kumpel mate *(ugs.)* [meɪt]
Kunde/Kundin customer ['kʌstəmə]
Kunst Art [ɑ:t]
Kunststück trick [trɪk]
kurz short [ʃɔ:t]; **zu kurz** too short [ʃɔ:t]
Kusine/Cousine cousin ['kʌzn]
Küste coast [kəʊst]

L

Lächeln smile [smaɪl]
lächeln smile [smaɪl]
lachen laugh [lɑ:f]

[ʃ] **sh**e [tʃ] tea**ch**er [dʒ] **j**eans [j] **y**es [θ] **th**ing [ð] **th**e [i:] h**e** [ɑ:] c**a**r [ɔ:] **o**r [u:] t**oo** [ɜ:] g**ir**l

Laden shop [ʃɒp]; **gut besuchter Laden** busy shop [bɪzi 'ʃɒp]
Lampe light [laɪt]
Land country ['kʌntri]; **auf dem Land** in the country [ɪn ðə 'kʌntri]; **(Bundes-)Land** state [steɪt]; **Landes-** national ['næʃənl]
landen land [lænd]
Landkarte map [mæp]
lang long [lɒŋ]
langweilen: Ich langweile mich. I'm bored. [aɪm 'bɔ:d]
langweilig boring ['bɔ:rɪŋ]; **dir ist langweilig** you're bored [jɔ: 'bɔ:d]; **du langweilst dich** you're bored [jɔ: 'bɔ:d]
Lärm noise [nɔɪz]
lärmend noisy ['nɔɪzi]
lassen leave [left]; **(stehen)lassen** leave [li:v]; **Lass(t) uns ...** Let's ... [lets]
laufen run [rʌn]; **um die Wette laufen** have a race [reɪs]; race against [reɪs ə'geɪnst]; **wie läuft's?** How are things? *(ugs.)* [haʊ ə 'θɪŋz]
laut noisy ['nɔɪzi]; loud [laʊd]
Lautsprecher loudspeaker ['laʊdspi:kə]
Leadsänger/Leadsängerin lead singer [li:d 'sɪŋə]
Leben life [laɪf]; **Renn/t um dein/euer Leben!** Run for your life! [rʌn fə jɔ: 'laɪf]
leben: leben von live off ['lɪv ɒf]
Lebensmittel food [fu:d]
leer empty ['empti]
Legende legend ['ledʒənd]
lehren teach [ti:tʃ]
Lehrer/Lehrerin teacher ['ti:tʃə]
leicht easy ['i:zi]
leid: Es tut mir leid. I'm sorry. [aɪm 'sɒri]
leihen rent [rent]
leise quiet ['kwaɪət]
lernen study ['stʌdi]; learn [lɜ:n]
lesen read [ri:d]
Lesen: (das) Lesen reading ['ri:dɪŋ]; **Basiswissen: Lesen** basic reading [beɪsɪk 'ri:dɪŋ]
letzte(r, s) last [lɑ:st]
Leute people ['pi:pl]
Licht light [laɪt]
Liebe love [lʌv]
Liebe(r, s) ..., Dear ..., [dɪə]
lieben love [lʌv]
lieber: Lieber spät als gar nicht. Better late than never. [betə 'leɪt ðən 'nevə]
Lieblings- favourite ['feɪvərɪt]
Lied song [sɒŋ]
liegen: liegen (auf) lie (on) [laɪ]
Limonade lemonade [lemə'neɪd]; **Irn-Bru** [ɜ:n 'bru:] schottisches Limonadengetränk
Lineal ruler ['ru:lə]
Linie line [laɪn]
Link link [lɪŋk]
links to the left [tə ðə 'left]; on the left [ɒn ðə 'left]; **nach links abbiegen** turn left [tɜ:n 'left / 'raɪt]; **auf der linken Seite** on the left [ɒn ðə 'left]
Liste: eine Liste schreiben make a list [meɪk ə 'lɪst]
Loch puncture ['pʌŋktʃə]; hole [həʊl]
Lokal pub [pʌb]
Londoner/Londonerin Londoner ['lʌndənə]
Luft air [eə]; **er wird an der Luft Gefallen finden** he will take to the air [hi wɪl teɪk tə ði 'eə]; **in die Luft jagen** blow up [bləʊ 'ʌp]
lustig funny ['fʌni]

M

machen make [meɪk]; do [du:]; **Fotos von ... machen** take photos (of) [teɪk 'fəʊtəʊz əv]; **wir machen (gerade)** we're making [wɪə meɪkɪŋ rɪ'pɔ:ts]; **Das macht doch nichts.** it doesn't matter [ɪt dʌznt 'mætə]; **macht nichts** never mind [nevə 'maɪnd]; **Mach(t) es so.** Do it this way. [du: ɪt 'ðɪs weɪ]
Mädchen girl [gɜ:l]
Mahlzeit meal [mi:l]
Mai May [meɪ]; **der erste Mai (1. Mai)** May the first (= 1st May) [meɪ ðə 'fɜ:st]
mailen email ['i:meɪl]
Mais maize [meɪz]
Mal time [taɪm]; **zum ersten Mal** first [fɜ:st]
mal times [taɪmz]
malen paint [peɪnt]
Mama mum *(BE)* [mʌm]; mom *(AE)* [mɒm]
manche: manche andere some others [sʌm 'ʌðəz]
manchmal sometimes ['sʌmtaɪmz]
Mann man (*pl.* men) [mæn, men]; **Mann!** Gee! [dʒi:] *(AE)*
Mannschaft team [ti:m]
Marke brand [brænd]
Markenzeichen, -name brand name ['brænd neɪm]
Markt market ['mɑ:kɪt]
Markthalle market hall ['mɑ:kɪt hɔ:l]
März March [mɑ:tʃ]
Maschine machine [mə'ʃi:n]
Maske mask [mɑ:sk]
Mathe(matik) maths [mæθs]
Mauer wall [wɔ:l]
Maus mouse (*pl.* mice) [maʊs, maɪs]
Meer sea [si:]; **am Meer** at the seaside [ət ðə 'si:saɪd]
mehr: mehr als over ['əʊvə]
Meile mile [maɪl]; **eine Meile hoch** a mile up [ə maɪl 'ʌp]
mein/meine my [maɪ]
meinen mean [mi:n]; **Was meinst du ...?** What do you think ...? [wɒt də ju 'θɪŋk]
Meinung opinion [ə'pɪniən]; idea [aɪ'dɪə]; **er änderte seine Meinung** he ate his words [hi 'eɪt hɪz wɜ:dz]
meisten: die meisten most [məʊst]
Menge: eine Menge a lot of [ə 'lɒt əv]; **eine Menge** lots (of) ['lɒts əv]
Mensch: Mensch! Gee! [dʒi:] *(AE)*; **Menschen** people ['pi:pl]; **Menschen-** human ['hju:mən]
menschlich human ['hju:mən]
merkwürdig funny ['fʌni]
Meter metre ['mi:tə]
mich me [mi:]
mieten rent [rent]
Milch milk [mɪlk]
Milchmann milkman ['mɪlkmən]
Million million ['mɪljən]
Mineralwasser mineral water ['mɪnərəl wɔ:tə]
Minigolf minigolf ['mɪnigɒlf]
minus minus ['maɪnəs]
Minute minute ['mɪnɪt]
mir me [mi:]
mit with [wɪð]
mitbringen bring [brɪŋ]; **Essen, zu dem alle Gäste etwas mitbringen** pot-luck meal [pɒt lʌk 'mi:l]

[i] sorry [u] July [ɪ] big [e] yes [æ] cat [ʌ] bus [ɒ] dog [ʊ] put [ə] again [eɪ] name [aɪ] time

Mitleid: Mitleid mit jemandem (jdm.) haben feel sorry for somebody (sb.) [fi:l 'sɒri fə sʌmbədi]
mitmachen join [dʒɔɪn]
Mitnehmen: ... zum Mitnehmen take-away ... ['teɪkəweɪ]
Mittag(essen) lunch [lʌntʃ]
Mitte middle ['mɪdl]
Mittelpunkt centre ['sentə]
Mittwoch Wednesday ['wenzdeɪ]
Mixer mixer ['mɪksə]
Mobiltelefon mobile ['məʊbaɪl]
möchten: Ich hätte gern .../Ich möchte ... I'd like ... (= I would like) [aɪd 'laɪk]
Mode fashion ['fæʃən]
Modelleisenbahn model train [mɒdl 'treɪn]
modern modern ['mɒdn]
mögen like [laɪk]; **gar nicht mögen** hate [heɪt]; **sehr mögen** love [lʌv]; **Ich mag ... nicht.** I don't like ... [aɪ dəʊnt laɪk]
Möglichkeit way [weɪ]; option ['ɒpʃn]
Möhre carrot ['kærət]
Monat month [mʌnθ]
Monster monster ['mɒnstə]
Montag Monday ['mʌndeɪ]
Morgen: Guten Morgen. Good morning. [gʊd 'mɔ:nɪŋ]
morgen tomorrow [tə'mɒrəʊ]
morgens in the morning [ɪn ðə 'mɔ:nɪŋ]; a.m. [eɪ'em]
Moschee mosque [mɒsk]
Motor motor ['məʊtə]
Mountainbike mountain bike ['maʊntən baɪk]; **Mountainbike fahren** mountain bike ['maʊntən baɪk]
müde tired ['taɪəd]
Müll rubbish ['rʌbɪʃ]; junk [dʒʌŋk] *(AE)*
Müllmann dustman ['dʌstmən]
mürrisch grumpy ['grʌmpi]
Museum museum [mju'zi:əm]
Musik music ['mju:zɪk]
müssen must [mʌst]; have to ['hæv/'hæf tə]; need to ['ni:d tə]
mutig brave [breɪv]
Mutter mother ['mʌðə]
Muttertag Mother's Day ['mʌðəz deɪ]
Mutti mum *(BE)* [mʌm]; mom *(AE)* [mɒm]

N

nach to [tu]; after *(zeitlich)* ['ɑ:ftə]; **Viertel nach ...** quarter to/past ['kwɔ:tə tə/pɑ:st]; **nach draußen** outside [aut'saɪd]; **nach Hause** home [həʊm]; **nach links/rechts abbiegen** turn left/right [tɜ:n 'left / 'raɪt]; **nach oben** up [ʌp]; **nach rechts** right [raɪt]
Nachbar/Nachbarin neighbour ['neɪbə]
nachmittags p.m. [pi: 'em]
Nachricht message ['mesɪdʒ]
nachschauen look [lʊk]
nächste(r, s) next [nekst]; **als Nächstes** next [nekst]; **Wo ist der/die/das nächst(e) ...?** Where's the nearest ...? [wəz ðe 'nɪərɪst]
Nacht night [naɪt]; **heute Nacht** tonight [tə'naɪt]
nahe near [nɪə]; **um dir nahe zu sein** to be near you [tə bi: 'nɪə ju:]
Nähe: in der Nähe von near [nɪə]; **um in deiner Nähe zu sein** to be near you [tə bi: 'nɪə ju:]
Nase: die Nase voll haben be fed up [bi fed 'ʌp]; **Asif hatte die Nase voll.** Asif was fed up. ['æsi:f wəz fed 'ʌp]
nass wet [wet]
national, National- national ['næʃənl]
natürlich of course [əf 'kɔ:s]
neben next to ['nekst tə]
neblig foggy ['fɒgi]
nehmen take [teɪk]
nein no [nəʊ]; **Nein (habe ich nicht).** No, I didn't (= did not). [dɪdnt]; **Nein (tut sie nicht).** No, she doesn't. [nəʊ ʃi 'dʌzənt]
nennen call [kɔ:l]
nervös nervous ['nɜ:vəs]
nett nice [naɪs]; friendly ['frend-li]
Netz (= Internet) Web (= World Wide Web) [web]
neu new [nju:]; **neueste(r, s)** latest ['leɪtəst]
neun nine [naɪn]; **neunte(r, s)** ninth [naɪnθ]
neunzehn nineteen [naɪn'ti:n]; **neunzehnte(r, s)** nineteenth [naɪn'ti:nθ]
neunzig ninety ['naɪnti]
nicht not [nɒt]
nichts nothing ['nʌθɪŋ]; **macht nichts** never mind [nevə 'maɪnd]; **Dein Team/Deine Mannschaft taugt nichts.** Your team is no good. [jɔ: 'ti:m ɪz nəʊ 'gʊd]
nie never ['nevə]; **ich bin (noch) nie gewesen, ich war (noch) nie** I've never been [aɪv nevə 'bi:n]
niedlich sweet [swi:t]
niemals never ['nevə]
niemand nobody ['nəʊbədi]
noch still [stɪl]; **noch einmal** again [ə'gen]; **Sonst noch etwas?** Anything else? [eniθɪŋ 'els]
Norden north [nɔ:θ]
Nordirland Northern Ireland [nɔ:ðən 'aɪələnd]
nördlich north [nɔ:θ]
normalerweise usually ['ju:ʒuəli]
Notiz note [nəʊt]
November November [nəʊ'vembə]
null zero / 0 ['zɪərəʊ]
Nummer number ['nʌmbə]
nun well [wel]
nur only ['əʊnli]; **nur so zum Spaß** just for fun [dʒʌst fə 'fʌn]

O

oben at the top [æt ðə 'tɒp]; at the top (of) [ət ðə 'tɒp (əv)]; **nach oben** up [ʌp]; **am oberen Ende** at the top (of) [ət ðə 'tɒp (əv)]
Obst fruit [fru:t]
obwohl though [ðəʊ]
oder or [ɔ:]
offen: Bus mit offenem Dach open top bus [əʊpən tɒp 'bʌs]
öffnen open ['əʊpən]
oft often ['ɒfn]
ohne without [wɪ'ðaʊt]
Oktober October [ɒk'təʊbə]
Öl oil [ɔɪl]
Oma grandma ['grænmɑ:]
Onkel uncle ['ʌŋkl]
online online [ɒn'laɪn]
Opfer victim ['vɪktɪm]
Orange orange ['ɒrɪndʒ]
Ordnung: in Ordnung, O.K. OK ['əʊkeɪ]
Organisation organisation [ɔ:gənaɪ'zeɪʃn]
Organisator/Organisatorin coordinator [kəʊ'ɔ:dɪneɪtə]
organisieren organise ['ɔ:gənaɪz]

[ɔɪ] **boy** [əʊ] **no** [aʊ] **house** [ɪə] **here** [eə] **chair** [ʊə] **sure** [b] **bike** [p] **pen** [d] **day** [t] **ten** [k] **book**

Ort place [pleɪs]; scene [siːn]; **am/vom Ort** local ['ləʊkl]
örtlich local ['ləʊkl]
Ostern Easter ['iːstə]
Österreich Austria ['ɒstriə]

P

Paar pair [peə]
paar: ein paar some [sʌm]; a few [ə 'fjuː]
Päckchen packet ['pækɪt]
Paket packet ['pækɪt]
Pakistan Pakistan [pækɪ'stɑːn]
Papa dad [dæd]
Paprika(schote) pepper ['pepə]
Park park [pɑːk]
Parkhaus car park ['kɑː pɑːk]
Parkplatz car park ['kɑː pɑːk]
Parkzeit: das Überziehen der Parkzeit late parking [leɪt 'pɑːkɪŋ]
Parlament parliament ['pɑːləmənt]
Partner partner ['pɑːtnə]; **eine(n) Partner/in fragen über/nach** ask a partner about [ɑːsk ə 'pɑːtnə əbaʊt]
Party party ['pɑːti]
passieren happen ['hæpən]
Pause break [breɪk]
Pence pence [pens] *(pl.)*
Persönlichkeit personality [pɜːsə'nælɪti]
Pfad path [pɑːθ]
Pferd horse [hɔːs]
Pforte gate [geɪt]
Pfund pound *(britisches Geld)* [paʊnd]
Picknick picnic ['pɪknɪk]
Pirat/in pirate ['paɪrət]
Pizza pizza ['piːtsə]
Plan plan [plæn]
planen plan [plæn]
Plasma-TV, -Fernseher plasma TV ['plæzmə tiː viː]
Platte: (Schall-)Platte record ['rekɔːd]
Platten puncture ['pʌŋktʃə]; flat [flæt]
Platz space [speɪs]
Player: MP3-Player MP3 player [(empiː'θriː)'pleɪə]
plötzlich suddenly ['sʌdnli]
Polizei police [pə'liːs]
Polizeirevier police station [pə'liːs steɪʃn]
Polizeiwache police station [pə'liːs steɪʃn]
Polizist policeman [pə'liːsmən]
Pommes frites: Fisch und Pommes frites fish and chips [fɪʃ ənd 'tʃɪps]; **Pommes-frites-Bude** chip shop ['tʃɪp ʃɒp]
Popgruppe pop group ['pop gruːp]
Popmusik pop music [pɒp 'mjuːzɪk]
Portion portion ['pɔːʃn]
Postamt post office ['pəʊst ɒfɪs]
Poster poster ['pəʊstə]
Postkarte postcard ['pəʊstkɑːd]
Postleitzahl postcode ['pəʊstkəʊd]
Präposition preposition [prepə'zɪʃn]
Preis prize [praɪz]; **(Kauf-)Preis** price [praɪs]
preisgünstig good value [gʊd 'væljuː]
pro per [pə]; **pro (Tag)** a (day) [ə 'deɪ]
probieren: (aus)probieren try [traɪ]
Problem problem ['prɒbləm]
Programm programme ['prəʊgræm]
Projekt project ['prɒdʒekt]
Prospekt brochure ['brəʊʃə]
Prozent per cent (%) [pə 'sent]
prüfen test [test]; **(über)prüfen** check [tʃek]
Prüfung test [test]
PS/Postskript(um) PS ['piː ɛs]
Punkt point [pɔɪnt]
Puppe doll [dɒl]
putzen clean [kliːn]; brush [brʌʃ]

Q

Quiz quiz [kwɪz]

R

Rad wheel [wiːl]; **Rad fahren** ride a bike [raɪd ə 'baɪk]
Radiergummi rubber ['rʌbə]
Radio radio ['reɪdiəʊ]
„rappen" rap [ræp]; **Reime „rappen"** rap rhymes [ræp 'raɪmz]
Rapper/Rapperin rapper ['ræpə]
rasen speed [spiːd]
Ratte rat [ræt]
rauchen smoke [sməʊk]
Raum room [ruːm]; space [speɪs]
rausgehen: mit dem Hund rausgehen take the dog for a walk ['teɪk ðə dɒg fə ə wɔːk]
Recht right [raɪt]; **Du hast Recht.** You're right. [jɔː 'raɪt]
recht quite [kwaɪt]
rechts right [raɪt]; to the right [tə ðə 'raɪt]; **nach rechts abbiegen** turn right [tɜːn 'left / 'raɪt]
Rede speech [spiːtʃ]
Redewendung phrase [freɪz]
Regel rule [ruːl]
regnen rain [reɪn]
regnerisch rainy ['reɪni]
reich rich [rɪtʃ]
Reifenpanne flat [flæt]
Reifenschaden puncture ['pʌŋktʃə]
Reihenfolge: alphabetische Reihenfolge alphabetical order [ælfə'betɪkl 'ɔːdə]
Reim: Reime „rappen" rap rhymes [ræp 'raɪmz]
Reise: (lange) Reise journey ['dʒɜːni]
Reiseführer guide book ['gaɪd bʊk]
reisen travel ['trævl]; ride [raɪd]
Rennen race [reɪs]
rennen run [rʌn]; **Renn/t um dein/euer Leben!** Run for your life! [rʌn fə jɔː 'laɪf]
reparieren repair [rɪ'peə]
reservieren book [bʊk]
Reservierung booking ['bʊkɪŋ]
Rest rest [rest]
Restaurant restaurant ['restrɒnt]
Revolution: industrielle Revolution Industrial Revolution [ɪndʌstriəl revə'luːʃn]
richtig right [raɪt]; **richtig oder falsch** Right or wrong? [raɪt ɔː rɒŋ]
Richtung: in unsere Richtung our way [aʊə 'weɪ]; **in Richtung auf** towards [tə'wɔːdz]
riechen smell [smel]
Rockband rock band ['rɒk bænd]
Rollschuhe skates [skeɪts]; **Rollschuhlaufen** skating ['skeɪtɪŋ]
rosa pink [pɪŋk]
rot red [red]

[g] **g**o [ŋ] mornin**g** [l] **l**ike [r] **r**uler [v] se**v**en [w] **w**e [s] **s**ix [z] hi**s** [ʃ] **sh**e [tʃ] tea**ch**er [dʒ] **j**eans

Ruf: (An-)Ruf (phone)call [('fəʊn)kɔ:l]
rufen shout [ʃaʊt]
Rugby rugby ['rʌgbi]
ruhig quiet ['kwaɪət]
Rundfunk radio ['reɪdiəʊ]

S

Sache thing [θɪŋ]
Sack bag [bæg]
Saft: (Frucht-)Saft fruit juice ['fru:t dʒu:s]
Sage legend ['ledʒənd]
sagen say [seɪ]; **man sagt** they say [ðeɪ 'seɪ]
Saison season ['si:zn]
Salat: (Kopf-)Salat lettuce ['letɪs]
sammeln: (ein)sammeln collect [kə'lekt]
Samstag Saturday ['sætədeɪ]; **am Samstag** on Saturday [ɒn 'sætədeɪ]
Sand sand [sænd]; **Sand-** sandy ['sændi]
sandig sandy ['sændi]
Sandwich sandwich ['sænwɪdʒ]
Sänger/Sängerin singer ['sɪŋə]
Satz sentence ['sentəns]
sauber clean [kli:n]
saubermachen: (das) Saubermachen cleaning ['kli:nɪŋ]
Säule column ['kɒləm]
Sauna sauna ['sɔ:nə]
Schachtel packet ['pækɪt]
schade: Das ist schade. That's a pity. [ðæts ə 'pɪti]
Schaf sheep (*pl.:* sheep) [ʃi:p]
scharf, cool cool [ku:l]
Schatz: Du bist ein Schatz! You're a star! *(ugs.)* [jɔ:r ə 'stɑ:]
schauen look [lʊk]
scheinen seem [si:m]; **die Sonne scheint** the sun is shining [ðə sʌn iz 'ʃaɪnɪŋ]
Scherz joke [dʒəʊk]
schicken send [send]
schieben push [pʊʃ]
Schiff boat [bəʊt]; ship [ʃɪp]
Schild sign [saɪn]
schlafen sleep [sli:p]
Schlafen: (das) Schlafen sleeping ['sli:pɪŋ]
Schlafzimmer bedroom ['bedru:m]
schlagen hit [hɪt]
Schlager hit ['hɪt]
Schlagzeug drums [drʌmz] *(pl.)*
Schlagzeuger/Schlagzeugerin drummer ['drʌmə]
schlau clever ['klevə]
schlecht: nicht schlecht not bad [nɒt 'bæd]; **schlecht in** bad at ['bæd ət]; **schlechter** worse [wɜ:s]; **der/die/das schlechteste** the worst [ðə 'wɜ:st]
schließen close [kləʊz]
schlimmer worse [wɜ:s]; **der/die/das schlimmste** the worst [ðə 'wɜ:st]
Schlittschuhlaufen skating ['skeɪtɪŋ]
Schloss castle ['kɑ:sl]
schlucken: Feuer schlucken eat fire [i:t 'faɪə]
Schlüssel key [ki:]
Schnee snow [snəʊ]
schneiden: in Stücke schneiden cut ... in pieces [kʌt ɪn 'pi:sɪz]
schneien snow [snəʊ]
schnell quick [kwɪk]; fast [fɑ:st]; **schnell fahren** speed [spi:d]
Schnur string [strɪŋ]
Schokolade chocolate ['tʃɒklət]; **heiße Schokolade** hot chocolate [hɒt 'tʃɒklət]
schon already [ɔ:l'redi]; **schon einmal** before [bɪ'fɔ:]
schön: (wunder)schön beautiful ['bju:tɪfəl]; **wird sehr schön sein** will be very nice [wɪl bi: verɪ 'naɪs]
Schottenrock kilt [kɪlt]
schottisch Scottish ['skɒtɪʃ]; **schottisches Gericht aus Schafsinnereien** haggis ['hægɪs]
Schottland Scotland ['skɒtlənd]
Schrank cupboard ['kʌbəd]
schrecklich terrible ['terəbl]
schreiben write [raɪt]; **eine Liste schreiben** make a list [meɪk ə 'lɪst]: **Schreiben** writing ['raɪtɪŋ]
Schreibung: (Recht-)Schreibung spelling ['spelɪŋ]
Schreibweise spelling ['spelɪŋ]
schreien shout [ʃaʊt]
Schulausflug (school)trip [trɪp]
Schule school [sku:l]; **in der Schule** at school [ət 'sku:l]; **Schule für 11- bis 14-Jährige** middle school ['mɪdl sku:l]
Schüler/Schülerin student ['stju:dnt]; pupil ['pju:pl]
Schulfach subject ['sʌbdʒɪkt]
Schulleiter/Schulleiterin principal ['prɪnsɪpl] *(AE)*
Schützer pad [pæd]
schwach poor [pɔ:]
schwarz black [blæk]
Schwein pig [pɪg]
schwer difficult ['dɪfɪkəlt]
Schwerkraft gravity ['grævɪti]
Schwester sister ['sɪstə]
schwierig difficult ['dɪfɪkəlt]; **schwierig(er)** hard(er) [hɑ:d]
Schwierigkeiten trouble ['trʌbl]
Schwimmbad swimming pool ['swɪmɪŋ pu:l]
Schwimmbecken swimming pool ['swɪmɪŋ pu:l]
schwimmen swim [swɪm]
Schwimmen: (das) Schwimmen swimming ['swɪmɪŋ]
sechs six [sɪks]; **sechste(r, s)** sixth [sɪksθ]
sechzehn sixteen [sɪk'sti:n]; **sechzehnte(r, s)** sixteenth [sɪks'ti:nθ]
sechzig sixty ['sɪksti]
See: (Binnen-)See lake [leɪk]; **die See** sea [si:]
segeln sail [seɪl]
sehen see [si:]
Sehenswürdigkeit sight [saɪt]; **Besichtigung von Sehenswürdigkeiten** sightseeing ['saɪtsi:ɪŋ]
sehr very ['veri]; really ['rɪəli]
Seifenoper: (TV-)Seifenoper soap ['səʊp]
sein be [bi]
sein/seine its [ɪts]; his [hɪz]; **auf der linken Seite** on the left [ɒn ðə 'left]
Seite page *(Buch)* [peɪdʒ]; side [saɪd]
Sekunde second ['sekənd]
selbstverständlich of course [əf 'kɔ:s]
seltsam strange [streɪndʒ]
senden send [send]
Sendung: (Fernseh-)Sendung programme ['prəʊgræm]; **(Fernseh-, Radio-)Sendung** show [ʃəʊ]
September September [sep'tembə]
Service service ['sɜ:vɪs]
setzen: sich setzen sit [sɪt]; **Setz dich hierhin.** Sit here. [sɪt 'hɪə]
Shake milkshake ['mɪlkʃeɪk]
Sheriff Sheriff ['ʃerɪf]
sicher safe [seɪf]; **sicher sein** be sure [bi 'ʃʊə]

[j] yes [θ] thing [ð] the [i:] he [ɑ:] car [ɔ:] or [u:] too [ɜ:] girl [i] sorry [u] July [ɪ] big [e] yes

sie she [ʃiː]; they [ðeɪ]; them [ðem]; **Sie** you [juː]; **sie ist** she's (= she is) [ʃiːz]; **sie sind** they're (= they are) [ðeə]
Sie: Sie sind you're (= you are) [jʊə]
sieben seven ['sevn]; **siebte(r, s)** seventh ['sevnθ]
siebzehn seventeen [sevn'tiːn]; **siebzehnte(r, s)** seventeenth [sevn'tiːnθ]
siebzig seventy ['sevnti]
siegen win [wɪn]
Sieger/Siegerin winner ['wɪnə]
sind: sind nicht aren't (= are not) ['ɑːnt]; **Sind sie ...?** Are they ...? [ɑː ðeɪ]
singen sing [sɪŋ]
Situation situation [sɪtʃu'eɪʃn]
sitzen sit [sɪt]
Skateboard skateboard ['skeɪtbɔːd]; board [bɔːd]; **Skateboard fahren** skate [skeɪt]; **zum Skateboarden gehen** go skateboarding [gəʊ 'skeɪtbɔːdɪŋ]
Skateboardfahrer/Skateboardfahrerin skateboarder ['skeɪtbɔːdə]; boarder ['bɔːdə]
„skaten" skate [skeɪt]
Skilaufen: (das) Skilaufen skiing ['skiːɪŋ]
Skisport skiing ['skiːɪŋ]
Slogan slogan ['sləʊgən]
SMS-Nachricht text message ['tekst mesɪdʒ]
Snack snack [snæk]
Snowboard: Snowboard fahren snowboarding ['snəʊbɔːdɪŋ]
snowboarden snowboarding ['snəʊbɔːdɪŋ]
so so [səʊ]; **nicht so beliebt wie ...** not so popular as ... [nɒt səʊ 'pɒpjʊlə æz]; **Mach(t) es so.** Do it this way. [duː ɪt 'ðɪs weɪ]
Socke sock [sɒk]
Sofa couch [kaʊtʃ]
Software software ['sɒftweə]
Sohn son [sʌn]
solange as long as [æz 'lɒŋ əz]
sollte: sollte/solltest/sollten/solltet should [ʃʊd]
Solo solo ['səʊləʊ]
Sommer summer ['sʌmə]
Sonderangebot special offer [speʃl 'ɒfə]
sonderbar strange [streɪndʒ]
Sonnabend Saturday ['sætədeɪ]; **am Sonnabend** on Saturday [ɒn 'sætədeɪ]
Sonne sun [sʌn]; **die Sonne scheint** the sun is shining [ðə sʌn ɪz 'ʃaɪnɪŋ]
sonnig sunny ['sʌni]
Sonntag Sunday ['sʌndeɪ]; **am Sonntag** on Sundays [ɒn 'sʌndeɪz]; **sonntags** on Sundays [ɒn 'sʌndeɪz]
sonst: Sonst noch etwas? Anything else? [eniθɪŋ 'els]
Sorge: Mach dir keine Sorgen. Don't worry. ['dəʊnt wʌri]
sorgfältig careful ['keəfl]
Sorte brand [brænd]; kind [kaɪnd]
Soße sauce [sɔːs]
Souvenir souvenir [suːvə'nɪə]
Spagetti spaghetti [spə'geti]
Spanien Spain [speɪn]
spannend exciting [ɪk'saɪtɪŋ]
sparen save [seɪv]
Sparkasse bank [bæŋk]
Spaß fun [fʌn]; **nur so zum Spaß** just for fun [dʒʌst fə 'fʌn]; **Spaß machen** be fun [bi fʌn]
spät late [leɪt]; **bis spät** till late [tɪl leɪt]; **er kommt zu spät** he is late [hiː ɪz 'leɪt]; **Lieber spät als gar nicht.** Better late than never. [betə 'leɪt ðən 'nevə]; **Wie spät ist es?** What time is it? [wɒt 'taɪm ɪz ɪt]; **Bis später.** See you later. [siː ju 'leɪtə]; **später** ['leɪtə]
spazieren: spazieren gehen walk [wɔːk]; **mit dem Hund spazierengehen** take the dog for a walk ['teɪk ðə dɒg fə ə wɔːk]
Spazierfahrt: eine Spazierfahrt machen go out in the car [gəʊ aʊt ɪn ðə 'kɑː]
Spaziergang walk [wɔːk]
Speicher memory ['meməri]
speien: Feuer speien eat fire [iːt 'faɪə]
Spiel game [geɪm]; match [mætʃ]
spielen play [pleɪ]; **ein Instrument spielen** play an instrument [pleɪ ən 'ɪnstrəmənt]; **spielen: Hast du mit ... gespielt?** Did you play with ...? [dɪd ju pleɪ wɪð]
Spieler: (mp3-)Spieler (MP3) player [(empiː'θriː)'pleɪə]
Spielkonsole games console ['geɪmz 'kɒnsəʊl]
Spielzeug toy [tɔɪ]
Spitze: an der Spitze at the top [æt ðə 'tɒp]; **an der Spitze (von)** at the top (of) [ət ðə 'tɒp (əv)]
Sport sport [spɔːt]; **verrückt nach Sport** crazy about sport ['kreɪzi əbaʊt 'spɔːt]; **Sport treiben** play sport [pleɪ 'spɔːt]
Sporthalle gym [dʒɪm]
sportlich sporty ['spɔːti]
Sportzentrum sports centre ['spɔːts sentə]
Sprache language ['læŋgwɪdʒ]
sprechen speak [spiːk]; **sprechen über** talk about ['tɔːk əbaʊt]
Spülbecken sink [sɪŋk]
spülen wash up [wɒʃ 'ʌp]
Staat: (Bundes-)Staat state [steɪt]
Stadt town [taʊn]; city ['sɪti]; **in die (Innen-)Stadt fahren** go to town [gəʊ tə 'taʊn]
Stadtplan map [mæp]
Stadtzentrum downtown ['daʊntaʊn] *(AE)*
Stand: (Verkaufs-)Stand stall [stɔːl]
Standbesitzer/in stallholder ['stɔːlhəʊldə]
Star star [stɑː]; idol ['aɪdl]
stark strong [strɒŋ]; **stark, cool** cool [kuːl]
starren: (an)starren stare [stæe]
Start start [stɑːt]
starten start [stɑːt]
Startseite home page ['həʊm peɪdʒ]
Statue statue ['stætʃuː]
Stau traffic jam ['træfɪk dʒæm]
Staubsauger vacuum cleaner ['vækjuəm kliːnə]
stehen stand [stænd]; **aufrecht stehen** stand up [stænd 'ʌp]; **sie stehen** they're standing [ðeə 'stændɪŋ]
stehlen steal [stiːl]
steigern raise [reɪz]
Stein rock [rɒk]
Stelle place [pleɪs]; job *(Arbeit)* [dʒɒb]
stellen: stellen (auf) put (on) [pʊt ɒn]
sterben die [daɪ]
Steuer tax [tæks]
Sticker sticker ['stɪkə]
Stiefmutter stepmother ['stepmʌðə]
Stiefvater stepfather ['stepfɑːðə]
Stil style [staɪl]
still still [stɪl]; quiet ['kwaɪət]
Stimme voice [vɔɪs]
stimmen: Stimmt. You're right. [jɔː 'raɪt]

[æ] cat [ʌ] bus [ɒ] dog [ʊ] put [ə] again [eɪ] name [aɪ] time [ɔɪ] boy [əʊ] no [aʊ] house [ɪə] here

Stinktier skunk [skʌŋk]
stolz proud [praʊd]
stoßen hit [hɪt]
Strand beach [bi:tʃ]
Straße road [rəʊd]; street [stri:t]
Straßenbahn tram [træm]
Strecke line [laɪn]
Struktur structure ['strʌktʃə]
Strumpf sock [sɒk]
Stück piece [pi:s]; **in Stücke schneiden** cut ... in pieces [kʌt ɪn 'pi:sɪz]
Student/in student ['stju:dnt]
studieren study ['stʌdi]
Stuhl chair [tʃeə]
Stunde hour ['aʊə]; **(Unterrichts-)Stunde** lesson ['lesn]
Stundenplan timetable ['taɪmteɪbl]
stürmisch stormy ['stɔ:mi]
stürzen fall [fɔ:l]
suchen look for ['lʊk fə]; **(durch)suchen** search [sɜ:tʃ]; **um Arbeit/Essen/... zu suchen** for work/food/... [fə 'wɜ:k 'fu:d]
Süchtige/r addict ['ædɪkt]
super super ['su:pə]; **super in** great at ['greɪt ət]
Supermarkt supermarket ['su:pəma:kɪt]
Suppe soup [su:p]
surfen: im Internet surfen surf the Internet [sɜ:f ði 'ɪntənet]
süß sweet [swi:t]
Süßigkeit sweet [swi:t]
Sweatshirt sweatshirt ['swetʃɜ:t]
Szene scene [si:n]

T

T-Shirt T-shirt ['ti:ʃɜ:t]
Tafel board [bɔ:d]
Tag day [deɪ]; **eines Tages** one day [wʌn 'dei]; **jeden Tag** every day [evri 'deɪ]; **besonderer Tag** special day ['speʃl deɪ]; **Guten Tag. (nachmittags)** Good afternoon. [gʊd a:ftə'nu:n]
Tagebuch diary ['daɪəri]
Tagesablauf timetable ['taɪmteɪbl]
Tagesausflug: einen Tagesausflug machen have a day out [hæv ə deɪ 'aʊt]
Tageskarte travelcard ['trævlka:d]
Tal valley ['væli]
Tante aunt [a:nt]
Tanz dance [da:ns]
Tanzen: (das) Tanzen dancing ['da:nsɪŋ]
tanzen dance [da:ns]
Tänzer/Tänzerin dancer ['da:nsə]
Tanzveranstaltung dance [da:ns]
Tapete wallpaper ['wɔ:lpeɪpə]
tapfer brave [breɪv]
Tasche pocket ['pɒkɪt]; **(Schul-)Tasche** bag [bæg]
Taschengeld pocket money ['pɒkɪt mʌni]
Taschenlampe torch [tɔ:tʃ]
Taschenrechner calculator ['kælkjuleɪtə]
Tatsache fact [fækt]
taugen: Dein Team/Deine Mannschaft taugt nichts. Your team is no good. [jɔ: 'ti:m ɪz nəʊ 'gʊd]
tausend thousand ['θaʊznd]
Tausende thousands ['θaʊzəndz]
Taxi taxi ['tæksi]
Team team [ti:m]
Techniker/Technikerin engineer [endʒɪ'nɪə]
Teddybär teddy bear ['tedi beə]
Tee tea [ti:]
Teenager teenager ['ti:neɪdʒə]; **Teenager-, für/von Teenager** teenage ['ti:neɪdʒ]
Teil part [pa:t]
Telefon telephone ['telɪfəʊn]
Telefonbuch phone book ['fəʊn bʊk]
Teller plate [pleɪt]
Temperatur temperature ['temprətʃə]
Tennis tennis ['tenɪs]
Test test [test]
testen test [test]
teuer: zu teuer too expensive [tu: ɪk'spensɪv]
Text text [tekst]
Theater theatre ['θɪətə]
Thema issue ['ɪʃju:, 'ɪsju:]
tief deep [di:p]
Tier animal ['ænɪml]
Tierhandlung pet shop ['pet ʃɒp]
Tipp tip [tɪp]
Tisch table ['teɪbl]
Tischgebet grace [greɪs]
Tischtennis table tennis ['teɪbl tenɪs]
Titel title ['taɪtl]
Toast toast [təʊst]
Tochter daughter ['dɔ:tə]
Toilette toilet ['tɔɪlət]
toll great [greɪt]; super ['su:pə]; terrific [tə'rɪfɪk]; fantastic [fæn'tæstɪk]
Tomate tomato *(pl.* -oes) [tə'ma:təʊ]
Tonfall intonation [ɪntə'neɪʃn]
Tor gate [geɪt]; goal [gəʊl]
töten kill [kɪl]
Tourismus tourism ['tʊərɪzəm]
Tourist/Touristin tourist ['tʊərɪst]
Tradition tradition [trə'dɪʃn]
tragen wear *(Kleidung)* [weə]; carry ['kæri]
Tram tram [træm]
Transport transport ['trænspɔ:t] *(no pl)*
Traum dream [dri:m]
treffen meet [met]; hit [hɪt]; **sich treffen (mit)** meet [mi:t]
Trick trick [trɪk]
trinken drink [drɪŋk]; have [hæv]
trocken dry [draɪ]
Trödelmarkt car-boot sale [ka: 'bu:t seɪl]
trotzen defy [dɪ'faɪ]
Tschüs Cheers [tʃɪəz]; Bye(-bye). [baɪ, bə 'baɪ]
tun do [du:]
Tür door [dɔ:]
Türkei Turkey ['tɜ:ki]
Turnhalle gym [dʒɪm]
Tüte bag [bæg]
typisch typical ['tɪpɪkl]

U

U-Bahn underground ['ʌndəgraʊnd]; tube *(besonders in London)* [tju:b]
übel sick [sɪk]
üben practise ['præktɪs]
über above [ə'bʌv]; about [ə'baʊt]; over ['əʊvə]; **(quer) über** across [ə'krɒs]; 'cross (= across) [krɒs (ə'krɒs)]; **sprechen über** talk about ['tɔ:k əbaʊt]
überall all over [ɔ:l 'əʊvə]; everywhere ['evriweə]
übereinstimmen agree [ə'gri:]
Überflieger economy flyer [ɪ'kɒnəmi flaɪə]
übernachten: Wir übernachteten (bei) we stayed (with) [steɪd]
überprüfen check [tʃek]
überqueren cross [krɒs]
überrascht surprised [sə'praɪzd]
Überraschung surprise [sə'praɪz]

[eə] chair [ʊə] sure [b] bike [p] pen [d] day [t] ten [k] book [g] go [ŋ] morning [l] like [r] ruler

Überschrift title ['taɪtl]
Überziehen: das Überziehen der Parkzeit late parking [leɪt 'pɑ:kɪŋ]
Übung exercise ['eksəsaɪz]
Uhr clock [klɒk]; **zwei Uhr** two o'clock [tu: ə'klɒk]; **um ... Uhr** at ... o'clock [ət ,,, ə'klɒk]
Uhrzeit time [taɪm]
ultra ultra ['ʌltrə]
um ... herum round [raʊnd]
umbringen kill [kɪl]
umdrehen: (sich) umdrehen turn [tɜ:n]
Umfrage report [rɪ'pɔ:t]
umziehen: ihre Famile ist umgezogen their family has moved [ðeə 'fæmɪli həz 'mu:vd]
umher around [ə'raʊnd]
und and [ænd]
Unfall accident ['æksɪdənt]
unfreundlich unfriendly [ʌn'frendli]
ungefähr about [ə'baʊt]
Ungeheuer monster ['mɒnstə]
ungeheuer: ungeheuer groß enormous [ɪ'nɔ:məs]
unglücklich unlucky [ʌn'lʌki]ə]
unglücklich unhappy [ʌn'hæpi]
Uniform uniform ['ju:nɪfɔ:m]
uns us [ʌs]
unser/unsere our ['aʊə]
unten below [bɪ'ləʊ]
unter under ['ʌndə]; below [bɪ'ləʊ]; **unter null Grad Celsius** below 0 °C [bɪ'ləʊ 'zɪərəʊ dɪ'gri:z 'selsiəs]
unterhalb (von) below [bɪ'ləʊ]
unterhalten: sich unterhalten wollen want a word [wɒnt ə 'wɜ:d]
Unternehmen company ['kʌmpəni]
Unterschied: (Zeit-)Unterschied (time)difference ['taɪm dɪfrəns]
unterwegs on the way [ɒn ðə 'weɪ]
Ureinwohner: amerikanische Ureinwohner Native Americans ['neɪtɪv ə'merɪkənz]
Urlaub holiday ['hɒlədeɪ]; vacation [və'keɪʃn] *(AE)*; **im Urlaub** on holiday [ɒn 'hɒlɪdeɪ]; **in Urlaub gehen/fahren** go on holiday [gəʊ ɒn 'hɒlədeɪ]
USA USA [ju: es 'eɪ]

V

Vater father ['fɑ:ðə]
Vati dad [dæd]
verändern change [tʃeɪndʒ]
verängstigt sein be frightened [bi 'fraɪtənd]
veranstalten organise ['ɔ:gənaɪz]
Veranstaltung event [ɪ'vent]
Verb verb [vɜ:b]
verbergen conceal [kən'si:l]
Verbindung link [lɪŋk]; **sich in Verbindung setzen mit** contact ['kɒntækt]; **das Verbindungskabel anschließen** fix the hook-ups [fɪks ðə 'hʊkʌps]
Verbrechen crime [kraɪm]
verbringen spend (time/money) [spend]
verdienen earn [ɜ:n]
verehren admire [əd'maɪə]
Verein club [klʌb]
vereinigt: die Vereinigten Staaten USA [ju: es 'eɪ]; **Vereinigtes Königreich** United Kingdom (UK) [junaɪtɪd 'kɪŋdəm]
Vergangenheit history ['hɪstri]; past [pɑ:st]
vergessen: Vergesst/Vergiss nicht! Don't forget! [dəʊnt fə'get]
verheimlichen conceal [kən'si:l]
verkaufen sell [sel]
Verkehr traffic ['træfɪk]; transport ['trænspɔ:t]
verlassen leave [left]; **das Haus verlassen** leave the house ['li:v ðə haʊs]
verletzt hurt [hɜ:t]
verlieren lose [lu:z]; **Verloren im Irrgarten.** Lost in the maze. [lɒst ɪn ðə 'meɪz]
vermischen: alles miteinander vermischen mix everything ['mɪks evriθɪŋ]
vermissen miss [mɪs]
vermuten expect [ɪk'spekt]
vernünftig: Sei(d) mal vernünftig! Grow up! ['grəʊ ʌp]
verpassen miss [mɪs]
verreisen go away [gəʊ ə'weɪ]; **verreist** away [ə'weɪ]
verrückt: verrückt nach mad about [mæd ə'baʊt]; **verrückt nach Sport** crazy about sport ['kreɪzi əbaʊt 'spɔ:t]
verschicken: als E-Mail verschicken email ['i:meɪl]
verschieden different ['dɪfrənt]
Verschmutzung: (Umwelt-)Verschmutzung pollution [pə'lu:ʃn]
verschneit snowy ['snəʊi]
verspäten: sich verspäten run late [rʌn 'leɪt]; **er verspätet sich** he is late [hi: ɪz 'leɪt]
Verspätung: Verspätung haben run late [rʌn 'leɪt]
verstehen understand [ʌndə'stænd]
Versuch experiment [ɪk'sperɪmənt]
versuchen try [traɪ]
Vertrieb distribution [dɪstrɪ'bju:ʃn]
verursachen cause [kɔ:z]
Verwandte/Verwandter relative ['relətɪv]
verwegen keen [ki:n]
verwenden use [ju:z]
Video video ['vɪdiəʊ]
Videorekorder video recorder ['vɪdiəʊ rɪ'kɔ:də]
Videospiel video game ['vɪdi:eʊ geɪm]
viel much [mʌtʃ]; **viel Glück** good luck [gʊd 'lʌk]; **wie viel?** how much? [haʊ 'mʌtʃ]; **viel, viele** lots (of) ['lɒts əv]; a lot of [ə 'lɒt əv]; **viele** many ['meni]; **wie viele?** how many? [haʊ 'meni]
vielleicht perhaps [pə'hæps]; **vielleicht werden** may [meɪ]
vier four [fɔ:]
vierte(r, s) fourth (= 4th) [fɔ:θ]
Viertel: Viertel vor/nach ... quarter to/past ['kwɔ:tə tə/pɑ:st]
vierzehn fourteen [fɔ:'ti:n]; **vierzehnte(r, s)** fourteenth [fɔ:'ti:nθ]
vierzig forty ['fɔ:ti]
Vogel bird [bɜ:d]
voll: voll (mit, von) full of ['fʊl əv]ə; **die Nase voll haben** be fed up [bi fed 'ʌp]
Volleyball volleyball ['vɒlibɔ:l]
von from [frɒm]; **von ... bis** from ... till [frəm ,,, tɪl]; **von ... bis** from ... to [frəm, tə]
vor in front of [ɪn 'frʌnt əv]; before [bɪ'fɔ:]; ago [ə'gəʊ]; **Viertel vor** quarter to/past ['kwɔ:tə tə/pɑ:st]
vorbeifahren pass [pɑ:s]
vorbeifliegen fly by [flaɪ 'baɪ]
vorbeigehen pass [pɑ:s]
vorbeiziehen pass [pɑ:s]
Vorhaben plan [plæn]

[v] seven [w] we [s] six [z] his [ʃ] she [tʃ] teacher [dʒ] jeans [j] yes [θ] thing [ð] the [i:] he

Vorhang curtain ['kɜ:tn]
vormittags a.m. [eɪ'em]
Vorort suburb ['sʌbɜ:b]
Vorschrift rule [ru:l]
vorsichtig careful ['keəfl]
vorspielen act [ækt]
Vorstellung idea [aɪ'dɪə]
vorüberfliegen fly by [flaɪ 'baɪ]
Vorwahl dialling code ['daɪəlɪŋ kəʊd]

W

Wachsfiguren(kabinett) waxworks ['wækswɜ:ks]
Wagen: (Pferde-)Wagen waggon ['wægən]
wählen: (aus)wählen choose [tʃɔ:z]; dial [daɪəl]
Wahnsinn! Wow! [waʊ]
wahr true [tru:]
Wald forest ['fɒrəst]; wood [wʊd]
Wales Wales [weɪlz]
walisisch; (die) Waliser Welsh [welʃ]
Walkman Walkman ['wɔ:kmən]
Wanderer hiker ['haɪkə]
wandern hike [haɪk]
wann when [wen]; **Wann bist du geboren?** When were you born? ['wen wə ju bɔ:n]
warm warm [wɔ:m]
warten wait [weɪt]
warum why [waɪ]; **Warum nicht?** Why not? [waɪ 'nɒt]
was: was für what kind of [wɒt 'kaɪnd əv]; **Was für ein/eine ...** What a ... [wɒt ə]; **Was geht hier vor?** What's happening? [wɒts 'hæpənɪŋ]; **Was ist ...?** What's? [wɒts]; **Was ist denn (los)?** What's the matter? [wɒts ðə 'mætə]; **Was ist los?** What's happening? [wɒts 'hæpənɪŋ]; **Was kannst du ...?** What can you? [wɒt kən ju]; **Was kostet das?** How much is it? [haʊ 'mʌtʃ ɪz ɪt]; **Was würdest du gern ...?** What would you like ...? ['wɒt wʊd ju laɪk]
Waschbecken sink [sɪŋk]
waschen: sich waschen have a wash [həv ə 'wɒʃ]
Wasser water ['wɔ:tə]
Wassersport water sports ['wɔ:tə spɔ:ts]
Webcam, Webcamera webcam ['webkæm]
Website website ['web saɪt]
wechseln change [tʃeɪndʒ]; **ein Wort wechseln wollen** want a word [wɒnt ə 'wɜ:d]
wecken wake [weɪk]
Wecker alarm clock [ə'lɑ:m klɒk]
Weg path [pɑ:θ]; **auf dem Weg** on the way [ɒn ðə 'weɪ]; **den Weg kennen** know the way [nəʊ ðə 'weɪ]
weg away [ə'weɪ]; **weit weg** far away [fɑ:r ə'weɪ]
Weihnachten Christmas ['krɪsməs]
Weihnachtstag: der 1. Weihnachtstag Christmas Day ['krɪsməs deɪ]
weil because [bɪ'kɒz]
weinen: ich werde ewig weinen I'm forever crying [aɪm fərevə 'kraɪɪŋ]
Weise way [weɪ]
weiß white [waɪt]
weit far [fɑ:]; **weit weg** far away [fɑ:r ə'weɪ]
weitere other ['ʌðə]; **ein/e weitere(r, s)** another [ə'nʌðə]
welche(r, s) which [wɪtʃ]; what [wɒt]
Welpe puppy ['pʌpi]
Welt world [wɜ:ld]
weltweit world wide [wɜ:ld 'waɪd]
wenden turn [tɜ:n]
wenig: ein wenig a little [ə 'lɪtl]; **wenige** few [fju:]; **weniger** less [les]
wenn when [wen]
wer who [hu:]; **wer ist** who's (= who is) [hu:z]; **Wer ist es?** Who is it? [hu: 'ɪz ɪt]
Werbeprospekt leaflet ['li:flət]
Werbespruch slogan ['sləʊgən]
werden will [wɪl]; become [bɪ'kʌm]; **vielleicht werden** may [meɪ]; **Wir werden keine Zeit haben.** We won't (= will not) have time. [wi wəʊnt hæv 'taɪm]; **werden/wird nicht** won't (= will not) [wəʊnt]; **wird sehr schön sein** will be very nice [wɪl bi: verɪ 'naɪs]
Werkzeug tool [tu:l]
Westen west [west]
Wettbewerb competition [kɒmpə'tɪʃn]
Wette: um die Wette laufen have a race [reɪs]; race against [reɪs ə'geɪnst]
Wetter weather ['weðə]
Wettkampf match [mætʃ]
Wettlauf race [reɪs]
Whisky whisky ['wɪski]
wichtig important [ɪm'pɔ:tnt]
widersetzen: sich widersetzen defy [dɪ'faɪ]
wie how [haʊ]; **(sein/aussehen) wie** be like [bi 'laɪk]; **(genau)so gut wie** as good as [æz 'gʊd əz]; **(genau)so freundlich wie** as friendly as [əz 'frendli əz]; **nicht so beliebt wie ...** not so popular as ... [nɒt səʊ 'pɒpjʊlə æz]; **Wie alt bist du?** How old are you? [haʊ 'əʊld ə ju:]; **Wie bitte?** Pardon? ['pɑ:dən]; **Wie geht es dir/euch/Ihnen?** How are you? [haʊ ə 'ju:]; **Wie geht's?** How are things? *(ugs.)* [həʊ ə 'θɪŋz]; **Wie heißt du?** What's your name? [wɒts jɔ: 'neɪm]; **Wie ist/war/waren ...?** What is/was/were ... like? [wɒt ɪz, wɒz 'laɪk]; **Wie läuft's?** How are things? *(ugs.)* [həʊ ə 'θɪŋz]; **Wie spät ist es?** What time is it? [wɒt 'taɪm ɪz ɪt]; **wie viel?** how much? [haʊ 'mʌtʃ]; **wie viele?** how many? [haʊ 'meni]; **Wie wäre es mit ...?** What about ...? [wɒt ə'baʊt]
wieder again [ə'gen]; **hin und wieder** every now and then [everi naʊ ənd 'ðen]
Wiese field [fi:ld]
wild wild [waɪld]
Willkommen! Welcome! ['welkəm]
Wind wind [wɪnd]
windig windy ['wɪndi]
Winter winter ['wɪntə]
wir we [wi:]; **wir sind** we're (= we are) [wɪə]
wirklich really ['rɪəli]
Wissenschaft: (Natur-)Wissenschaft science ['saɪəns]
Witz joke [dʒəʊk]
witzig funny ['fʌni]
wo where [weə]; **Wo ist der/die/das nächst(e) ...?** Where's the nearest ...? [wəz ðe 'nɪərɪst]; **Wo kommst du her?** Where are you from? [weə ə ju: 'frɒm]
Woche week [wi:k]
Wochenende weekend [wi:k'end]
Wochentag weekday ['wi:kdeɪ]
wohnen live [lɪv]; **Wohnt dein Cousin/deine Kusine ...?** Does your cousin live ...? [dʌz jʊə kʌzn 'lɪv]; **wir wohnten (bei)** we stayed (with) [steɪd]

[ɑ:] car [ɔ:] or [u:] too [ɜ:] girl [i] sorry [u] July [ɪ] big [e] yes [æ] cat [ʌ] bus [ɒ] dog [ʊ] put

Wohnmobil motorhome ['məʊɪtəhəʊm]
Wohnung flat [flæt]
Wohnwagen-Campingplatz caravan park ['kærəvæn pɑ:k]
Wohnzimmer living room ['lɪvɪŋru:m]
Wolke cloud [klaʊd]
wolkig cloudy ['klaʊdi]
wollen want [wɒnt]
Wort word [wɜ:d]; **ein Wort fehlt** one word is missing [wʌn wɜ:d ɪz 'mɪsɪŋ]; **ein Wort wechseln wollen** want a word [wɒnt ə 'wɜ:d]
Wörterbuch dictionary ['dɪkʃənri]
wunderbar terrific [tə'rɪfɪk]
wünschen: Ich wünschte, du wärst hier. Wish you were here. ['wɪʃ ju wə hɪe]
würde: Was würdest du gern ...? What would you like ...? ['wɒt wʊd ju laɪk]
Wurst sausage ['sɒsɪdʒ]
Würstchen sausage ['sɒsɪdʒ]
wütend angry ['æŋgri]

Z

Zahl number ['nʌmbə]
zahlen: zahlen (für) pay (for) ['peɪ fə]
zählen count [kaʊnt]
Zähne teeth [ti:θ]
Zaubershow magic show ['mædʒɪk ʃəʊ]
zehn ten [ten]
zehnte(r, s) tenth ['tenθ]
zeigen show [ʃəʊ]; **Zeig(t) es mir bitte.** Show me, please. ['ʃəʊ mi pli:z]
Zeit time [taɪm]; **Zeit haben** have time [həv 'taɪm]; **Wir werden keine Zeit haben.** We won't (= will not) have time. [wi wəʊnt hæv 'taɪm]
Zeitschrift magazine [mægə'zi:n]
Zeitung newspaper ['nju:zpeɪpə]
Zelt tent [tent]
zentral, Zentral- central ['sentrəl]
Zentrum centre ['sentə]
zerbrechen break [breɪk]; **zerbrochen** broken ['brəʊkn]
Zeug stuff [stʌf]; **altes Zeug** junk [dʒʌŋk] *(AE)*
ziehen: (um)ziehen move *(Wohnort)* [mu:v]
ziemlich quite [kwaɪt]
Zigeuner/Zigeunerin gypsy ['dʒɪpsi]
Zimmer room [ru:m]; **Zimmer mit Frühstück** B&B (Bed & Breakfast) [bed ənd 'brekfəst]
zirka: (um) zirka at about [ə'baʊt]
Zoo zoo [zu:]
zu to [tu]; closed *(geschlossen)* [kləʊzd]; **ab und zu** every now and then [everi naʊ ənd 'ðen]; **bei ... zu Hause** at ... house [ət haʊs]; **zu teuer** too expensive [tu: ɪk'spensɪv]
zuerst first [fɜ:st]; at first [ət 'fɜ:st]
Zug train [treɪn]; **im Zug/Bus/...** on the train/bus/... [ɒn ðə 'treɪn 'bʌs]
Zugabe extra ['ekstrə]
Zukunft future ['fju:tʃə]
zulächeln: jemandem (jdm.) zulächeln smile at somebody (sb.) ['smaɪl ət sʌmbədi]
zumachen close [kləʊz]
zurück back [bæk]
zurückkehren return [rɪ'tɜ:n]
zurückkommen/-finden get back [get 'bæk]
zurücklegbar walkable ['wɔ:kəbl]
zurücktreten retire [rɪ'taɪə]
zurückziehen: sich zurückziehen retire [rɪ'taɪə]
zusammen together [tə'geðə]
zusammensetzen put together [pʊt tə'geðə]
Zusatz extra ['ektrə]
zuschauen watch [wɒtʃ]
zusteigen get on [get 'ɒn]
zustimmen agree [ə'gri:]
zwanzig twenty ['twenti]; **zwanzigste(r, s)** twentieth ['twentiəθ]
zwei two [tu:]
zweimal twice [twaɪs]
zweite(r, s) second (= 2nd) ['sekənd]
zwischen between [bɪ'twi:n]
zwölf twelve [twelv]; **zwölfte(r s)** twelfth [twelθ]

[ə] again [eɪ] name [aɪ] time [ɔɪ] boy [əʊ] no [aʊ] house [ɪə] here [eə] chair [ʊə] sure [b] bike

Wichtige Wörter zur Grammatik

Grammatical terms	Grammatische Begriffe	Beispiele
noun	Nomen (Substantiv)	*car, town, school, sister, dog*
singular	Singular (Einzahl)	*a car, a school, a sister, a dog*
plural	Plural (Mehrzahl)	*some cars, a lot of schools*
verb	Verb (Tätigkeitswort)	*have, eat, goes, went*
infinitive	Infinitiv (Grundform)	*have, eat, go*
regular verb	regelmäßiges Verb	*repair → repaired*
irregular verb	unregelmäßiges Verb	*make → made*
modal verb	modales Hilfsverb	*must, have to, should*
article	Artikel (Begleiter)	*the, a/an*
adjective	Adjektiv (Eigenschaftswort)	*easy, small, big, quiet, good*
adverb	Adverb (Umstandswort)	*often, never, today, there*
preposition	Präposition (Verhältniswort)	*after, before, at, next to*
personal pronoun	Personalpronomen	*I, you, he, she, it, we, they*
conjunction	Konjunktion (Bindewort)	*and, but, so, because, when*

sentence	Satz	*I have a big car.*
question	Frage	*Do you have a car?* *Where did you buy your car?*
answer	Antwort	*Yes, I have. I bought it in Spain.*
phrase	Satzteil	*last year, at school*
word order	Wortstellung	

tense	Zeitform	
simple past	Präteritum (einfache Vergangenheit)	*He went home yesterday.*
simple present	Präsens (einfache Gegenwart)	*He goes home every day.*
present progressive	Verlaufsform der Gegenwart	*He's going home now.*
will-future	Futur	*He'll go home after school.*

LIST OF NAMES

GIRLS/WOMEN

Abbie	[æ'bi]
Alice	['ælɪs]
Amy	['eɪmi]
Ann	[æn]
Anna	['ænə]
Anne	[æn]
Belle	[bel]
Beth	[beθ]
Cindy	['sɪndi]
Claire	[kleə]
Daisy	['deɪzi]
Donna	['dɒnə]
Ella	['elə]
Emily	['emɪli]
Emma	['emə]
Erin	['erɪn]
Eve	[i:v]
Faye	[feɪ]
Grace	[greɪs]
Haley	['heɪli]
Heather	['heðə]
Holly	['hɒli]
Jenny	['dʒeni]
Jill	[dʒɪl]
Jo	[dʒəʊ]
Julie	['dʒu:li]
Karen	['kærən]
Kate	[keɪt]
Katie	['keɪti]
Kylie	['kaɪli]
Madonna	[mə'dɒnə]
Megan	['megən]
Pat	[pæt]
Rebecca	[rə'bekə]
Sally	['sæli]
Samantha	[sə'mænθə]
Sue	[su:]
Tamsin	[tæm'sɪn]
Tina	['ti:nə]

BOYS/MEN

Alan	['ælən]
Ben	[ben]
Bobby	['bɒbi]
Darris	['dærɪs]
Dave	[deɪv]
Dean	[di:n]
Freddie	['fredi]
Gary	['gæri]
Graham	['greɪəm]
Jack	[dʒæk]
Jake	[dʒeɪk]
Jamie	['dʒeɪmi]
Jody	['dʒəʊdi]
Joe	[dʒəʊ]
John	[dʒɒn]
Luke	[lu:k]
Mohammed	[mɒ'hæməd]
Paul	[pɔ:l]
Rick	[rɪk]
Sam	[sæm]
Tim	[tɪm]
Tom	[tɒm]

FAMILIES

Bates	[beɪts]
Evans	['evənz]
Fernandez	[fɜ:'nændez]
Gale	[geɪl]
Gray	[greɪ]
Green	[gri:n]
Hall	[hɔ:l]
Hill	[hɪl]
Inman	['ɪnmən]
Lang	[læŋ]
Miles	[maɪlz]
Murray	['mʌri]
Nelson	['nelsn]
Patel	[pə'tel]
Walker	['wɔ:kə]
Weston	['westən]

PLACES

Aberdare	['æbədeə]
America	[ə'merɪkə]
Baker Street	['beɪkə stri:t]
Brixton	['brɪkstn]
Camden Town	[kæmdən 'taʊn]
Cardiff	['kɑ:dɪf]
Chester	['tʃestə]
Chicago	[ʃɪ'kɑ:gəʊ]
Colorado	[kɒlə'rɑ:dəʊ]
Covent Garden	[kɒvənt 'gɑ:dn]
Denver	['denvə]
Detroit	[dɪ'trɔɪt]
Edinburgh	['edɪnbrə]
England	['ɪŋglənd]
Europe	['jʊərəp]
Glasgow	['glɑ:zgəʊ]
Greenbridge	['gri:nbrɪdʒ]
Greenville	['gri:nvɪl]
Highlands	[ðə 'haɪləndz]
Italy	['ɪtəli]
Loch Ness	[lɒk 'nes]
London	['lʌndən]
Manchester	['mæntʃɪstə]
Miami	[maɪ'æmi]
Michigan	['mɪʃɪgən]
New York	[nju: 'jɔ:k]
North Sea	[nɔ:θ 'si:]
Notting Hill	[nɒtɪŋ 'hɪl]
Pembroke	['pembrəʊk]
River Thames	[ðə rɪvə 'temz]
Scotland	['skɒtlənd]
Skerry Beach	[skeri 'bi:tʃ]
South Kensington	[saʊθ 'kenzɪŋtən]
South Wales	[saʊθ 'weɪlz]
Southfields	['saʊθfi:ldz]
Springfield	['sprɪŋfi:ld]
St. Louis	[sənt 'lu:ɪs]
Sundale	['sʌndeɪl]
Trinidad	['trɪnɪdæd]
UK	[ju:'keɪ]
United Kingdom	[jʊnaɪtɪd 'kɪŋdəm]
USA	[ju:es'eɪ]
Wales	[weɪlz]
Westminster	['westmɪnstə]
Wimbledon	['wɪmbldən]

OTHER NAMES

Auld Lang Syne	[ɔ:ld læŋ 'saɪn]
Barry Gates	[bæri 'geɪts]
Benjamin Zephaniah	[bendʒəmɪn zə'feɪniə]
Big Ben	[bɪg 'ben]
British Museum	[ðə brɪtɪʃ mjʊ'zi:əm]
Buckingham Palace	['bʌkɪŋəm 'pæləs]
Charles Dickens	[tʃɑ:lz 'dɪkɪnz]
Charlie Chaplin	[tʃɑ:li 'tʃæplɪn]
Crown Jewels	[ðə kraʊn 'dʒu:əlz]
Dash	[dæʃ]
Dave Blue	[deɪv 'blu:]
Dean Road	[di:n 'rəʊd]
Diwali	[dɪ'wɑ:li]
Eid	[i:d]
Eminem	['emɪnəm]
Greyfriars Bobby	[greɪfraɪəz 'bɒbi]
Hampton Court Palace	[hæmptn kɔ:t 'pæləs]
Henry Ford	[henri 'fɔ:d]
Hogmanay	['hɒgməneɪ]
Howe Road Youth Club	[həʊ rəʊd 'ju:θ klʌb]
iwalk	['aɪwɔ:k]
James Bond	[dʒeɪmz 'bɒnd]
Kate Star	[keɪt 'stɑ:]
London Eye	[ðə lʌndən 'aɪ]
London Transport Museum	[ðə lʌndən 'trænspɔ:t mjʊzi:əm]
London Zoo	[lʌndən 'zu:]
Madame Tussaud's	[mədæm tʊ'sɔ:dz]
McFly	[mək'flaɪ]
MI6	[emaɪ'sɪks]
Mikey Mike	[maɪki 'maɪk]
Mile High City	[maɪl haɪ 'sɪti]
Millenium Stadium	[mɪleniəm 'steɪdiəm]
Model T	[modl 'ti:]
Motor City	[məʊtə 'sɪti]
Motown	['məʊtaʊn]
Museum of London	[ðə mjʊzi:əm əv 'lʌndən]
Nessie	['nesi]
New Year	[nju: 'jɪə]
Pembroke Centre	[pembrəʊk 'sentə]
Queen	[ðə 'kwi:n]
Rainforest Café	['reɪnfɒrɪst kæfeɪ]
Robert Burns	[rɒbət 'bɜ:nz]
Rockies	[ðə 'rɒki:z]
Rocky Mountains	[ðə rɒki 'maʊntənz]
Science Museum	[ðə 'saɪəns mjʊzi:əm]
Sherlock Holmes	[ʃɜ:lɒk 'həʊmz]
Sistas	['sɪstəz]
Stockwell Park	[stɒkwel 'pɑ:k]
Teenmag	['ti:nmæg]
Time Out Magazine	[taɪm aʊt 'mægəzi:n]
Tower	[ðə 'taʊə]
Tower Bridge	[taʊə 'brɪdʒ]
Tower of London	[ðə taʊə əv 'lʌndən]
Welshpark Centre	[welʃpɑ:k 'sentə]
Willie Nelson	[wɪli 'nelsən]
Windsor Castle	[wɪndzə 'kɑ:sl]
Winston Churchill	[wɪnstən 'tʃɜ:tʃɪl]

CLASSROOM PHRASES

Sorry, I'm late.	Entschuldigung, dass ich zu spät komme.
Sorry, I've forgotten my book.	Entschuldigung, ich habe mein Buch vergessen.
I'm sorry. I don't have my homework.	Entschuldigung. Ich habe meine Hausaufgaben nicht.
Sorry, I can't find it. What page?	Entschuldigung, ich kann es nicht finden. Auf welcher Seite?
Sorry, I haven't finished.	Entschuldigung, ich bin noch nicht fertig.
I don't understand this exercise.	Ich verstehe diese Übung nicht.
I don't know.	Ich weiß es nicht.
Can I say it in German?	Kann ich es auf Deutsch sagen?
Can I open/close the window, please?	Kann ich bitte das Fenster öffnen/schließen?
Can you help me, please?	Können Sie mir bitte helfen?
Can you write it on the board, please?	Können Sie es bitte an die Tafel schreiben?
Can you say that again, please?	Können Sie das bitte wiederholen?
Can you speak louder, please?	Können Sie bitte lauter sprechen?
Can we listen to it again, please?	Könnten wir es noch einmal hören?
Can we work together, please?	Können wir bitte zusammen arbeiten?
Can I read the next sentence?	Kann ich den nächsten Satz lesen?
Can we act the dialogue?	Können wir den Dialog spielen?
What's "..." in English / in German?	Was heißt „ ... " auf Englisch / auf Deutsch?
Is this right?	Ist das richtig?
How do you spell that word, please?	Wie wird das Wort geschrieben?
Excuse me. What's the homework?	Entschuldigung. Was haben wir (als Hausaufgabe) auf?